Classification Struggles

Pierre Bourdieu

Classification Struggles

General Sociology, Volume 1

Lectures at the Collège de France (1981–1982)

Edition established by Patrick Champagne, Julien Duval, Franck Poupeau and Marie-Christine Rivière

Translated by Peter Collier

polity

First published in French in *Sociologie générale. Volume 1. Cours au Collège de France (1981–1983)* © Éditions Raisons d'Agir/Éditions du Seuil, 2015

This English edition © Polity Press, 2018

Polity Press
65 Bridge Street
Cambridge CB2 1UR, UK

Polity Press
101 Station Landing
Suite 300
Medford, MA 02155, USA

ISBN-13: 978-1-5095-1327-7

A catalogue record for this book is available from the British Library.

Library of Congress Cataloging-in-Publication Data
Names: Bourdieu, Pierre, 1930-2002, author.
Title: Classification struggles : General sociology, volume 1 / Pierre Bourdieu.
Other titles: Sociologie g?en?erale. Volume 1. English
Description: Cambridge, UK ; Medford, MA : Polity Press, [2018] | Includes bibliographical references and index.
Identifiers: LCCN 2018019602 | ISBN 9781509513277 (hardback)
Subjects: LCSH: Sociology--Study and teaching (Higher)--France. | Classification. | Sociology.
Classification: LCC HM578.F8 B68213 2018 | DDC 301.071--dc23 LC record available at https://lccn.loc.gov/2018019602

Typeset in 10.5 on 12 pt Times New Roman by
Servis Filmsetting Ltd, Stockport, Cheshire
Printed and bound in the UK by CPI Group (UK) Ltd, Croydon

The publisher has used its best endeavours to ensure that the URLs for external websites referred to in this book are correct and active at the time of going to press. However, the publisher has no responsibility for the websites and can make no guarantee that a site will remain live or that the content is or will remain appropriate.

Every effort has been made to trace all copyright holders, but if any have been overlooked the publisher will be pleased to include any necessary credits in any subsequent reprint or edition.

For further information on Polity, visit our website: politybooks.com

Contents

Editorial note

With this book, we continue the publication of Pierre Bourdieu's lectures at the Collège de France. A few months after his final lecture in this institute in March 2001, Bourdieu published a condensed version of the last year of his teaching (2000–1), entitled *Science of Science and Reflexivity*.[1] Since his death, a further two volumes have been published, *On the State*, in 2012, and *Manet: A Symbolic Revolution*, in 2017, corresponding to his lectures for 1989–92 and 1998–2000 respectively.[2] The present volume inaugurates the publication of the 'course of lectures on general sociology' that Bourdieu had chosen for the first five years of his teaching at the Collège de France. It presents the lectures for the first year, that is, eight one-hour lectures given between April and June 1982. A second volume, to appear later, will contain the thirteen two-hour lectures delivered between October 1982 and January 1983. Further volumes will collect the lectures from the three following years.

Our edition of this 'course of lectures on general sociology' follows the editorial conventions that were defined for the publication of the lectures on the state, in order to reconcile fidelity with readability.[3] The text published here is a transcription of the lectures as they were actually delivered. However, in transposing from the oral to the written mode we have introduced some minor revisions, while respecting the approach that Bourdieu himself adopted when he revised his own lectures and seminar papers: making stylistic corrections and smoothing the rough edges of oral delivery (such as repetition, and other linguistic tics). Only on exceptional occasions have we suppressed the development of an argument, sometimes because it was too hastily improvised, but more often because the sound recording was not clear enough for us to establish a convincing text. In general, we have placed inaudible words and passages, or interruptions to the recording, where we were unable to obtain a secure reading, between square brackets [. . .].[4] The division of the text into paragraphs is the work of the editors, as are the subheadings and the punctuation. The 'parentheses' where Bourdieu digresses from his main argument have been handled in different ways, according to their length and their relation to the context. The shorter ones have been placed between dashes. When these digressions acquire a certain autonomy and imply a break in the thread of the argument, they are placed between brackets, and when one is really too long, it may be given the status of a separate section in its own right. The endnotes are mostly of three different kinds. Some mainly indicate the texts to which Bourdieu refers explicitly or implicitly, when it has been possible to identify them; in those cases where it seemed helpful, short quotations from these texts have been added. Others aim to indicate to the reader those writings by Bourdieu, whether predating or postdating the lectures, that develop the points under discussion. The third kind of note provides contextual information, for example explaining allusions which might escape the contemporary reader or a reader unfamiliar with the French cultural context of the period.

We have reproduced in an appendix the summaries of the lectures, as published in *L'Annuaire du Collège de France – cours et travaux*.

Acknowledgements

The editors would like to thank Bruno Auerbach, Donald Broady, Christophe Charle, Johan Heilbron, Thibaut Izard and Remi Lenoir for their contributions to this book.

Lecture of 28 April 1982

Teaching research – The logic of research and the logic of exposition –
What is classification? – Classifying the classifying subject – Constructed
divisions and real divisions – The insult

I have given the course of lectures that I am going to teach over the
next few years the title 'A course of lectures on general sociology'.
This might sound distinctly pretentious if we emphasize the universal
nature of 'general sociology' yet extremely modest if we draw attention to the 'course' as a series of lectures. The very notion of teaching
a course, as I would define it in sociological terms, necessarily implies a
modicum of modesty. My aim might best be understood as a study of
my own research. I am obviously not the best-placed person to lecture
on what I do, because there is, it seems to me, a certain contradiction
between teaching and research, between the complex and subjective
nature of research and the simplification demanded by the very nature
of a taught course. Thus what I propose to offer will not be a course in
the strict sense of the term, yet it will be a course in the more modest
sense of the term. In fact, to explain more clearly the title that I have
chosen, I would call it an axiomatic view of my own research, showing
the articulation between the fundamental concepts and the structure
of relations that connects these concepts. Basically, I have taken the
liberty of using the excuse of teaching a course, in the ordinary social
sense of the word, in order to do something that I would not normally
risk undertaking, that is, attempt to present the major lines of force of
my whole research enterprise.

Over the next few years I shall explore a certain number of key
concepts, both in terms of their conceptual mechanisms and in terms
of their technical function for research. I shall take the notion of a
field, and, on the one hand, situate this notion in relation to the notion

of a material field, and, on the other hand, examine the relationship between the material field and the field defined as a site of conflict. Then I shall go on to examine the relationship between the notion of field and the notion of *habitus*, which will lead me to investigate what motivates and determines practices; more specifically, I shall attempt to explain what seems to me to be the logic of action that emerges from the articulation of the notion of field with the notion of habitus. And, finally, I shall try to show the relations between different types of field and different types of capital. These are only the chapter headings. But I wanted to mention them in order to provide the framework for my reflections this year on something that seems to me to be an essential precondition for any attempt to establish a theory in the social sciences, that is, the relation between the scientific subject and his or her object, and more precisely the relation between the scientific subject as subjective intelligence, and the object of his or her studies, which is a set of subjects in action.

In order to formulate these questions without being unnecessarily theoretical, I propose to examine one of the procedures fundamental to all the social sciences, the operation of classification. Any social science that needs to use statistical analysis, and draw on it in order to make comparisons between different constructed classes, is obliged to divide the populations that are its objects into classes, and I intend to examine this procedure by comparing it to what we find in the natural sciences, for example in biology, zoology or botany, and by trying to determine more precisely the relations between the classifications produced by scholars, the conditions that led them to produce these classifications, and the classifications that social agents put into practice in their everyday lives.

Teaching research

I would like to take advantage of the fact that this is my first lecture in order to attempt a *captatio benevolentiae* – as classical orators used to call it – to try to justify my approach in advance. I don't know if the approach that I propose to follow is ordinary or extraordinary, but it is the only way that I can operate. Although I readily admit that a lecture is never more than a teaching exercise, I shall endeavour to make mine as unlike a taught course as possible. I hope to be able to neutralize the neutralization effect that teaching almost inevitably engenders, for, even when called 'direction of research', teaching creates something of a fiction – an 'artefact' – we work in a vacuum, for we present the results of our research rather than explain our methods of research. I cannot escape the general rule, if only because of the structure of the space within which I am speaking, and the diversity of my audience. But as far as I can, within the limits of the freedom allowed to me as a social agent, I would like to neutralize these effects by anticipating them in two ways: on the one hand, by drawing on concrete examples, that is, my experience as a scholar and the research that I am engaged in, or on social experiences directly accessible to the majority of my audience; and on the other hand, by counting on the complicity of my audience: I shall of course be obliged to conduct a monologue – this is the very logic of our situation here – but I would like to encourage a form of dialogue, for example by way of questions put to me either orally at the end of a lecture or in writing at the start of the next lecture, so that I can wherever possible clear up misunderstandings and reply to objections or questions – or say that I am unable to answer the question, which will no doubt often be the case. This is not a mere rhetorical flourish; I really would welcome any kind of feedback, whether in conversation at the end of the lecture if you feel so bold, or in the form of written notes for those less brave.

This concern to avoid following the logic of the taught course, as far as I can, will have an impact on the rhetorical style of my discourse. The paradigm of the lecture is the *agrégation* lecture, which I have analysed elsewhere in sociological terms, and which I wish to avoid.[1] It is an exercise designed to be impregnable; the professor who delivers it is quite unassailable. Engaging in research is quite the contrary, for rather than taking every possible precaution, it implies laying oneself bare, with all one's weak points and insecure arguments; since scientific progress by definition requires us to lower our guard and prepare to be criticized. Breaking with French-style teaching will lead me to use a different mode of expression, sometimes hesitant or pedestrian, one that experts in French rhetoric might call 'laborious', 'long-winded', or 'cumbersome'. I shall not hesitate to be pedestrian when the situation calls for it, although I shall not do so on purpose. French-style teaching insists so much on wit, elegance, distinction and lightness of touch that it accustoms its audience to be satisfied with arguments that gloss over the truth, particularly social truths, as long as it produces a cosy feeling of shared intelligence and equal intellect: both speaker and listener enjoy a feeling of mutual understanding, and both feel that they are colleagues collaborating in a significant intellectual event.

In scholarly research, as I understand it, we have to be prepared quite often to feel foolish, incapable, idiotic even (I shall return to the word 'idiotic', which has considerable social importance). The best kind of philosophy teaches us to open ourselves up completely and adopt a stance of absolute ignorance. Many theses and treatises hope to impress by claiming to do this ('I know that I do not know . . .'), but few scholars actually put this into practice. In sociology this virtue of ignorance, this 'learned ignorance', as Nicholas of Cusa called it,[2] is especially important if we wish to investigate the most basic topics, as I shall do today, in questioning for instance the notion of law, of the right and the just (what is 'the law'? what do we mean when we refer to someone as doing something 'in the name of the law'?), and the notion of nomination (what does the word 'nomination' mean in the kind of sentence that we read casually every day, but which ought to make us stop and think, such as 'the President of the Republic has nominated one of his friends Director of the Banque de France'). This laborious process of argumentation – the very antithesis of the elegant style as defined by classical and scholarly tradition – will sometimes be thrust upon me, but will almost always be intentional, and since I am in a position of authority here, will have to be accepted by my audience.

In the material that I am about to discuss, I freely admit that my conclusions are only provisional, some more, some less; however, they seem to me to matter less than a certain manner of thinking. I shall invoke the example of a book by Benveniste, *Dictionary of Indo-European Concepts and Society*,[3] which was the end product of several years of lectures at the Collège de France, and for me is the epitome of everything that this institution does best. Of course, I find this book admirable for the conclusions it reaches, but also for the mode of thinking it uses. You can read it in any order, or even start at the end; for the structure of the book does not reflect the sequence of the lectures; the order is unimportant, but in each of its fragments we find the same modus operandi at work. Once this has been assimilated by the reader, it becomes a tool which they can then apply to objects of study that Benveniste – unfortunately – did not address, and continue the book themselves. The goal of the ideal course of lectures is, I think, to successfully transmit what we tend commonly to call a method (although we overwork this word so much that we tend to forget what it signifies: it is not a dogma or a thesis – there was a time when philosophers promulgated theses, but that is not my style . . .). My aim is to articulate modes or styles of thinking that we may otherwise assimilate without being consciously aware of the process, by taking you through the simple experience of seeing them at work, with all their imperfections. You see the strategy underlying my argument: I am asking you to accept in advance all the flaws in my argument, and even believe that they are intentional, which will certainly not always be the case. If I had wished to follow a fashionable line of argument – for anything can be argued in an ethereal, or let us say 'Parisian' way – I could have held forth at length on the notion of the sketch. I would have said that 'I am going to draw sketches, I am going to be sketchy', and so on. However, I shall not structure things in this way, because this would dematerialize something that is undeniably real and true.

I propose to close this preamble with one last remark. I intend to approach one of the most fundamental exercises of research, that is, nomination or classification, but I shall do so in order to find a roundabout way of attacking a fundamental problem for sociologists, that of social class. There is a pedagogical contradiction here, but for my demonstration to function properly, you will have to try to forget my underlying intention (which is to attempt, in your company, to solve the problem of social classification), and yet at the same time recognize my hidden agenda, so that you understand what it is I am looking for. In fact, I would like to encourage you to practise ignorance and engage in learning at one and the same time.

There are numerous treatises on the social classes, and if any among you are disappointed with my teaching, I can offer some excellent bibliographies on the problem. What we are lacking, it seems to me, is research that aims, if not to solve the problem, as people rather pretentiously claim to do, at least to reformulate it, so that at the end of the day we are no longer certain of what we thought we knew at the outset. If I may invoke another late, great master, it has to be Wittgenstein: we need this type of thinker, who makes us unlearn everything that we know or think we know, and who makes us realize, when confronted with an issue like that of social class, that we know nothing, or very little, although any sociologist worthy of the name is capable of delivering a dazzling course of lectures on the social classes.[4]

Here we might call for a sociological analysis of the part played in the intellectual education of all intellectuals by the required initiation, however diverse in depth, commitment or passion, into Marxism. In fact we need a sociology of knowledge to enable us to study the impression we may have in our twenties that we know perfectly well how to think about what there is to know on the subject of social class: this is a collective experience shared by almost everyone, and is so completely institutionalized that it renders formidably difficult something that should be routine, that is, to approach the issue of classes in general virtually from scratch, and reconsider what it means to classify. What is the relation between a social class and a biological or botanical class?

The logic of research and the logic of exposition

These are the rather simplistic questions that I shall address in this first lecture. In order to present the most persuasive and convincing picture, I shall progress from the more obvious to the more unexpected. I shall today merely try to put the questions, although I obviously have to admit that this is a slightly artificial procedure, in so far as I have only been able to formulate some of these questions after the event, that is, after due reflection and analysis. One of the difficulties in transmitting scientific knowledge is precisely the fact that, for the purposes of communication, we are often obliged to describe things in a sequence that was not the sequence of their discovery. All epistemologists agree that the logic of research and the logic of a narrative exposition of research are completely different, but the logic of exposition has its own impetus and imperatives that create a kind of discourse on research which has very little to do with what really happens in the process of research. I myself, when engaged in this kind of work (*The Craft of Sociology*),[5] have had to mark out separate stages (for instance: 'you have to gain control of the object, and then construct it'), which never occur in that guise in practice. Similarly, we are frequently unable to formulate clearly the problems we have been addressing until we have found the answers: the answers help us to rephrase the question more accurately, and, in so doing, to refocus the debate. This dilemma is the perfect illustration of what I was saying just now: my course of lectures will be a compromise between the reality of research (it might occur to me to wonder: 'Well, what does naming actually imply, what is a nomination?') and the requirements of my exposition, which will lead me to elaborate as a series of problems something that did not proceed in that sequence at all.

What is classification?

To put it briefly, I shall focus today on the following questions: 'What does classification imply? What does classification imply when it concerns the social world?' A logician may find a solution to the problem of classification in general; and the biological systems of zoology or botany solve it very well, even in a way that can indeed be very useful for us as sociologists, by making us realize that things are not so simple in the social sciences.[6] For when we come to consider the social world, classification in fact classifies subjects who classify in their turn;[7] it classifies objects that have the property of being classifying subjects. We must therefore call into question the classifications that are made by the social subject. Do these resemble botanical or zoological classifications, or another kind of classification? Do all classifications have the same import? (You will very soon appreciate how far a problematic constructed after the event is actually a fiction, because it necessarily contains its own answer. It is very difficult to put a question without giving the answer and proving that the question and answer had not been constructed in that order, otherwise, by definition, there would have been no research, or it would be too good to be true.)

The question of classification, as it is treated in sociology, obliges us to ask who does the classifying in this social world. Does everyone classify? Do we classify all the time? How do we classify? Do we classify in the same way as a logician does in using concepts or definitions as the basis of a classification? And then, if everyone classifies, do all these classifications and all their classifiers along with them have the same social weight? To take some examples from very different contexts, does an official at the INSEE (National Institute of Statistics and Economic Studies) who uses a scholarly or semi-scholarly taxonomy to classify, have the same status as an inspector of taxes who says: 'Above this particular band of income, you will pay this particular rate of tax'? Are the classifications used by sociologists, when they construct the category of agents who have such and such a property, commensurate with the classifications imposed by the preacher in distinguishing between heretics and true believers?

If we start by asking whether all classifications have the same social import, we are led to ask a very difficult question: are all acts of classification equally prone to be self-validating? Politicians, for instance, are able to formulate arguments about the social world which seem highly likely to be true, since they invest them with a kind of self-validating authority. We can plot social classifications from the entirely gratuitous (I shall return to this point, using the example of the insult) to those which, as the saying goes, lay down the law.

Now, what is there in common between the classifications made by the sociologist or the historian (by any social scientist, in fact) and those made by the botanist, for example? I shall speak of botanical classification in very basic terms, because it is not my profession and it is not the direct object of my research. I refer to it, as I said just now, only to shed light on what is specific to sociological classification. Botanists establish classes based on criteria that, in their own terms, may be more or less natural or artificial. Botany and zoology distinguish between two major branches of classification, and this is a useful distinction for a sociologist – the artificial, which they call systems, and the natural, which they call methods.

The classification that they call *artificial* takes as criterion a characteristic chosen either arbitrarily, or according to a deliberately decided purpose, with the principle of the choice being facility or rapidity in determining a species. As the ideal is to classify as rapidly as possible, they take a visible characteristic, an external property, such as the colour of the eyes. If they take a deeper criterion, like the level of urea in the blood, classification is much less straightforward.

Natural classification, however, draws, not on some more or less arbitrary, convenient criterion, but on a whole set of criteria. It takes as criteria all the organs considered in the order of their real importance for the organism. Natural classifications take into account several elementary characteristics: for instance, structure, form, morphology, anatomy, function, physiology and ethology. And the most natural classifications are those which manage to take into account the correlations between the different criteria chosen.

Thus, on the basis of this ensemble of criteria with a strong correlation among themselves, they establish classes which they call 'natural' (the word 'natural' is treacherous and will present problems for sociology): these classes are grounded in the nature of things, or, as they said in the Middle Ages, *cum fondamento in re* ('with a basis in the things themselves'). All the elements of a class established in this way will bear more resemblance to each other than to the elements of any other class, and a natural classification will be a search for sets of characteristics responsible for the greatest possible proportion of the variants observed. One of the problems for classifiers is therefore to find what they call the 'essential characteristics', that is the most powerful distinctive traits, so that the important properties may all in some way be deduced from this interrelated set of criteria. A certain type of system may be used, drawing on methods of factor analysis and correspondence analysis, in order to try to produce classifications that combine the universe of pertinent criteria with the reciprocal relations between these criteria. This summary will seem very cursory to the cognoscenti, but I believe that it is sufficient to explain my comparison of the social sciences with the natural sciences.

Classifying the classifying subject

To a certain extent, we could take everything that has just been said and apply it to sociology. The sociologist, like the botanist, seeks to identify criteria sufficiently correlated among themselves to make it possible, when there are enough criteria, to try to assimilate and integrate them all, and thus reproduce the universe of all the variants established. This is what I attempted to do for instance in *Distinction*, with the notion of a constructed class[8] that combines a whole system of criteria: economic, social, and cultural, as well as gender. Using a finite system of interrelated criteria that I have tried to define in the most economical fashion (any criterion that did not add supplementary information to the system of criteria chosen was rejected), it should be possible to provide a complete but economical explanation for the totality of the pertinent differences recorded. So far, so good, there is no difference between the two disciplines.

The true difference seems to me to lie in the fact that, among the criteria they can use to elaborate their system of criteria, their taxonomy and their division into classes, sociologists find two different categories of criteria. As an example: if I am studying the professors of the University of Paris, I choose criteria such as age, gender, the establishment in which they teach, whether they hold the *agrégation* or not, whether they belong to one or other teachers' union, whether they write student handbooks ('Que sais-je?'), whether they publish with Klincksieck or Les Belles Lettres, and so on.[9] But as soon as I take criteria as objects, and not as instruments for the dissection of reality, I discover considerable differences between the instruments that I use for my dissection: for instance, the terms '*agrégés*' or '*non agrégés*' refer to groups.[10] Some criteria are constituted in reality (the word 'constitute' is important, it contains 'constitution'), they are constitutive of reality, they divide it into units, and there are people who have an interest in the existence of this division: there is a president of the *Sociétés des Agrégés* who has plenipotential powers and is authorized to speak on behalf of all the *agrégés*.

At the other extreme, before the feminist movement, the masculine/feminine divide was the one that caused the least difficulty for the statisticians, although if we stop to think, we can see that there is a continuum and that the divisions between the sexes are drawn arbitrarily by society; to match the detail of the real structures, we would need much subtler distinctions. Another example is the age groups, which generally don't cause the statisticians to lose much time. (An interesting point to study is the correlation between the social position of the classifiers and the social characteristics of their classifications. The administrative classifications that INSEE and others use seem quite unproblematic to those who produce them, but they start causing problems as soon as you start to think about them. Alphonse Allais was amused by the fact that you got a discount on train travel for a child under the age of three, but you lost it as soon as the child was older, and he wondered what would happen if a father was travelling on the birthday of his child: should the father press the alarm button to declare that his child is now over three, and ask to pay a supplement?[11] Comedians are the allies of the sociologist because they ask questions that our everyday routines lead us to forget.) In all the cases where there is a continuum, legal taxonomies and classifications draw clear lines: below/above, masculine/feminine. The law decides and divides, cutting across the continuum.

Constructed divisions and real divisions

When sociologists fail to question the relation to reality of the classifications they use or the juridical standing of their criteria, they inevitably confuse two kinds of classes. Most of the sociologist's 'typologies' are the result of some such confusion, which I consider to be an epistemological monstrosity. I remember for instance a piece of research on academics which confused formal oppositions of the kind 'cosmopolitan/local' with oppositions grounded in reality and linked to real divisions (such as 'jet sociologist', which establishes an opposition between 'itinerant professor' and 'stay-at-home professor').[12] In other words, these typologies often conflate constructed divisions with divisions taken from reality. I remember how, at the time of the first American imitations of structural anthropology, Lévi-Strauss commented on an article by an ethnologist which treated oppositions taken from the reality of mythology or ritual ('wet/dry', etc.) on the same level as very complex oppositions (which I would have found it difficult to invent myself, such as 'pure/impure', for example), that have a completely different level of construction and elaboration. In sociology, if we do not question the 'ontological' status of the classifications we use, we will be led to put in the same basket principles of division which do not have the same standing in reality at all.

To return to the comparison with biological classification, I should say that the sociologist encounters 'things', whether individuals or institutions, that are already classified. For instance, if you classify university professors by institution, you have to be prepared to categorize the universities themselves, and the more prestigious institutes as well. In general, one of the methods we can use to handle these classifications is to trace their history: when did they emerge, or when were they created? Are they a recent bureaucratic or technocratic invention? Do they have different kinds of history? Whether people or institutions, the objects of sociological study present themselves as already classified. They bear names and titles that signal their membership of certain classes and give us an idea of how we classify in everyday life. If what the sociologist encounters comes in already classified form, it is because classifying subjects are involved.

In everyday life, an institution (or an individual) never presents itself as a thing – it never presents itself purely in itself and for itself – but always as something endowed with qualities, always already qualified. For example, a person who acts as we say 'in virtue of office' (I shall return to this expression which seems to me to contain a profound social philosophy), whether professor, preacher or civil servant, presents themselves as endowed with social properties and qualities which may be underlined by all sorts of signs that identify what kind of social agent they are, such as formal dress, insignia, decorations, epaulettes, and so on. These signs or insignia may also be incorporated and therefore virtually invisible, such as distinguished behaviour, stylistic verve and eloquence, or received pronunciation. This is extremely important: incorporated qualities are almost invisible, almost natural (and that would bring us back to natural classification). They provide us with a basis for social interpretation. I am anticipating the answers here somewhat, although I intended only to put the questions, but it is obvious that social life is only possible because we constantly classify, that is to say, we constantly make assumptions about the class (and not only in the sense of social class) into which we have classified the person we have to deal with. As the saying goes, 'you have to know who you are dealing with'. These properties may be even more invisible if they are located outside the person who bears them: they may be found in a situation connecting two people in their relationship, as is the case with signs of respect. The term 'respect' involves the notion of perception, for the properties that form the basis of classifications are properties that strike the eye and demand to be seen in a certain light, and in so doing, demand the appropriate behaviour in return.

In everyday life, social individuals classify. You have to classify to live, and, to parody Bergson's saying that 'it is grass in general which attracts the herbivorous animal',[13] we might say that what the social subject most usually encounters is other people in general. In other words, we have to deal with social individuals, that is particular, named individuals (taking the word 'named' in its widest sense, to include 'nominated', as in 'the President of the Republic has nominated . . .'), who are designated and indeed constituted by a name that not only designates them, but makes them become what they are. I shall return to this point.

To help you understand this, I shall use the insight provided by the analogy of 'attribution'. When a work is judged as 'attributed to', the word 'attributed' has a very specific meaning in art history: it is the fact of giving a name to a picture and its painter. Everyone knows that, depending on the painter to whom a picture is attributed, our perception of the work changes, and with it, our subjective appreciation, as well as its objective value in terms of a quantifiable market price. The collectors or professional art historians who are able to change the attribution of a third-rate Dutch painting exercise a remarkable power of classification which has important social consequences. Some of the classifications that we find at work in the social world are of the same nature. For instance, the nominations of officials by the government are binding executive acts, which have the force of law and entail all sorts of palpable consequences: enhanced respect, salary, pension, contributions and other benefits – all sorts of social benefits in the widest sense of the term. The classifications that we handle in the social world, which are the qualities that the sociologist encounters in the shape of properties given in advance, are therefore denominations which in a sense generate the properties of the object they nominate, and create its status.

The insult

In order to illustrate this first theme, I propose to refer briefly to an article that has just been republished in a book by Nicolas Ruwet: *Grammaire des insultes et autres études*.[14] In fact I shall be asking the same questions again but from a different angle (with the ulterior motive of showing to what extent the boundaries between disciplines are artificial; what I am about to say will expose the vacuity of certain divisions that people are ready to die for, divisions between sociology, pragmatics, the sociology of language, linguistics . . .).

In this article, Nicolas Ruwet replies to a text by Milner dealing with insults[15] and what he calls 'qualifying nouns'. These qualifying nouns are typically what Aristotelian logic would have called *categorems*. Categorem comes from *katégoreisthai*, which, etymologically, means 'to publicly accuse':[16] that is, quite clearly, to insult. A category, a categorem, is a public accusation. The word 'public' is crucial: it means 'unashamed', 'daring to state its name' as opposed to denunciations that are ashamed to show their face. The categorem, then, is a public accusation that takes the risk of being acknowledged, or rejected. Ruwet notes in passing that when I call someone an 'idiot', I take the responsibility for this upon myself, whereas when I call someone 'professor', I am not taking much of a risk (although it is true that if a left-wing intellectual says 'you are only a professor', that may be taken as an insult!). As a result, 'qualifying nouns' differ semantically from common nouns like 'gendarmes' or 'teachers' by the fact that they do not classify. Ruwet goes on to say that 'teachers' and 'gendarmes' have a specific 'virtual reference', they refer to a 'class "whose members are recognizable by certain common objective characteristics"'.[17]

To be brief: the census (as an inventory of the population) attracts a consensus; everyone agrees to think of a gendarme as a gendarme, whereas not everyone would agree to label as idiot the person that I call an idiot, unless – and this is what the linguist forgets – I have the authority to say that other people are idiots, if I am a teacher for instance [*laughter*], in which case it has obvious social consequences. (I said a teacher to tease, but we could say a psychiatrist . . . and that would be far worse . . .). Ruwet rejects Milner's distinction between 'qualifying nouns' and, shall we say, names of professions. He argues that this is not a lexical difference and that on a semantic level we could dispense with Milner's analyses. I let the linguistic debate stand, but I note the problem presented, which in my opinion is crucial. Austin's famous text on performatives had a considerable impact on me.[18] It woke me a little from the dogmatic slumber in which we sociologists lie, since, like all human beings, we are dependent on words. We fail to be surprised by anything that the everyday usage of words routinely imposes upon us.

Just as Austin revitalized the discussion of speech that claims to enact (of which the insult is a particular case), so the debate between Milner and Ruwet has the merit of capturing the attention of the sociologist, who might be tempted to forget that the classes he handles are ultimately categorems, one of which is the insult. For example, when obliged to use certain insulting categorems taken from everyday life, the sociologist uses quotation marks (as does *Le Monde* when it quotes statements likely to be perceived as defamatory). When the sociologist encounters the insult as a categorem that engages the personal responsibility of the speaker, a categorem lacking authority, he takes his distance by placing it between quotation marks; but when he writes the word 'teacher', he will not use quotation marks, because he knows that he speaks for the whole social world.

To quote Milner: 'There is no class of "idiots" or "bastards" whose members would be recognizable from shared objective characteristics; the only common property that we may attribute to them is that they are subjected on some particular occasion to the insult in question.'[19] These speech acts are performative, they perform an insult. What is most interesting is that the very word 'idiot' follows this logic: 'idiot' comes from the Greek *idios,* which means 'singular'. The idiot is someone who insults all and sundry, without being authorized to do so. He is liable to be dismissed as an eccentric, condemned to the absolute solitude of someone who has no one to support him.

This is the opposite to a successful performative utterance, which has to be articulated in conditions mandating the speaker to say it, in which case he has every chance of seeing his utterance translated into action. In other words, the classifications made by the insulter are very likely to backfire, with a typical rejoinder like: 'And the same to you!' The insult backfires against the idiot; as a child might say: 'it takes one to see one'. In other words, there are classifications which are the sole responsibility of the speaker – which are published at the authors' expense, as it were. If this author is a prophetic author who has *auctoritas*, who is the author of his own authority, his classification may impose itself, but apart from this case, any act of imposition of meaning that is authorized only by the singular subject who proffers it is bound to appear idiotic. I propose to show next time how the logic of the insult and the logic of scientific classification represent the two extreme poles of what a classification may be in the social world.

Lecture of 5 May 1982

The act of institution – The insult as magical behaviour – Coding individuals – Dividing reality – The example of socio-occupational categories

In his argument, Nicolas Ruwet indicated that Milner's distinction between qualifying nouns and common nouns implied basically ignoring what semantics could contribute to the problem. And, contradicting Milner, he points out that the distinction between non-classifiers and classifiers like 'teacher' or 'gendarme' is based on extreme cases. Thus Ruwet reproaches Milner with choosing the extreme poles of a continuum, whose extremities run from 'teacher' and 'gendarme', that is, professional names, at one end, to obvious insults like 'idiot' or 'bastard'. Milner insists on the fact that 'idiot' or 'bastard' are not clearly defined classes on which a random sample of speakers could concur; by the same token, anyone who proffers an insult becomes vulnerable, being the only guarantor of that classification. In other words, the insulter is a classifier who takes extreme risks.

I shall not deal with the theme of the insult in greater depth, even if I were capable of doing so. What interests me in this example is how it reminds us of something that sociologists and others often forget, which is that problems of classification are not necessarily and exclusively conceptual issues. The insult is typically one of those practical classifications in which the classifier commits their whole being, and their whole sense of self; the classifier takes a risk without consciously intending to. We need this kind of *in vitro* observation, because it contradicts the impressions that sociologists frequently record when they ask the object of their enquiry to become classifiers. I wish I could have brought you some questionnaires produced by titular, accredited sociologists, who ask the objects of their enquiry to classify themselves (unfortunately we sometimes consign to the waste bin things that are bad research, but would be extremely useful documents). The sociologist is in a way imposing his status as teacher of the social world onto the objects of his scientific analysis when he asks them to classify themselves: 'What class do you think you belong to?' 'How many classes do you think exist . . .?', 'If we divide society into five classes, where do you think you would fit in?', 'Do you think that you belong to the middle classes?' In these cases, what people reply does not reveal anything very much: to dismiss a stupid question, we reply in terms that minimize the likelihood of seeming stupid – the news for anyone here who is a sociologist is that the objects of your enquiry have a thousand ways of telling you that you are an idiot, generally very politely and euphemistically.

The problem of the insult makes us realize that the process of classification in everyday life is a practical operation with concrete aims, and consequences that implicate the person who pursues those aims. It is a risky operation, in which the person who judges lays himself or herself open to being judged; as I mentioned last time, the child's counterattack – 'It takes one to see one' – shows that there is a whole rhetoric of the insult. This kind of symbolic struggle, of which the insult is one example, reminds us of something we ought not to forget – that the problems of classification are something more than what scholars make of them in their research, when they treat them merely as problems of analysis and judgement.

The act of institution

To continue for a moment, using one of Ruwet's notes:

> '*You're an imbecile*, according to Milner, is not, despite appearances to the contrary, a parallel to *You're a teacher*. The first sentence differs from the second in that its very utterance necessarily produces pragmatic effects: it is an insult.' Whence the assimilation to the performative, made by Milner. But we should note that, if we think of the (rather uncommon) cases where it would be natural to speak the words *You're a teacher*, this sentence could also include a performative (although not necessarily insulting) implication – for instance it might mean something like *I appoint you to be a teacher*.[1]

This observation is at the heart of what I would say if I had to construct a theory of the insult (I find it interesting that the linguist consigns to a note in passing something that seems crucial to me: this is rather a good example of the relationship between two neighbouring disciplines that virtually ignore each other's perspective).

Ruwet's remark seems important to me because the phrase 'You're a bastard' could have a status equivalent to 'You're a teacher', but only if 'You're a teacher' were used in a very specific case. In fact, the language would not be so familiar (i.e., would not use the 'tu' form of address in French). To nominate someone as a teacher, you would say: 'You are appointed Teacher', handing them a parchment scroll, as in certain American universities, where in a ritual ceremony, the candidate receives a title giving them the right to exercise the function of teacher. If you say, 'You are a teacher' in an act of nomination, you accomplish an act of institution. Ruwet's remark, if you take it literally, means that the insult ('You're an absolute idiot') and the nomination ('You're a teacher') are two elements of the same class. This is the class of acts of nomination that I shall call the 'class of acts of institution', that is, acts whereby one signifies something to someone, understanding the term 'to signify' to include both its sense in linguistic theory as a synonym of 'to communicate' ('I signify this or that' by making certain gestures) and the sense whereby 'I signify something to you' means: 'I call on you', 'I expect you' or 'I order you' to be what I tell you that you are. I think this is the correct definition of the performative. (I shall not get involved in the subtle differences between the different meanings of the word 'performative'; I shall stay for the moment with the original meaning that Austin gave to the word, while he still had control over it, before the word became the subject of hair-splitting squabbles among linguists. I state this for anyone among you who might find my initial hypothesis too simplistic.) In this light, the insult and nomination would belong to the same class of acts that we might call 'institutional', whether positive or negative. The positive institutional act, for instance, consists in designating someone as worthy of holding a position. Negative institutional acts (it would be better to call them acts of destitution, or degradation) consist in depriving someone of the dignity that has been granted them. Insult or abuse would then be a subclass of acts of destitution, itself a subclass of positive or negative institutional acts in general.

I would like to use these examples in order to investigate the nature of those acts through which an individual or a group, or, more often, an individual delegated by a group, establishes another individual or entity as consecrated, as nominated. This question, although very general, is central to the issue of classification, as you will see, because the sociologist will constantly encounter among the objects of his studies individuals who are already instituted and classified. The difficulty for the sociologist, as I said the other day, lies in the fact that the social agents he gets to study have been classified in advance, and the sociologist must recognize that he is dealing with people already classified. You will see that this has important consequences.

As the insult belongs to the class of performatives understood as a rite of institution – following Austin's original formulation – so abuse occupies a special position within this particular class of rites of institution. A remark by Ruwet shows that he was well aware of this, although he is not concerned with sociology (I think in fact that he practises sociology without realizing it, which shows that you need to know what you are doing when you practise linguistics, and especially pragmatics): the person who pronounces the insult takes a risk. The insult then has a special status within the category of the rites of degradation, which have been described by an American ethnomethodologist, Garfinkel, in an article where he analyses the rite where an officer is stripped of his epaulettes.[2] The official rite of degradation can only be accomplished by an official personage. We might say that, in order to degrade someone, you need rank – say the grade of general – whereas, to insult a car driver in the street, you can be a simple *idios*, a mere man in the street. By saying: 'You're an idiot', I am saying that I am an individual, I lay myself open. Thus abuse or insult imply a private ritual, *idios*, a singular rite committing no one but its author – the ethnologist is familiar with this kind of ritual: there are for instance the rituals of amorous magic which are practised under cover of darkness, usually by women in societies where the division of labour between the sexes assigns a negative role to women, as is often the case. And these private rituals are opposed to the public, official rituals performed by the whole group, at any rate in the presence of the whole group and by an individual mandated by the group, who is authorized to speak on behalf of the group and has the authority to practise an act of degradation on behalf of the group.

The other day I invoked Heidegger's reference to the etymology of the word 'category': category comes from the Greek *katégoreisthai*, which means 'publicly accuse', and we think of our public prosecutor.[3] The public prosecutor is someone who classifies and who says: 'You are sentenced to so many years', 'You are demoted', etc., and that classification carries the force of law. Someone classified by a public prosecutor delegated by the whole group, and pronouncing the verdict before and in the name of the whole group, has no right to argue. That person is objectively stigmatized, whereas someone classified by a mere individual venting their spleen is entitled to answer back.

We see that behind the problem of classification there lies the absolutely fundamental problem of the authority wielded by the classifier in their act of classification. Our analysis of the insult allows us to raise a certain number of questions: classifications may be practical; we can make classifications when engaged in the most everyday, commonplace and insignificant practice. We need to look into the relations between these acts and the scholar's acts of classification; such acts lead us as sociologists to wonder whose authority it is that authorizes these classifications. In other words, when we raise the question of classification, we need to know that there is a question of authority at stake. This is what we can learn from the examples of insult or abuse.

We might take the analysis of insult or abuse further (it would be interesting to discuss whether the two words are perfectly synonymous, although I do not intend to do so here). Abuse, in this perspective, appears to be an attempt or a claim to exercise authority – as Ducrot argues when discussing the performative.[4] The word 'claim' is important, for it has psychological connotations. Abuse thus appears to be an attempt or a claim to destitute – that is, to perform the opposite of instituting – to disqualify and discredit (an important word in which there is reference to 'credence', or belief: to discredit someone is to strip them of what they have been granted by common credence), by a magical act of nomination (I shall return to this 'magic') that engages only its author, but implicates that author entirely, to the point where they risk coming to an untimely end. You can risk your life by trading insult for insult: in a society of honour, insulting someone's mother, for example, may put your life at risk – these are very serious matters. And if we moved beyond the insult, and went on to look into the question of the relations between scholarship and politics (often considered in rather rhetorical and ritualistic terms), I think that we would see more clearly that a scholarly classification does in fact implicate its author profoundly as scientific subject, but hardly at all as political subject.

The insult as magical behaviour

The insult may then be described as magical behaviour – with properties that I shall return to later. What I have been saying about the insult, once we consider it as a performative, may be valid for the whole set of performatives: it is magical behaviour that aims to act, but symbolically, without resorting to action, like a curse or a blessing. Furthermore, it is magical activity that is conducted by and for the individual. Unlike the ritual of degradation, it has no institutional guarantee, authorization or authority – just like judgements of taste, which constitute another form of classification, and are often judgements of distaste. Most often, when I express 'disgust' or 'distaste', what I am actually saying is that I dislike someone else's tastes. You can confirm this by looking at the fashion columns in your magazines or newspapers, or any other articles where judgements of taste are involved. Judgements of taste are nearly always indirect judgements of distaste. Like insults, they implicate and compromise their author, who acts as a classifier, but is exposed as aggressor. This magical action then is a private act, as opposed to an official ritual of destitution or a legitimate accusation levelled by the public prosecutor.

A third characteristic is that this magical action, although performed in a personal capacity, with no institutional guarantee, does have a certain force (I shall return to this notion, which Austin and later linguists called the 'illocutionary force', that is, the force inherent in discourse). The force of this symbolic act depends partly (albeit only partly) on its form. Oddly enough, the (fairly numerous) linguists I have read forget that the social force of an insult, its power to strike home, depends on its form. I take an example from a book by Jacques Cellard, *Ça ne mange pas de pain* [That won't cost you], which collects a whole series of popular expressions with their historical origins.[5] Cellard records a ritual snub that I am sure you all know: *Arrête ton char, Ben Hur!* [literally, 'Stop your chariot, Ben Hur', with the sense here being: 'Get off your high horse']. This saying has evolved from *Arrête ton charre!*, where *charrier* meant to split hairs: hence: 'stop being clever-clever', 'stop rabbiting on', 'get off your high horse'. This is a classic case of the evolution of a popular saying, acknowledged by all ethnologists: these sayings come down over the centuries, but are constantly transformed, which is in fact why they last so long. We no longer understand *charre* (hair splitting), but hear it as *char* (chariot). This evolution is normal, but the insulter wants the audience to join in the mockery in order to give more force to the insult, and as this force can only be derived from the audience, the form of the insult has to be adjusted; in adding *Ben Hur* to *Arrête ton char*, the insulter claims a kind of spurious authority by using the classical reference in a jocular context, at once mocking it and turning it into a sort of inverse barbarism, or chic rhyming slang. Its power derives from the complicity this creates.

What I am saying about the function of insult or abuse is exactly similar to what we know of the role of the bard in archaic societies. It seems strange to describe the insult in this way, but, without wishing to be too populist, I think there is a popular inventiveness which springs from the same source as poetic creation and which consists in making a personal variant of an impersonal, common, well-known theme, while clearly remaining within the norms of the group. In so-called archaic societies, the poet is someone who is able to take a well-known formula and make it their own (in Greek verse, it might be a line from Simonides of Ceos that has come down through the centuries and is reworked and slightly reformulated each time);[6] the poet is someone who knows how to choose the right moment to take a well-known formula and modify it to suit present circumstances, thus earning the approval of the audience, and pleasing them at the same time.

This is the classical definition of charismatic behaviour – for anyone not in the know, the term 'charismatic' is taken from Weber (*charisma*, the blessing or the gift of being able to say things simply). Charismatic authority is the opposite of the administrative type of authority.[7] The general who degrades an officer is mandated by the group and he need have no charisma: he may be misshapen, lame or a hunchback and nonetheless accomplish an act of degradation, because he does not do so in his own name, but accomplishes this magical action on behalf of the group mandating him. In the case of the *idios logos*, the singular idiot, who has no resources but his own to draw on, the only way to have a modicum of illocutionary force is to use charisma, which is in this case a sort of virtuosity (Weber speaks of 'religious virtuosity'[8]) that for the case in point consists in taking a hackneyed figure of speech or trope and converting it into something personal, but at the same time, obviously, something that is common knowledge, because if no one knew who Ben Hur was, and no one understood the play on words, the joke would fall flat. It has to be at once personal and common, and that is how the individual idiot, the author of the successful insult which sends the whole pub into fits of laughter, gets their support and acquires an authority that is necessarily collective, the authority of the group. I shall not take this further, but I think that this argument opens up an important debate. In the case of the insult, the classifier asserts their claim to a symbolic authority and claims it on their own account, through the linguistic dexterity that earns them a reputation as a master of language. This is important for a social history of the insult and, obviously, for the problem that I want to discuss.

I do not propose to take this summary analysis of the insult further, since it is not my principal concern. I remind you of what I said last time: I wanted to compare the problem of classification as encountered by the sociologist with the form in which the problem is encountered by zoologists or botanists, taking the example of the insult in order to highlight one specific difficulty, and also to give a more concrete and less scholarly face to the whole argument that I was putting forward, which is that, for the sociologist, the act of classification means playing a social game consisting partly in an exercise in reciprocal classification. In order to convey something of the nature of this infinitely spiralling game, where everyone is both classifier and classified, classified by their own classifications, I chose the example of the insult. The function of this example was to show how the scientific act of classification, as practised by the sociologist, has to deal with pre-existing acts of classification, which are not necessarily inspired by the desire for knowledge that motivates the sociologist, but may be driven by a desire for action, influence, or the imposition or abolition of power.

Another question: how does the classification operated by the sociologist stand in relation to those of the botanist on the one hand and the insulter on the other? Is the sociologist closer to the insulter or the botanist? One difficulty with the narratives produced by sociologists is that they are often read with the same dispositions that we commonly employ to interpret the sense of any ordinary classificatory discourse, so that they are very often read as insults. We should look at more specific examples, but I shall leave it up to you to find them.

The analysis of the insult thus seems to me to raise the question of the status of sociological discourse on the social world, that is a science aiming to provide the neutral, universal discourse that Austin calls 'constative', which claims, not to transform the world, but to state 'what is the case', as philosophers of language say.[9] Ordinarily, the everyday social world is the place of the performative. I may be rushing into this rather too hastily, but I am ready to defend the thesis that the statements we make in everyday life are hardly ever merely constative. Even in the most anodyne utterances there are effects of imposition, intimidation and symbolic bluff; in other words, symbolic power relations are hidden – in an adjective, a silence or a grimace – beneath the surface of the apparently most rigorously constative speech. This being the case, we may say that scientific discourse will be a discourse aiming to subject the performative to its own constative ends. However, in a universe designed for the performative – to repeat in different terms what I said just now – it will be liable to revert to its performative function.

Let me give you an example. Linguists who analyse the expression 'the meeting is open' show how this expression may be understood in two different ways. Firstly, as a constative – I am someone in the room and I say: 'You know, the meeting is open'; I state a fact. Or, alternatively, I may be the chair of the meeting and say: 'The meeting is open.'

I have used a different tone of voice, but I could use the very same tone. In saying 'the meeting is open' in the performative mode, in using the verb in the performative mode, that is, with authority, with a mandate to do so, having the authority to do so and being authorized to do so, I am not merely noting that the meeting has begun, I actually make the meeting begin. And this phrase immediately becomes an inaugural rite, opening the meeting, which would not be open or even exist without it.

You could summarize my whole lecture series for the year as follows: the statement 'There are two social classes' could be heard, just like 'The meeting is open', in two ways: we might be saying 'there are two social classes, it's a given fact', we are merely noting that there are two social classes; or I may say 'there are two social classes' if I have the authority to say it, and if the fact of saying it helps to bring them into being. When, for example, in the name of a certain Marxism, some people feel authorized to say 'there are two social classes', they are adopting a performative logic, and deciding on the truth of the proposition is a problem of verification far more than validation. In other words, when it functions as a performative, the phrase 'there are two social classes' claims to verify itself, and if it is pronounced by the proper person, that is, the person who is able for example to trigger a class struggle, it will be verified. The question then is whether the performative power to verify it, to make it come true by virtue of saying it, is independent of the constative function? In order to bring the social classes into being, is it sufficient for me to have the authority to affirm their reality, or should the premise of their true existence be out there in the real world? So I wish to highlight this crucial problem immediately, at the risk of seeming enigmatic or oracular, because I want you to bear it in mind throughout my lecture course – even though I shall certainly stray away from it, I shall constantly have it at the back of my mind: what is the meaning of the expression: 'there are two social classes'?

Coding individuals

This is still part of the preliminary stage of my argument. Having analysed the relationship between sociological classification and zoological classification, and the problem of the insult, I would like to raise another issue, to introduce a third and last case which will present us with another set of problems that I believe are implicated when we speak of classes – whether social class, the gender divide or age groups. I wish to present an extremely simple problem. It is faced by any

sociologist who uses systems of coding. Coding is a typical classification procedure, because it entails allocating individuals to classes and
assigning properties to them; we take an individual who is a composite
reality (each and every one of you is an individual who has a name, a
title, and other distinctive personal attributes), but coding that individual then implies decomposing and atomizing them, analysing them out
into a series of independent, autonomous properties, capable of being
translated into singular categories. For a very ordinary enquiry, like
the study of teachers that I am working on at the moment, the process
of coding draws on the fact that the individuals who have been interviewed have revealed a certain number of properties; they have stated
their age, gender, profession, their parents' professions, their educational qualifications and the institution where they studied, and in
some cases their political opinions. What are the criteria that I should
establish in order to allocate this population to categories that correspond to its own internal articulations? This is the problem facing the
code maker: you cannot just slap down formal divisions and divide up
things that shouldn't be separated; you should divide them into classes
that are really separate in the real world. We can only code a reality if
we know it already, which raises the question of the hermeneutic circle,
a problem as old as the human sciences, but which each new generation
of ignorant beginners rediscovers as if it were a profound mystery that
threatened the progress of the social sciences. I have to say that it is in
fact a problem that is very easy to resolve – which doesn't mean that
it isn't a very serious problem – as long as we treat it in the way that I
propose to deal with it.

What, therefore, are the criteria of classification that we should
choose? Age, gender, and so forth? Any serious scholar who has
worked on a number of investigations will have a repertory of codes,
and be tempted to use age, gender, and the like on each and every occasion. There is a repetitive side to research, which tempts us not to question everything that we should question. I said this last week, but I say
it again, although I know that it is likely to annoy those of you who are
hearing it for the second time, but I accept this, because I believe that
I am right to repeat it. Contrary to received wisdom, I think that this
reflexive turn of the gaze to look back into our own scientific practice is
neither a display of spiritualist virtue by the scientist indulging in epistemological fancies in order to salvage his soul as he reaches the end of
his career, nor a waste of time, intelligence and scholarship, at least in
the social sciences (I can't speak for other disciplines, but it seems to
me to be crucial in the social sciences). In any case, it is my experience
that all important scientific progress arises from reflections apparently

unrelated to what seems to be the most urgent, immediate priority, which is, how to code in the most economical manner. Should the code cover fewer than 15,000 people, 15,000 to 70,000, 15,000 to 30,000, or 30,000 to 40,000? Is it representative of the whole population? Does my graph include . . .? and so on.

Dividing reality

My own experience leads me to believe that such reflections have unde-niable scientific fertility. They are not merely philosophical musings in the pejorative sense of the term. The problem is how to discover which criteria are pertinent (I shall return to this term), which criteria will divide up reality according to the divisions that are pencilled in, so to speak, in the real world. We need to find criteria that really distinguish groups in the real world, rather than formal criteria devised to suit the needs of the cause. But do the criteria we can draw on all have the same status in social reality, do they all have an equal operational impact? In my choice of criteria, should I rate, say, *'agrégé de l'université'* on the same level as 'only son'? Will these criteria have the same social import and the same predictive power? One of the major problems for the sociologist is how to maximize the return on their questionnaire. Anyone who devises a questionnaire knows that the main rule – which I must insist on, in case anyone here does not know how important it is – is to obtain the maximum amount of information that we consider pertinent to our quest, while using the minimum number of questions: we mustn't waste questions, we need a strategy; and if we don't have both an explicit principle of maximizing the return on the questions and also clear strategic principles directing an enquiry designed to obtain the most information with as few questions as possible, there is a risk of creating hopeless questionnaires that will not even be usable for other enquiries. To maximize the benefit of the enquiry we must therefore consider the power of the indicators we use.

What does 'the power of the indicators' mean? If you turn your minds to what I said just now about the insult and official degrading, you might see a link with the social power of indicators. To take one example: there is a difference between the numbers of years spent in study and the certificates awarded. I realize that you may not grasp the difference straight away, because it only occurred to me when I reflected along the lines that I have just suggested to you, although I had used both of these indicators for some time without questioning them. The number of years spent studying is a very good indicator, when you want to measure certain types of things such as the degree of exposure (in the sense of a photosensitive plate) to education. The diploma is something quite different; it measures a social award. Imagine two equally cultivated people: one absolutely self-taught, with no academic qualifications, certificates or credentials, and another, who has acquired the same amount of cultural knowledge, but in a form measurable by theses and educational qualifications. When it comes to the social uses of these equivalent cultures, there will be enormous differences: in the one case the simple mention of the title will give access to posts, with their salaries, privileges, perks and other advantages, and this will apply even if the candidate's culture has withered away (which does happen); in the other case, the candidate will be required to give evidence of their culture, to display it. As with the insult, the candidate will be out on a limb, will be an *idios*. But, when I choose my criteria, am I not obliged to rely on pre-existing social classifications, and the most powerful among them? What I long used to call a 'good questionnaire' (that is a questionnaire that gathers the greatest amount of pertinent information with the least possible number of questions and the least possible ambiguity and loss) would surely have to be a questionnaire capturing information that preserved all the strongest social classifications, among which, in a society like our own, academic classifications have a very special place. This is not a problem in itself, but I think that we should be aware of it. To continue with the corps of teachers: I might choose as one of my indicators the title of *agrégé*, for example. I mentioned this last time: it is a socially established qualification; the procedure of certification provides the *agrégé* with a legally guaranteed property. The whole social world conspires to invest in this title and the guarantee that it provides (I shall return to this point later). Moreover, the whole set of individuals thus designated and constituted as *agrégés*, that is, set apart from the herd (the operation of classification is expressed in the word itself),[10] and consecrated (another term that I shall return to) by the type of magical social act that is implied in any act of division, will feel themselves bonded with all the other individuals in this class. There is a Société des Agrégés, that is, a group with a spokesperson who can speak in the name of the group, which means that the members of the group thus constituted can consider it in their interest to belong to the group. This is one criterion to bear in mind.

Another example: gender as an almost inevitable criterion. Is the status of this indicator the same since the emergence of the feminist movement? I leave you to think about that. Might the emergence of a feminist movement have brought the masculine/feminine indicator closer to the *agrégé* indicator? Another example, the age group. Here the professional classifiers are happy because there is no apparent problem, but it is normally a purely arbitrary class, based on a purely formal criterion; there are no groups like those formed by the '*agrégés*' or '*normaliens*' behind this criterion.[11] In certain periods debates opposing youth to maturity do of course arise, constructed in general by adults who want to use them as a means of manipulation (we think of youth movements in the pre-Hitler era for example), but it is obvious that this criterion does not have the same predictive, constitutive status as the others. I could continue with religion, a criterion on which I could easily talk for two hours,[12] but I fear that I would bore you and repeat things that I have already dealt with. A criterion like religion is very difficult to handle, because it can function either as a badge of honour or as a stigma. The logic of the stigma and the logic of abuse ('You're nothing but a . . .') are obviously very similar and the stigmatized groups are often used as scapegoats for abuse. Another example: geographic origin.[13] As with gender, a few years ago regionalist movements were not understood in such a way as to make you think of a region south of the Loire as being in 'Occitania'. I could continue . . . This example is becoming long-winded, but I am thinking of those among you who are professional practitioners of sociology and who know what I am talking about but are tempted to forget it. In any case, the fact that I myself have often forgotten to take the advice I have just given you makes me feel authorized to say all this.

The example of socio-occupational categories

I shall take one last example from these problems of classification: that of the socio-occupational category. A time-honoured debate divides the world of sociologists, or, more precisely, those who are professional enough to consider classification as problematic (unfortunately, this is not the whole of the class . . .). Some say that they are partisans of social classification in the Marxist sense, others prefer the CSP (socio-occupational category), that is the cold, complex, bureaucratic system used by INSEE ('middle management', 'office employment', 'service sector', 'retail business', etc.). It is an academic debate and I am ready to bet that 50 per cent of the pedagogic energy spent on teaching sociology in France is devoted to this distinction – so you will allow me to spend five minutes on the subject [*laughter*]. Here too there are entire bibliographies on this CSP-versus-social-class debate, seemingly so important. Everything that I shall argue throughout this lecture series will be an attempt to undermine this opposition and to question it as I have done for the other categories (age, gender, *agrégé*, etc.). We need first to ask what kind of groups are produced by these classifications. Do they correspond to real groups, to something like the Société des Agrégés, for example? And then, do the classes produced by these two principles of classification ('class' and 'CSP') match the 'reality' we see in groups displaying the signs by which we recognize a group, such as the existence of a more or less stable administrative structure, an official delegate, plenipotentiary or spokesperson mandated to speak on behalf of the group, and so on?

Secondly, where do these classifications originate? Who devises them? Where do we situate the producers of these classifications in the space of classifiers. Are they considering things in sociological terms (enquiries into the 'social classes' tend to be more of an academic exercise), or are they dealing with 'socio-occupational categories' (which is more the province of INSEE and the administration)? These two principles of classification correspond to different social aims and functions. The CSP are constructed for the needs of economic administration, that is, to predict as accurately as possible trends in things like patterns of consumption, and so on. The social classes have a different social origin and function; they are situated in a different space, and yield benefits on another level, that of Marxist debate. In discussing this third case, that of coding, I wanted to say, as I have already shown in the case of the insult, that there are considerable differences depending on the categorems that I use when I categorize, when I classify, when I devise an ordinary code for an everyday enquiry. Categorems are enabling powers; they are *credentials*, as the English say. They are titles which function as bonds (a diploma is a certificate of credit), they are shares or investments in society; to have an academic title means that, in a wide range of circumstances – which we should define – they are officially guaranteed by the state, they allow their holders to make a legitimate claim to the advantages associated with these titles (academic position, high rank, property ownership). Among the properties that I shall select in order to characterize these individuals, some are powers (think of the English word *knowledge*, it can imply power, in the sense of 'knowledge is power', or an 'acknowledged representative empowered to act'). I think that, for a sociology of power, the use of the word 'power' in this sense is important – who guarantees these powers? The question is important. We return to the problem that I raised in the case of abuse, where the insulter is their own sole guarantor but the degrader is sponsored by the whole social order. The holder of a universally accredited academic title is guaranteed by the whole social order. The holder of an in-house qualification issued by an employer, such as the privately qualified engineer, has a certificate of passage of only local validity. The self-taught person who has followed an open-access correspondence course has no guarantee at all.

There is then a continuum among the socially guaranteed properties, from those that are universally guaranteed to those that have almost no guarantee, are accredited only in small circles, and whose only function is to impress friends and family. That is one factor. Then, alongside these socially guaranteed criteria, which from the sociologist's point of view are the most effective for understanding and classifying the real world and its articulations, there are others produced by scholars, whose knowledge of reality makes them introduce them because they believe that, although they are not officially certified, they are efficient.

Lecture of 12 May 1982

Objective classification and objectivity – Objective indicators and strategies of self-representation – Parenthesis on monumental history – The ruses of sociological reason – An objective definition of objective indicators? – The objectivist moment – The geometrical point of convergence of all perspectives – The problem of sampling

My rather long preamble may well have left more questions than answers in your minds. But, at the risk of making the list even longer, I would like to offer some justification, because I suspect that we have not yet finished with these questions, given the nature of what I believe to be their objective difficulty. I shall return to these questions and I remind you, as I said in my first lecture, that my intention is not really to transmit a complete and closed body of knowledge but rather a manner of thinking, a manner of asking questions. Something that makes what I am going to say today difficult is the fact that most of the questions we call methodological or epistemological are at the same time political questions. I shall try to show you that perfectly theoretical and procedural questions (for instance, how to select a sample? Should we include such and such a given population in the sample, etc.?) are also political questions, and this, it seems to me, is one of the difficulties specific to sociology. Even when we are not aware of it, we are always engaging in politics when we engage in sociology. It is important to realize this, in order to avoid being 'political' in the pejorative sense of the term, and as you will often see from my way of raising the issues I discuss, it is very difficult to practise sociology and have a clear, positivist conscience. A sociologist cannot practise their profession with serenity and pride. I may be generalizing from individual experience, but I prefer to admit this explicitly, because you were bound to notice it, so I wanted you to be sure to know that I am aware of it.

Objective classification and objectivity

I intend to today to launch into the first phase of my analysis of classification: what is an objective classification? Briefly, the procedure that I shall follow is to approach the question from a viewpoint that we might call objectivist, or one that adopts the logic of a social physics and assumes that the problems of classification present themselves to the sociologist in the same terms that they do to a physicist, or at least to anyone who deals with matters that may be treated as physical realities. I shall then proceed to try to show how this objectivist perspective becomes dangerous if we forget that, in practice, the objects classified also classify in their turn. I shall therefore take a critical look at the objectivist posture in order to lead on to a description of the practical logic of classification. I then hope to show how we may construct a theory of classification that integrates both the objectivist and the practical perspectives. That is my basic approach. What is an objective classification? As sociologists, we use the word 'objective', in the French sense, in very different circumstances. We may say for example that 'a diploma is an objective indicator of a person's position in the distribution of cultural capital', that 'pronunciation is an objective indicator of membership of a class', and so on. We speak of the 'objective meaning' of a practice, of the 'objective truth' of a practice. As an example, I intend in a moment to read you a text where I find to my surprise that I have used the word 'objective' three times. This banal word, which rolls so easily off the tongue, is laden with a whole social and political philosophy, and someone really ought to write a history of its social usage. In its political usage it is usually a very tendentious word. It is a 'categorem', in the full sense of the word, it is an accusation; when we tell someone that they are 'objectively' something, it is not good news for them. It is very important to know this because it is one of the reasons why sociologists are so tempted to use the term, but it is also one of the objective reasons why so many people are quite justifiably infuriated by sociologists.

If we didn't bear in mind these very important social connotations, the word 'objective' would function as a kind of political law-enforcement agency. We could elaborate a bogus sociological discourse that would preserve appearances and yet would be based on all sorts of impressionistic senses of the word 'objective'. After listing the ways in which I see terms such as 'objective', 'objectivism', 'objective meaning', 'objective guilt' or 'objective error' working, I would like to judge how far I find their use for ordinary scientific practice legitimate. For example, the term 'objective indicators' designates by and large the characteristics, indices, signs and symbols, among other things, which reveal something that the person showing them is unaware of. What we are aiming to do, then, is to draw attention to what a certain kind of behaviour reveals, rather than what it proclaims. This is a right claimed by all the social sciences and this is where the logic of the objectivist stage of research resembles that of a trial. We need to bear in mind that social science does in many ways have much in common with a trial. When I was teaching sociology, I often commented on a very interesting text where Claude Bernard discusses the relationship between the biologist and nature and says: 'We often need to preach what is false in order to know what is true.'[1] I consider that a good sociologist, at some stage or other of his work, must obviously conceal what he is looking for in order to have some chance of finding it. He must extract from his respondent things that are practically unknown to the object of his enquiry.

An objective indicator is therefore an indicator that causes people to reveal something they are unaware of. I think, for example, of Panofsky's formula for the flying buttress, which, until the final flowering of the Gothic, was hidden beneath the roof: 'There comes a moment when we discover what the flying buttress is disguising and therefore what it is stating.'[2] The role of all science is to try to go beyond what the thing in question reveals of itself: this is valid for a flying buttress, a manuscript, an interview, someone's style of behaviour or choice of vocabulary, and so on. This is all the more important when the object of study resists: when it is the church, the episcopate, or a secretary general of the episcopate, that is, people who hold powerful positions at the heart of such institutions and whose incorporated strategies constitute these institutions, it is obvious that the enquiry engages in a symbolic struggle where the sociologist seeking the truth must conceal the aims of their quest. There are many different ways of tackling sociological research, but we often approach it with a kind of naive humanism, believing that we may discover the truth by talking face to face with the object of our enquiry. I think that we have to renounce this vision, which is morally comforting but scientifically sterile. We have to choose between deceiving or being deceived. When we interview a business executive about business management or a bishop about the episcopate, we have every likelihood of being symbolically manipulated.[3] Using objective criteria means this: a person tells me the whole story, but I look away and study their shoes, or some such thing, and reflect on what it is they are not telling me.

Objective indicators and strategies of self-representation

Having made this point, we may now proceed more rapidly. An objective indicator basically represents something that allows us to sidestep the strategies of presentation of self, as Goffman describes them.[4] These strategies may affect individuals – I think of one of Balzac's heroes who, whenever he goes to meet someone, strikes a pose. There are in life situations where we draw ourselves up as if posing for a portrait. There is also a sociology of collective strategies of self-presentation. As individuals we elaborate our own personal strategies by drawing on an arsenal of collective strategies acquired from here, there and everywhere.

And there are also strategies of self-presentation that are more formidable for the sociologist, and these are group strategies, which complicate the problem. I shall give you an example of what an objective indicator is, analysing the presentation of self that any group uses in trying to impose its own objective self-definition. I have written somewhere that what defines a dominant individual is their ability to impose their own perception of themselves on others.[5] This is the role of the portrait, the bust, or the equestrian statue: the dominant individual is the one who, as in Byzantine mosaics, is able to oblige you to look at them from near or far, but whether from a distance or close up, always with respect. They are the master of the subjective relationship that others may entertain with them. This is in fact the very definition of symbolic violence. It is true of individuals as it is *a fortiori* of institutions, which, when they present themselves, are presenting the norms according to which we should perceive them, and are saying: 'I insist on being considered with respect, that is, from a distance, from here or there, in this way or that, in profile rather than full face . . .'. As soon as we realize that it is through strategies of self-presentation that individuals or institutions elude objectification, it is these strategies of imposition of the image of the self that become the indicators. We can learn a lot about an individual or an institution through an analysis of the strategies they use to prevent us from learning what it is they don't want to tell us. One might make an excellent comparative study of the strategies of self-presentation, for example in portraits, official correspondence or *Who's Who*, where 'celebrities' are asked to present themselves. A celebrity is someone who should present himself or herself in a certain way, who should say some things about themselves and not reveal others.

Managing to bring to light what I call the objective indicators is not at all easy. If you take a group like the bishops that I am studying at the moment, for example, or teachers in higher education,[6] the sociologist is immediately confronted with images which may legitimately be perceived as strategies that have to be acknowledged, precisely because they are designed to pre-empt the sociologist's vision. For example, the bishops 'advance in disguise',[7] sheltered by their image of unity. Commenting on a sociological enquiry in *Informations catholiques internationales*, a canon says that bishops are all the same, that there are just minor differences between them, but nothing very important. Sociologists echoing *Informations catholiques internationales*, using the same statistics, will repeat that 'it is a very homogeneous population',[8] retranslating it into scholarly language and speaking of 'mean' and 'median', rather than simply 'average'. This is what the sociologist is up against. This strategy of manipulating one's self-image can be very sophisticated when handled by an institution aware of itself, and aware of the fact that its power base is rooted in the symbolic. An institution whose mastery of the social world depends on symbolic power has the utmost interest in being the master of its self-image, which is the foundation of its symbolic power. At the same time, in the case of the church, we encounter strategies operating on two different levels: there are strategies of presentation (such as press conferences, whose spokespeople will be carefully chosen), but there can also be strategies of manipulation within the group itself. For instance, you might appoint an archbishop with a regional accent to Paris, if it is useful for the Archbishop of Paris, as a representative of the church, to seem to be born of the people. Faced with this, sociologists have to give themselves the means to look behind this screen of received ideas – it is part of their job not to be naive, which does not mean that they are necessarily reductive, hostile or suspicious.

I have spoken of the conscious and explicit manipulation of the terms in which the institution may be discussed, as well as the manipulation of the institution itself, which is achieved by the choice of the individual agents who are presented up front or who lurk in the background. I refer you to the article by Sylvain Maresca in *Actes de la recherche en sciences sociales* on the different styles of dress adopted by the representative of the farmers' trade union:[9] he dresses differently depending on whether he is meeting another farmer, or negotiating with an official. This manipulation then does not just involve ideology, that is, 'ideas', 'arguments' and 'language' – it is embodied in the very material of the performance prepared for perception.

Parenthesis on monumental history

There is a further level, which will be of particular interest to any historians among you. Historians find manuscripts that are memorials, or monuments – I refer you to Nietzsche's text on monumental history.[10] Monuments are memorials that we leave behind in order to remind those who come after us how good and just and beautiful we were. We are left with something that is the result of an operation, whether conscious or unconscious, which we might suppose to be motivated by the desire to produce a legitimate image of the self. In a book on Roman civilization by Paul Veyne,[11] there is a description of Augustus's work, which shows how those in power manipulate in advance the way they are perceived both *in vivo* and *post mortem*. Augustus is a very interesting example because he worked as it were for posterity. There are people who are able to produce an everlasting image in order to assure themselves a worldly form of eternal life, which is the eternal life of the document, memorial or monument.

Institutions spend a lot of time preparing their heritage, and the sociologist is constantly faced with two contradictory pitfalls: either an institution offers you documents and says: 'Look at this, you will find it interesting, do look.' Or it withholds documents, telling you 'this one is confidential', 'this one is no good', or 'come back later'. Or, even worse, it has no documents to show you, and, if you fail to ask certain questions, there is a whole slice of reality that fails to materialize. I have said this rather rapidly but it is very important, at any rate in my experience of research. I think for example that the whole sociology of the church (you should handle with care propositions that are introduced by 'the whole' . . .) is to a considerable extent controlled by these two types of manipulation, which the 'church' (in quotation marks, to remind us that it refers to a complex ensemble) performs on the data available to study the church, its clergy and lay members, its practising and non-practising congregation.

To be more precise, I wish simply to say that one of the central problems of the church, which was the first institution to provide itself with a team of in-house sociologists (the university still does not have one), is to understand the behaviour of its lay members:[12] Why do fewer and fewer Catholics attend mass? Why do some continue to attend? Faced with this kind of problem, the church has mobilized its resources, and also enlisted the help of its congregation, to catalogue the characteristics of the faithful; it has indulged in market research into religious practice. In so doing, it immediately attracts the attention of sociologists by providing them with ready-made statistics, which sociologists love, because they find it so much easier than having to calculate them for themselves. But by providing documents or material, the church avoids all consideration of any questions that it neglects to raise. For example, there is no investigation at all of how the numbers of priests or members of religious orders may be changing according to gender or age. There is therefore a whole raft of potential requests for information swept aside by the fact that the institution comes to greet you offering its own information about itself. This is why it is so vital to insist that the object of research must be constructed. This is not an arbitrary methodological precept. (The drama is that so much of the most successful historical research is a 'gift of the gods' – we 'happen upon'[13] the archives of a major eighteenth-century Genevan publisher, who published the *Encyclopédie*. And Darnton proceeds to make a very fine analysis of it.[14] But, since we find such things ready-made, we don't ask ourselves questions like: 'If I had intended to look for this, what sort of model would I have needed to construct?' or 'What resources would I have had to draw on in order to discover what was interesting?', and so on. I think that this is the fundamental trap for the sociologist, and *a fortiori* for the historian, who is not free to choose. I shall now close this parenthesis, which is slowing the progress of my lecture, but is a useful exercise in practice.)

The ruses of sociological reason

I return to the indicators that are called 'objective' in the legitimate jargon of research teams. These indicators provide the information on individuals, institutions and groups that they are either unwilling to reveal or are unaware of; the most crucial point being that most of the information that interests the sociologist is not really secret, but merely remains in a latent, practical state, where nobody actually possesses it. It is in the interaction between the person who reveals something without realizing it and the person who records it that scientific truth may emerge. People give this information sometimes unwittingly, sometimes unwillingly. For example, in dialogues with members of the church, one of the objective ruses of sociological reason is to exploit the fact that the respondents hide things that they are not asked and do not hide the things that the sociologist is seeking to find: they are mistaken as to what they should hide. This supposes a carefully calculated strategy, and also poses the problem – to which I shall return – of the myth of the sociologist's unbiased interview, a sort of 'sounding board' that merely listens and records. If what I have argued is right, you will

immediately see that this myth of neutrality is in fact designed to legitimize all the effects of imposition exerted by the object of the enquiry on
the would-be scientific subject.

Objective indicators are therefore things that people reveal
unwittingly. Sociolinguists, who delve much deeper than the most
sophisticated sociologists, manage to grasp the most elusive facts: The
number or the type of liaisons, the fact of using the genitive case or
not, addressing people with the formal 'vous' or the informal 'tu'.[15]
Sociolinguists therefore adopt from the outset an approach that
admits their loss of control. All social behaviour is necessarily 'mul-
ticoded'. (I borrow this barbarous term from the linguists: it implies
that it is impossible for a speaker to control every level of the code: if
you control your syntax you lose your grip on the vocabulary; if you
control the vocabulary you cannot check your pronunciation, and in
addition your gestures may contradict your pronunciation or syntax
or semantics.) So, however hard you try, the sociologist will always
have something to work on, *a fortiori* if he makes you discuss matters
of taste, for example: if you are cautious over your tastes in music, you
will let slip your tastes in painting, and when you talk of cuisine you
will betray the truth of your musical tastes. This is what makes sociology possible, this is how it works.

I now return to the ways of announcing oneself. The practices of
self-representation are not neutral; they do yield information; even
the refusal to respond is very interesting. As soon as you are faced
with a scientific enquiry – or in fact any enquiry in general – as soon
as someone asks you a question, you've had it, even if you refuse. You
are caught up in the 'dialectic of honour':[16] as soon as you are challenged, whatever you do, you fall into the trap. In this way the sociologist launches an aggressive assault that forms a stranglehold you can
only unlock by releasing objective information. I shall return to this
question.

I should have spent less time on this rather basic topic, but I want
to take it a little further. I want to look at what it is to question people
about what they are, what it is to try to discover facts they are unaware
of or try to conceal. Taking this to be the problem of classification I
mentioned at the outset, I can approach individuals, groups, institutions or their representatives, I can arrange to conduct interviews
with individuals or with groups. Among the things that sociologists
often forget to question are the form and method of their enquiry.
For instance, if we are trying to investigate a group, what is the status
of an enquiry that focuses on the individuals who compose or belong
to those groups? To confirm what I have already suggested: most

epistemological questions are also political questions. For instance, when there is a strike, there is often a debate over how representative the union delegates representing the working class or some particular group are: the conservative authorities challenge the union delegates by resorting to an electoral type of consultation, that is, an individual scenario, where each individual voter is isolated in the polling booth. They hope to use the true opinion that should emerge from the sum of the intentions of the individuals, expressed in their individual choices, in order to challenge the truth put forward by the group, or on its behalf, as it emerges from the arguments of the spokespeople mandated to speak for them. This is the famous debate over the relation between the political apparatus and the grass roots: does what Georges Marchais[17] says coincide with what we would find if we polled a representative sample of all the members of the Communist Party? This typically political question lies at the heart of the problem that I intend to discuss in this series of lectures.

The sociologist who wishes to study 'social classes', 'age groups' or 'generations', and who chooses as the object of the experiment a sample of individuals drawn at random, is adopting a methodological but also a political and social bias towards the reality being investigated; he runs the risk of becoming the objective transmitter of a theory that is implicit within the group, which is a problem if the aim is to study what it is that constitutes a group. This is what I want to argue: in the case of enquiring into the nature of a group like the church, I should ask myself whether the best idea is to question all the lay members, or all the clergy. Here we already have a problem of definition. In the history of the sociology of religion, some say that 'the church is all of the clergy', others that 'the church is all of the clergy and its lay members'. This is a bone of contention within the internal politics of the church, and it presents us with a scientific dilemma. To choose whether to question individuals or representatives is a scientific gambit. In medieval canon law, it was the bishops who were declared to be the church; today we would not put it in quite those terms. Should I question just the bishops, all of the clergy, or the whole congregation of the faithful? Many people, I imagine, will think: 'But this is child's play, I do hope that Bourdieu is aware that there are theories of sampling.' However, it is not a question of sampling at all. In fact, theories of representative sampling will provide statistically representative answers, but is statistical representation not precisely something that any institution worthy of the name can outmanoeuvre by appointing representatives who may be representative, without being statistically representative? History is full of declarations that would not stand up to the most elementary poll.

Questioning people one by one is an important means of grasping at least *one* aspect of the objective truth of allegedly representative institutions. But it would be a serious mistake to believe that this objective truth of the institution as represented is the whole truth of the institution, in so far as the whole truth includes the fact that its representatives may not be representative. So it may be important, in an enquiry worthy of the name, to add to a survey of individuals questioned separately, a survey addressed to their spokespeople, who are also, in another guise, the institution.

I have chosen this example deliberately because I wanted to demonstrate how, in the very process of deciding who or what to question, the problem that I propose to discuss throughout this lecture series is already virtually formulated: what is a group? When does a group start to exist? Does it start to exist when someone can say that they are the group and they can speak on its behalf? This problem presents itself in the very manner of approaching the object of the enquiry, and there is a danger of providing a catastrophically bad solution to the problem before it has even been formulated. There is then an objective truth to be detected in the practice of the sociologist. And, as I always say, one way we can hope to avoid scientific error is to constantly pay attention to the objective truth that sociologists may unwittingly reveal to be at work in their practice, both in their research and in their conclusions.

To recapitulate this first point, I would like to say that, in order to try to escape the pressures imposed whether consciously or unconsciously by the object of the enquiry, the sociologist can either turn towards the statistical type of survey where the individuals are taken one by one and questioned in such a way as to make them reveal truths that they are unaware of, or proceed in what we might call an ethnographic or ethnological way and analyse all sorts of things: the discourse produced by the institution, legal systems (such as canon law), ritual procedures (the consecration of bishops). These two approaches, which are rarely undertaken by the same person, are often seen as contradictory for the silliest of reasons: because of the historical tradition of the French education system, we have ethnologists on the one hand and sociologists on the other, and both parties, whether to disguise their limitations or to transform their limitations into methodological virtues, are proud of not doing what the other does. These two procedures, which seem to me to be complementary, are both inspired by the concern to grasp an objective truth. More precisely, I think that it is in the confrontation of the two objective truths revealed by two different approaches that we may discover the true nature of what constitutes a group, a truth involving a complex relationship between what is on display and what actually happens, both at an individual level, and at the level of the state, the church, and the various administrative bodies.

An objective definition of objective indicators?

My questions about objective indicators contain in embryo a further series of questions, which I hope you may already have thought of: is there an objective definition of objective indications? When I include in my questionnaire 'has written "Student Guides"', what right have I to make such an act of 'constitution' (the word constitution being taken either in the traditional philosophical sense or in the sense of constitutional law), what right to constitute this factor as worthy of being detected, noted and recorded as pertinent when it comes to understanding what takes place in a university institution?

When I say 'objective', even before I start to think about it I have in mind something that all sociologists worthy of the name (I insist, those 'worthy of the name') would agree on. We might expect objectivity to be exemplified in the act of 'saying the same thing': *homologein*, for the Greeks. '*Homologein*' is an important word in so far as there is a kind of social 'homologation' or consensus that is in competition with scientific consensus; and one of the main problems for the social sciences is the balance of power between scholars and society when each accredits something different as most pertinent and important. If I accept that the objective criteria are defined by the agreement of scholars worthy of the name, I am postulating that there is in a way a judge to judge the criteria; so either I am trapped in a circular argument – which may be embarrassing – or I am engaging in a sort of pyramidal logic, with a supreme judge somewhere out there, an agency able to judge judgements on the legitimacy of criteria.

I started with an abstract formulation, now I shall try to be more concrete. In fact, I think that this '*homologein*', this 'saying the same thing', or consensus, does not exist. A *trend report*[18] on the social classes – and our libraries are full of them – would show that all attitudes towards them are possible: for some people social classes do not exist at all, for others they are omnipresent, and there are those who say that there is only one class, and so on. Since all attitudes are possible, the sociologist cannot appeal to the *consensus omnium*, a consensus of the scholarly and scientific community endorsing the social community's consensus on what should be called 'objective'. This is a long-running debate that I feel honour bound to raise, because it is important not to disguise the state of the debate within the social sciences and because it is capital, given the particular status of the social sciences, to know that there is no minimal consensus on such a fundamental topic. To give you my honest opinion, the fact that someone can still say that there is no such thing as social class without being disqualified as a sociologist seems to me to reveal how detached the scientific universe and particularly its social sciences are from the rest of the intellectual universe. But I don't want to launch into this all too familiar debate; it is rather too reminiscent of the debate on social class that takes place in hung-over Monday morning seminars.

How does the problem of ratification by society of the scholars' objective judgement of objective criteria arise in practice? A criterion can be said to be objective if all the scholars consulted were obliged to consider it inevitable, pertinent and indispensable. But is it the force of a true idea that compels them to concur? Or is it the polite social conventions that rule the scholarly universe (if the group considers my opinions ridiculous, I lose status and respect)? This would be enough to sustain an entirely false science. To take the two extremes, is the constraint purely social or purely scientific?

To take this debate on social class within the scientific universe a stage further, we might say that 'a criterion is objective when it is not subjective, that is, when it is neutral, and does not involve any value judgement on my behalf': this is what Weber calls 'ethical neutrality'. This thesis, which I have made seem rather ridiculous and caricatural, can obviously have a social function, and be a political weapon at certain moments in time, given that the universe of sociology is constantly obliged to reassert its autonomy in the face of external pressure. In this occasional text, Weber [19] wanted to affirm that there was such a thing as ethical neutrality, and that it concerned the scholar. But that is as far as it goes. It is a laudable political strategy, which is morally respectable, noble even, but I doubt whether we can build a science on something as meagre and disappointing as ethical neutrality.

The objectivist moment

So, how then does the scholar proceed in doing research? As a zoologist. It cannot be enough to use the argument that: 'The criteria are objective because they are neutral.' When I say that I classify teachers of classical literature according to whether they publish with Klincksieck or Les Belles Lettres, I have no personal stake in the matter. I have no connection with either publisher, I am not myself a teacher of classical literature, I have no friends in either camp; moreover, I'm not at all sure what this criterion corresponds to, but it seems pertinent to me because it appears to divide people. There I touch upon what I believe to be an objective meaning: it is a criterion that seems to me to split people into opposing factions, and does so through a set of criteria linked to one another in a pertinent and meaningful way, in such a way that it is out of my hands, I am no longer the classifier, I am caught up in a network of interrelated criteria that are linked by correlations that I can measure. I can draw up a table, distribute people as individuals or even institutions, since we might be looking at the Collège de France, the École des Hautes Études en Sciences Sociales, the École des Chartes, the École Polytechnique, or government ministries, for instance. In this way I can distribute social phenomena across an objective space so that the relations arising between the things thus constituted can be called objective because they are both necessary and independent (independent, obviously, in the eyes of the observer). For example, if I construct the space of teachers in higher education, we could reasonably admit that the fact that I belong to this space myself is not an obstacle and does not affect my perception, except in so far as it has helped me discover the hidden indices which, if I were an ignorant outsider, I would not have known how to exploit.[20] Thus I can construct a space in which I am fully present, and yet at the same time where I am not an active participant, and this objective space will enable anyone in my place, that is, equipped with my data and my computer, to discover exactly what I have discovered. This would then be proof of my objective scholarship, the supreme triumph of the scientific enterprise. I shall return to this, but I have taken too long already. Next time I shall take this further, but also return to the sources of the argument.

This objectivist, would-be scientific search aims to constitute a space endowed with a quasi-material objectivity, within which individuals are distributed according to laws that escape them, but which our research makes apparent even to those who are the very object of that research. Within this space, there may arise artificial divisions (resulting from certain methods of classification), once the programme and the algorithms have been set. The classification may be made independently of any subjective individual, and consequently the classifications take on the firmness and the opacity of material objects; in fact, they are laws, rules, constants and relations absolutely analogous to those established by the physicist. We are therefore in the world of the physicist and we have sets of criteria related to each other by relations that may be weighed and measured – here I am thinking of Antoine-Laurent de Jussieu's criticism of Linnaeus's classification: 'non numeranda, sed ponderanda' ('it is not sufficient to count up, one should weigh up').[21] We can assign a weight to each of these criteria and say to what extent it contributes to delivering the class, and the relationships that define that class. This type of objective classification assigns a position to each social agent, and enables us to deal with objective social classes. The social classes constructed in this way in *Distinction*[22] are thus objective classes, that is, units obtained by applying a set of interrelated criteria, and in this way we obtain the whole set of classes by applying to the population concerned the whole set of the criteria and the principles of distribution or hierarchization that are required to generate the real structure of this population.

The geometrical point of convergence of all perspectives

At this hyper-objectivist and rather frightening level the sociologist becomes a returning officer, or accountant, commanding an overview of the situation. My description of the sociologist would then match Hegel's definition of absolute knowledge, where he says that each social subject has a different perspective on the world, and the fact that any kind of social knowledge is necessarily perspectival is what we mean by 'ideology'. And science, that is, philosophical or scientific knowledge, would then be, as Leibniz would have said, the fact of being able to place ourselves at the 'geometral', the geometrical point of convergence of all perspectives,[23] that is at the geometrical position where all of these perspectives meet in a divine viewpoint where there is no point of view. I can cite the example of what I call the intellectual field, that space within which what we see as intellectual prizes (publications, celebrity, etc.) are played for. I might, as has so often been done in the past, write *L'Opium des intellectuals*[24] – that is to say, present a particular view of left-wing intellectuals. I might equally, as Simone de Beauvoir did in an important article that appeared at more or less the same time, 'La pensée de droite, aujourd'hui',[25] discuss only the intellectuals of the other persuasion. In other words, it is possible to base a viewing position of the intellectual field on an opposition within the intellectual field itself. On the other hand, I might construct the intellectual field as a competitive space within which the very concept of the intellectual is called into question – one of the challenges of the intellectual field consists in saying: 'This person *is* an intellectual, but a right-wing "intellectual" is not an intellectual at all.' As soon as I construct the notion of a field, I can adopt a viewpoint overlooking these points of view and construct even the very idea of a struggle to establish this intellectual field. I thus place myself in a quasi-divine position, which, I must insist, does not prevent me from being a player involved in the game, and my analysis of the game will immediately be recycled within the game according to people's positions in the game, and even better understood by those who occupy a subordinate position in the intellectual field, who generally have a greater interest in learning the scientific truth.

(This is a most interesting and very important problem: I think that there is an affinity, declared by Marx in quasi-theological terms, between the position of the dominated and the scientific position. I think that there can be scientific grounds for this, which does not mean that it is sufficient to be dominated in order to see the scientific truth. But once the scientific truth is produced, those in the space who are dominated hear it more clearly, and immediately make use of it, reworking and recycling it so that it expresses them more fully. This is a parenthesis, but it is relatively important, and I may return to it.)

I am in a divine position, I have an overview of all the viewpoints, and I constitute each and every viewpoint as a partial, singular, unilateral vision, taking its essential structure from its position in the space that I have constructed. In other words, I construct both the viewpoint adopted and the position from which this viewpoint is adopted, by reconstructing the perspective. To construct the viewpoint as viewpoint, we obviously have to construct the space. The characteristic of a viewpoint is not to see itself as a viewpoint, but to believe itself to be absolute. Sociologists see different views – I have explained how this works for the intellectual field, but the same would apply for the social classes – and will have their own particular view of the struggle to view the social world, as well as an overview of the viewpoint from which we view the social world. I can construct the universe of viewpoints, with all its structures and limits, and I can say: 'From this overview of the social world, I understand everything there is to see, and I understand people who can see nothing in another person's viewpoint other than that "They are all bastards", for instance.'

That having been said, is this the alpha and the omega of science? Is this the point of no return? Is the objective viewpoint that I have tried to describe an absolute viewpoint? Is the sociologist finally able to contemplate the spectacle as if it were a photograph? To survey the scene, empowered by modern techniques and statistics, and see what everyone is doing now, what they will be doing tomorrow, and predict where people in one place today will be in five years' time, etc. This is one of the great temptations for the sociologist; if you want to be a sociologist, it is because you want to enjoy that vision, to feel that you are almost God (taking the word to stand for whatever you happen to believe in, of course . . .).

I would however like to indicate where the flaw in this lies, and this will be the starting point for my next session. Just now I asked: 'Is there a judge able to judge the criteria of judgement?', and I propose finally to read a splendid text by Wittgenstein, where he speaks of the standard metre in Paris and says: 'There is one thing of which we can neither say that it is one metre long, nor that it is not one metre long, and that is the standard metre in Paris'.[26] This is a good metaphor for philosophical analysis. It is a distinctly unusual manner of thinking for our climes . . . It is the same problem as when someone asks whether there is a judge to judge the judges,[27] a principle to legitimize the principles of legitimacy, or a criterion for evaluating criteria.

This vision may appear absurdly theoretical, but it occurs quite concretely in scientific practice, when we face the problem of dividing up the objects of our studies. To take the example that I started to answer just now, it is precisely this: one of the contentious issues within the intellectual field is how to identify an intellectual. When someone starts an article by writing 'I shall call an intellectual whoever is this, or that', it's a lost cause, there is no point in reading any further, we know that they will find nothing that they themselves have not placed in their own article, that is, not very much . . . In fact, what is at the heart of an intellectual field – and you only need to have met one intellectual to know this – is precisely the struggle to discover what an intellectual is, that is, to impose the legitimate definition of an intellectual, which can admit only one legitimate representative: the person who is formulating the definition. But although I say this tongue in cheek, it is normal, it is the name of the game. However, the rules of the game also mean that it has to be hidden.

The problem of sampling

Let me finally take a simple example. For my research into management, I took a population of two hundred employers from the most important businesses, and, in my definition, I included bankers and industrial tycoons. One of my colleagues in History (this was no accident: the suggestion would never have come from a sociologist because sociology does not seek out this degree of *homologein*) had taken the precaution, before coming to discuss management with me, of reviewing my statistical analysis; and he had to reluctantly admit that he agreed with me, except on one point that he failed to understand, one where there was a mismatch among the populations. That seemed very interesting to me, for I had deliberately included bankers in my space, whereas he had excluded them.[28] Which proves that, using the would-be scientific definition that I gave just now, it is possible to *homologein*, to code the same criteria, and come to the same conclusion at the end of the analysis, while this *homologein* may yet allow a kind of fundamental disagreement to remain, that is, the initial bias to study one thing rather than another, in this case whether or not to include financial capital. The topic was the degree of domination by financial capital, with the simple problem of choosing a sample, but behind this choice there was another, scientific, choice to be made. However, in this case we can say that the debate could still be settled on scientific grounds, that we could *homologein*, and ask: 'Which one of you gave the right explanation for what happens in the space that both of you have constructed?'

I can also take the example of university academics, an even clearer example. I shall be brief, because it is exactly similar. Among the indicators used for teachers in higher education, I can introduce membership of the editorial board of a literary review. But, in the eyes of a certain number of academics, an academic who publishes with the *NRF*[29] is no longer an academic; an academic who writes for *Critique*,[30] or worse, for *Libération*,[31] is no longer worthy of the title of professor. The act of nomination and constitution operated by the sociologist: 'I call professor someone whose profile includes the fact of being a member of an editorial board', is thus quite an act of aggression, it is taking sides in the very struggle to discover where the dividing line should be drawn. This is a test case, as was financial capital, but even in less extreme cases, the very fact of selecting criteria that will reveal the conflict between teaching and research, and the very way in which we construct our object, will themselves operate a critical break not only with the representations familiar to the population concerned, but also with reality, because in the real world one of the issues at stake is precisely to identify who is engaged in research. If everyone is involved in some form of research or other, how do you devise a code without taking sides?

There comes a moment when you will have the choice either to accept that all things are equal (and then you can no longer classify anything) or, precisely, to take sides and say: 'I shall call "genuine research" research that has been translated into five languages, for example' (and then you will transgress all the norms of ethical neutrality). This is the issue that I would like to return to next time: we cannot construct a social space, with all its divisions and so on, and forget that the objective categories which we use to establish what is objective are themselves a contentious issue, and that they can at any moment be overturned.

Lecture of 19 May 1982

The legitimate definition of the principle of definition – Operations of research as acts of constitution – Classification as an object of conflict – Objectifying objectivism – Good classification and scholastic bias – Theoretical classification and practical classification

Today I would like to draw some first conclusions from my lectures to date. I have tried to show that we might call 'objective classification' a classification obtained by using a set of criteria linked to each other to varying degrees, which can be measured statistically and thereby determine classes that we might call objective, that is, existing in material reality in a latent state. These classes, that we might call 'latent classes',[1] after Lazarsfeld, are constructed classes which do not necessarily exist in the conscious minds of the individual subjects concerned. They may even be rejected or repressed by them, and are often constructed despite their intentions or claims. These objective or latent classes can be derived through perfectly rigorous procedures; 'scale analysis',[2] for instance, allows us to produce mechanical and automatic forms of classification and provide a technical solution to the problem of the relations between the criteria chosen and between the classes. I contrasted this objective classification with the practical classifications that the individual social subjects actually make use of in practice. In passing, I pointed out a certain number of questions that any classifier faces on passing from objective classification to practical classification, even while often failing or refusing to notice them.

The legitimate definition of the principle of definition

One of the charges that people often level against sociology, especially sociology driven by consciously theoretical intentions, is that it finds in reality what it has put there: which means that the constructions of the sociologist (for example, correspondence analysis, or analysis of consumption according to class) would be the product of a sort of vicious circle. The argument more or less explicitly advanced in scientific debates is that if the sociologist had not been looking for what he found, he would not have found it. This is an important consideration since it affects the limits of any objective classification: classifiers disagree over the legitimate principles of classification and here I have evoked Wittgenstein's paradox of the standard metre: 'There is one thing of which one can state neither that it is one metre long, nor that it is not one metre long, and that is the standard metre in Paris. But this is, of course, not to ascribe any remarkable property to it, but only to mark its peculiar role in the game of measuring with a metre rule.'[3]

As I pointed out last time, the problem of the criterion needed to judge the right criterion arises even at the level of relations between scholars, whereas the problem of legitimacy in general is that there is no judge to judge legitimacy. This hermeneutic circle, which is at the same time a circle of legitimacy, is constantly encountered (I analysed two or three examples in my last lecture) both on the level of the construction of the population – this was the example of whether or not to include the bankers in the study of management – and on the level of the construction of criteria. One example that particularly struck me and was the basis of my sociological research in the years 1962–1963 was this: the students of UNEF (a student union classified as left-wing) had themselves organized an enquiry into the student milieu and had entirely ignored the criterion of social origin. This is a good example of a group imposing its own definition, by the simple omission of a criterion that might introduce divisions that the group refused to admit. At that time students, or at least some of their spokespeople, wanted to affirm themselves as a class, in any case as a 'group on the move', and the simple fact of suppressing social origins in their questionnaire, and *a fortiori* in the statistical treatment of the results, produced a very significant ideological effect.[4] Examining analogous examples, like that of the bishops, which I mentioned, would show how the researcher can exercise his objectifying action by the simple fact of introducing a criterion rejected by the indigenous members, and thereby reveal divisions that are unsuspected, denied or repressed by them.

This problem of the legitimate definition of the principle of definition is encountered at every turn in even the most mundane enquiry. Let me give you a very naive and ordinary, but real example. During a discussion with the statisticians of INSEE over the coding of patterns of consumption, I pointed out that, if they constructed a class of 'fruit' which lumped together bananas, oranges, mandarins, lemons and apples, for instance, or a class of 'beans' that included both French beans and baked beans, they would prevent themselves from finding the slightest correlation with social class or income, given that the banana is the anti-apple and what leads to eating lots of bananas leads to eating very few apples, and vice versa. The same is true for French beans and baked beans.[5] This seemingly insignificant example is in fact absolutely central: if you don't have the hypothesis that there could be a pertinent heterogeneity within the class 'fruit' or the class 'beans', and that this heterogeneity is significantly related to social class, you will fail to record this heterogeneity. But, if you do note it, you will immediately be suspected by those who would not have noted it of having introduced it *a priori*, tendentiously, as if to adapt reality to suit your desires.

There are in the social world a great many facts that you can only see if you solicit them; otherwise anyone could call themselves a sociologist. Durkheim himself denounced the illusion of transparency as the principal obstacle to social knowledge.[6] There are many things in the social world which are only revealed when they are discovered. And the work of the sociologist, like the work of the philosopher in certain definitions of philosophy, consists in the labour of bringing to light, dis-covering, things whose existence you can only suspect if you already know something about them.

Operations of research as acts of constitution

Of course, this way of imposing classification can always be denounced as biased, even if it is validated by the facts. This is a problem that I shall tackle in the second part of this course, in my next lectures: that there is a relation between the approach to the social world entailed by a research project and the researcher's position in the social world. I did mention this problem briefly the other day, when I raised the question of whether there was a link between the scientific viewpoint and the world view held by the dominated, and what the nature of this link might be. More generally, we might wonder whether our position in the social space predisposes us to see, or not see, the hidden side of the social world. Classifications of the kind 'fruit' or 'beans', which are the result of automatic thinking rather than any serious reflection, are particularly common among people occupying administrative positions in the social space, and they are something that the sociologist must constantly combat. The bureaucracy of research is drawn to formal, 'neutral', apparently self-evident classifications.

What I want to repeat is that what seems to be an act of aggression committed by any adequate taxonomic classification is epistemologically justified. The whole tradition of epistemology (Bachelard, etc.) supports this. In the specific case of sociology, any adequate construction of the social world must be won through a break with the preconstructed versions, that is, with the classifications based on those already current in ordinary social usage. In other words, epistemological *laissez-faire*, which is often the product of institutionalized research or hyper-empiricist positivism, is almost always scientifically sterile and a political accomplice of the established order (the word 'accomplice' being used in the most neutral way possible). There is no way of making progress in the social sciences without resorting to the epistemological violence that consists in imposing choices composed in advance. There are certain relations that we cannot find unless we have constructed reality in such a way as to find them.

But in the social sciences it is not enough to justify the legitimacy of the theoretical *a priori*, because classification itself is an object of discussion and discord. What I want to argue today is that a truly objective theory of classification must build into its theory the fact that objective classification is itself a matter for debate. In other words, there is a conflict over systems of classification, where objective classification itself is involved, even if it does map out the ground of the positions adopted in the struggle.

The procedures that enable us to establish alternatives, to separate things normally amalgamated by common sense or even common scientific sense (such as French beans and baked beans, or 'no answer' due to oversight and 'no answer' from refusal to reply) are themselves an act of constitution. (I am using the word 'constitution' deliberately in a twofold sense: both that of the philosophical tradition – to constitute something as such is to move it from the non-thetic or implicit level to the thetic or conceptualized level – and that of political science, as when we speak of the Constitution of the French Republic.) The scientific act of classification is an act of constitution in both of these senses (as I said the other day when arguing that scientific approaches to the social world are always political): whether intended or not, any act of coding, however anodyne, is seen by society to involve or imply an attempt to impose a classification of the social world, and, thereby, a legitimate mode of perception or authorized vision of the social world.

Thus to argue that the basic procedures of research are acts of constitution is to admit that unconscious social interests can very often infiltrate the most elementary acts of research. This is one of the errors of political criticism of what we might call 'positivist' scientific research: very often people who have never led an enquiry themselves believe that they are able to mount a powerful challenge to scientific research work in the human sciences – which is often the case with philosophers, who are completely ignorant of the hard graft behind the scenes that is involved in research (cf, Goldmann's book)[7] – when they have no idea what an impact some omission or ignorance in the elementary stages of research can have, and they aim their criticism at a stage where the research is almost over and done with, and the harm already done. For example, a systematic criticism of the work produced by INSEE ought to look at their codes rather than their commentaries, at their programmes of mathematical analysis, rather than their justifications, which are often a superfluous excrescence.

If we insist on the fact that the elementary procedures of research are acts of constitution – that is, that they aim objectively, even if their author is unaware of it, to impose a world view, which is a political act – we are entitled to suspect that their authors are driven by hidden interests, by a social unconscious. It is in this area for example that we should look for the roots of the relation between a manner of conducting science and the researcher's position in the social space. The person who puts bananas and potatoes in the same bag, preventing themselves at a stroke from finding any significant correlation between social class and consumption, is perhaps moved by a social unconscious that overrides their will and intellect. In so doing they eliminate considerations of class from the debate more effectively and powerfully than through long theoretical discussions, since the classification of these products seems perfectly scientific, because no critical consciousness intervened at any moment.

If it is so difficult to impose social science in the rigorous terms I have prescribed, it is largely because it is in a position of weakness. It does what should be self-evident for a science, but it finds itself, through a sort of inversion of values, suspected of prejudice and *a priori* judgements. Contrariwise, unconscious, unthinking or automatic reactions (whose extreme limit would be totally automatic classifications, where the social unconscious of a conformist researcher would join forces with the mechanical procedures of an automated classification programme) can appear to be obviously right: appearances inevitably appear to argue in favour of appearances. I shall take this analysis no further, for fear of insisting too much. But it is vital for understanding the relations between a truly rigorous science and a science rigorous merely in social terms: as opposed to the latter, the rigorous science that I hope to formulate has no chance of social success. This sounds very pessimistic, but this is what the inextricably linked sociological and epistemological arguments I have expounded lead me to think.

Classification as an object of conflict

As I said last time, this objective classification could be both an aim and a means to an end in the rivalry between researchers; but it is also both weapon and target for social individuals in general – there is no social classification which is not both. The problem of establishing a pertinent system of classification that divides social scientists is therefore just as present and controversial in the real world studied by this field of experts, which does not mean to say that scientists fighting to establish their classification are able to consciously take into account the existence of their own internecine warfare. We must acknowledge that classification is a bone of contention in science, and that it is also socially controversial to make scientists accept the fact that all classification is an object of conflict, both in science and in society. A complete science of classification must include this conflict over classification.

We may take one example from the apparently neutral domain of technical nomenclature. It is the discussion provoked at INSEE by an article by Guibert, Laganier and Volle on industrial nomenclature.[8] The authors of this study, which appeared in *Économie et statistiques* in February 1971, set out to discuss current taxonomies of business (how do we classify different kinds of business?); they note that some classes of business can remain valid for the social agents who belong to them without there being any connection with real economic structures: 'These industrial branches have undergone such technical transformations that, in fact, from the point of view of pure economics, we ought to break down the aggregate, redistribute most of their activities under different headings, and only retain under the initial denomination the hard core of their activity' (p. 34). If we adopt an economic perspective, we will not find any real connections between such broad sectors as textiles and watchmaking, for instance. 'The economist, armed for the encounter with his criteria of association, is ready to make peremptory divisions: but the management are likely to be hostile' (p. 34). These are the views of a government economist, employed by a state

institution, whose distinctions have a certain legal force – this is important for our understanding of one of the problems that I shall define
later. The economists would like to decide on grounds of economics
alone, in the light of real connections, but the management running
the branch is likely to resist. In fact, the sector which no longer exists
at an economic level still exists as an institution. The industrial executives, united by a kind of family spirit, continue to bond together in the
comfort of a professional organization, which is at one and the same
time their club and their representative when faced with the government, the trade unions, and other associations affiliated to the CNPF
[Conseil National du Patronat Français – National Committee for
French Employers], colleagues and foreign competitors; this organization disposes of a professional journal that is read by and influences the
profession [. . .] so that the institution itself would be very reluctant to
disappear as an economic aggregate, and is very well able to voice its
opposition' (pp. 34–5).

This is a splendid piece of writing. Its authors are academics, but
their scholarship is not always entirely conscious. It is interesting to
note that in describing the real group that refuses to die they use words
which have pejorative connotations: a 'club', a 'kind of family spirit',
etc. The scientist who makes distinctions in this way makes them
sound all the more real, and declares them to be grounded in material
reality, but in the real world the people concerned say: 'We disagree,
we exist as a group because we have spokespeople who can speak in
our name to the government, the trade unions and other associations.
In addition, we are linked together by bonds that are stronger than
economic connections.' We can see from this example that objective
and objectivist classification, which appears to be less tendentious than
classifying by social class, is in fact highly controversial; behind an
appearance of pure scientific neutrality, it passes judgement on a contentious issue where identities, interests and personalities are at stake.
What is the nature of this interest in belonging to a group? What is the
nature of the interest that links you to a group such as the branch of a
profession?

Another example is the classification of property into three categories: consumer goods, capital equipment, and semi-finished goods,
There has been quite a debate over which goods fit into the semi-
finished category, which is in fact a catch-all category where anything
awkward may be filed away. This point would merit further reflection.
Laurent Thévenot, in an article in *Actes de la recherche en sciences
sociales* on the topic of the vagueness of classifications, tries to reflect
on those unclassifiable things that statisticians place as 'other', those

things that have no name in the language of classification and therefore drop out of their universe.[9] Semi-finished goods fall into this category. However, the classifiers still struggle to agree, for as soon as they really stop to think – as Bony and Eymard-Duvernay do in a study of the watchmaking sector[10] – they discover that even the most technical divisions based on chi square calculations[11] and other neutral measurements may require choices to be made because the location of the boundaries between the groups is a contentious issue.

The objective or objectivist classification that I described just now, which associates a statistician's unconscious with a well-programmed computer, is seen as natural. I shall return to this, but one of the forces inspiring ideological conflict in discussion of the social world is the desire to impose one's world view as legitimate, and there is no world view more legitimate than the natural one. If I manage to naturalize my vision of the world, I have won. Culture no longer matters – culture becomes synonymous with the arbitrary and the violent, it suggests that there are alternative ways of proceeding. If I manage to impose my classification of capital equipment, or gender, for instance, as natural, no further discussion is warranted. The question of how far objectivism should adopt technology is in fact a highly controversial political issue, and if I wanted to launch a debate on technocracy, I would initially examine the powers exercised by certain kinds of classifier, starting with an empirical consideration of the status of INSEE. Objectivist statisticians will try to engineer divisions into sectors as clear-cut as possible, that is to say, in their jargon, those producing goods as similar to each other as possible, so that the association between these products or between the people who produce, sell and distribute these products, appears as it were mechanical. Thus the working of the world may be described as a sort of vast machine where all human perspective has disappeared. In other words – and this is the question that I formulated rather clumsily at the outset: is there not a link between a viewpoint based on pure economics and the institutional view of the technocrat who wings his way over the social world, deploying a science that transcends individual interests, reminding us of the viewpoint claimed by Durkheim, who placed sociology on the same plane as that designated by Spinoza as a 'knowledge of the third kind'?[12]

Objectifying objectivism

What I call objectivism is the claim – which in certain historical circumstances may well be likely to succeed – to make the least arbitrary
classification possible, basing it on a knowledge of the relations imma-
nent in the real world and presenting it as a classification so natural
that it is self-evident, and no longer a subject of debate, dispute or
dissent. By reintroducing the debate over classification that is integral
to the scientific field and thereby to the social field, I was reintroducing,
with the examples that I quoted, the problem of the relation between
what we call objective or objectivist classification and the practical
classification that social subjects use in their everyday life. For those
who are familiar with my argument, I refer you to the first part of *The
Logic of Practice*, where I tried to show the stages through which all
scientific procedures must pass: the objectivist stage, the subjectivist
stage, and the stage that I consider to be truly scientific, where we can
integrate into a complete science both the knowledge acquired through
the objectivist approach and the realities against which it has been constructed.[13] I feel bound to refer to these analyses, because what I want
to do now follows on from there.

Objectivism, that is classification with claims to be objective, is an
inevitable stage in scientific procedure. We cannot get to know a social
universe without appropriating the means to acquire knowledge of
the type I have described: objective indicators, objective criteria, and
objective relations between these objective criteria. It remains the case
however that this objective truth is constructed in opposition to the
practical truths employed by individuals engaged in the real world
and that, for elementary sociological reasons (such as the division of
labour, for instance), the objective knowledge obtained by the scholar
is beyond the reach of the social subject. The scholar's multicriterial
knowledge of the space of teachers in higher education is thus a kind
of knowledge unavailable even to those individuals most at ease in this
universe: when I say 'at ease in this universe', I am suggesting that they
have a different form of knowledge of this universe, a practical knowledge, they have a practical mastery of things that objective knowledge
expresses in explicit, objectified terms, delivered in the form of schemas,
diagrams, reports and commentaries, etc. That having been said, there
is a qualitative difference between the practical knowledge that enables
us to live our daily lives perfectly adequately, and happily negotiate an
academic career, and a scientific knowledge of this universe. I can only
refer briefly here to what could be a protracted debate. The objective
truth produced by objective classifications based on objective indica-

tions contrasts with the truth of practical classifications; the objective truth is systematic and multiple, as opposed to the practical truth, which, as I said earlier when referring to Hegel, is essentially perspectival, for it is a viewpoint that does not see itself as a viewpoint, and because of this, passes itself off as universal and absolute.

That having been said, reminding ourselves that classifications are a site of conflict allows us to turn around and look at the classifier through the eyes of practice: just as the objectivist viewpoint allows us to see practical struggles as monocriterial and unilateral, so reflecting on the existence in practice of a conflict over different types of classification allows us to discover an objective truth behind objectivism, and in so doing to raise the question of the social conditions that make this objective viewpoint possible. Admitting that classifications are a site of conflict allows us to objectify the work of objectification. Our starting point is the simple realization that people are engaged in a constant struggle to insult or classify each other – no need to give further examples – and that the daily struggles over classification are struggles to impose the dominant criterion. For instance, conflicts within the dominant class, which are often misread as a class struggle, are conflicts over the dominant principle of classification within the dominant class: is it money, or intelligence or cultural capital that should matter most to the dominant class?[14] The fact of knowing that the social world is an area of conflict for classification allows us to question the work of the classifier, like the INSEE classifier just mentioned, who, believing himself to be neutral, is in danger of forgetting that he is imposing his cut-and-dried options on complex dramatic feuds, where the criteria no longer function as criteria, but as insults and aggression. Thus if in my investigation I assign codes to 'no. 328 *agrégé*', 'no. 329 *capésien*',[15] 'no. 330 former student at the ENS (École Normale Supérieure)', for instance, I am dealing with criteria (the word 'criterion' comes from *crisis*: it implies passing a judgement), for there are things I need to know: I want to know who to associate with whom, I want a classification that requires only four criteria to provide me with all the rest: a good classification will allow me to use their social origin and their branch of study, combined with the fact of being a *normalien* or *agrégé*, to predict a professor's attitude to May 1968, his or her political opinions and attitude towards the third world, etc.

Good classification and scholastic bias

A good classification will allow us to construct the generative matrix from which we may predict behaviour and attitudes. Thus I am faced with a problem of knowledge, which is how to maximize my theoretical mastery of the social world: how to find the most powerful and efficient instrument to gain insight into the social world. This is a purely theoretical question, but in the real world the people who ask these kinds of question never put them as purely conceptual questions: which creates an enormous difference, for questioning a classification always has a *function*. This is why I spent so much time on the example of the insult, an extreme case, where we declare the terms of our classification openly, and apply them aggressively, with the intention of doing as much harm as possible. In everyday life, classifications have a social function, where the criteria for classification are no longer critical criteria, instruments of *crisis* and *diacrisis*, division and separation, but are powers – as when we say of someone that they are 'empowered' to act.

The archetypal intellectualist error is failing to recognize that theoretical classification is theoretical. I refer you to *The Logic of Practice* where I develop this argument in relation to ethnology;[16] but what I am saying here about classification can equally apply to genealogy, kinship, and so on. This primordial error leads us to attribute to the objects of our study the awareness and knowledge that we have of their practice, projecting our own scholarly understanding into their practical minds. This is the supreme example of scholarly illusion. The sociology of knowledge, invented by Marx, traditionally relates the stance adopted by any agent to their position in the social space, but what I am trying to say today is that there is a more fundamental issue. Even before he starts to skew his material by classifying people – say as employers, or as dominant or subordinate intellectuals – the scholar, whether working for INSEE or the CNRS (Centre National de la Recherche Scientifique), whether sociologist or economist, introduces an even more important bias, because of the fact that he is unaware of the implications of his scholarship, ignorant of the fact that he has his own theoretical agenda. This ignorance leads to practical errors in the construction of a questionnaire and in the analysis of results, among other things.

We may criticize the objectivist illusion on two levels. Firstly, there is everything implied by the fact that the scholar is unaware of his condition as a scholar. Being outside the game, having no stake in the game, his engagement with the world is limited to using its material for study. For example, the fact that he is studying kinship, not in order to make a better marriage for his daughter, but to understand what kind of a marriage someone else is making, introduces an essential effect of distortion into the relationship between the investigator and the respondent: this is not how people consider the question of kinship; they look at it in this way only when questioned by a scholar. Secondly, a grand bourgeois responding to an enquiry by a petit bourgeois scholar is bound to have an imposing effect on the latter. This 'imposition' effect is something fairly evident, which everyone has noticed but is never taken into account in manuals of methodology.

What I now want to discuss is more serious, because it goes entirely unnoticed, and for good reason, for it is the identity of the scholar as scholar that is at stake. It is when the scholar asks the respondent: 'How many classes are there?' or: 'Do you think that there are different social classes?' (I have tested this, when I myself distributed a questionnaire to some old school friends, who did not share the same relationship with me that a sociologist would normally share with the 'object' of his enquiry. They replied; 'But that's your job!') In this case the sociologist invalidates his work as sociologist, albeit without realizing it, because if he was aware that he was pursuing theoretical ends, he could not unconsciously project his theoretical aims onto his respondent and ask the object of his enquiry to become his own sociologist. I might invite you to conduct an enquiry into a questionnaire: how many questions are there in the questionnaire that are designed, not to gather information about the respondent in order to draw a sociological portrait of them, but rather as a simple record of the kind of sociological view of himself that he has constructed? I could develop this further, but my main point here is that the experimental status of the enquiry situation tends to generate works of fiction – 'artefacts'. The positivist illusion consists in believing that whatever has been recorded is the reality that we should analyse – I asked a question, held out the microphone and recorded the answer. This illusion, as in the case of the bananas and apples that I mentioned just now, is particularly blatant in enquiries into social class, where the respondent is asked to situate himself by saying how many social classes there are and which one he belongs to. The enquiry situation, being an artificial situation, where one of the interlocutors is led by his social function and milieu to adopt a theoretical stance, inviting the other – who may or may not be aware of what is happening – to become the theoretician of his own practice, is a situation that engenders artefacts. How does this come about?

Firstly, this effect of theoretical imposition operates very differently depending on the social class of the person questioned. The higher the social status and level of education of the respondents, and the more practised they are at answering questions they haven't considered beforehand, the more they seem likely to be able to find an answer;[17] the 'artefact effect' is thus more veiled, yet at the same time less important, since people who have passed through the education system are bound to use well-rehearsed replies. But there are other cases where some respondents may reply using Marxist ideas and terminology if they have heard of Marx, and others, if they have INSEE's taxonomies in mind, will say 'middle class', or 'upper class', for instance. They resort to topoi that they have learnt, which means that they are concealing two things. Firstly, what they say is a *flatus vocis* – a commonplace – of little interest, since it records only their knowledge of fashionable taxonomies. You are merely testing their knowledge, while you think that they are answering your question. But then they are also hiding something more important: they give significant information about their social class in their manner of answering the question, if they are intimidated, or ashamed, for instance. Their sense of being classified, their sense of 'knowing their place' in the social space,[18] means, for example, that, from your way of speaking and putting your questions, and those particular questions, they know straight away that you are not one of them. And straight away you lose out on something important, which is being able to assess their 'sense of class', or sense of classification, everything that leads someone to behave appropriately in a social space without even giving it a second thought, using clues that are not actually conceptualized or formalized and are in fact completely unconscious.

Theoretical classification and practical classification

This apparently abstract discussion leads us to consider problems that are fundamental from the point of view of scientific practice itself and from the point of view of the political effects of discussing matters of class. A reflection on the artificial nature of the enquiry situation and its tendency to generate artefacts ought to yield important insights into the nature of practical classification and theoretical classification. To know what theoretical classification is, we have to understand what practical classification is, and vice versa.

Practical classification, the sort that you would use in a railway carriage to weigh up the situation and judge whether you can start a conversation or not, whether you can discuss politics, and so on, functions at a subconscious, often sub-verbal level. Otherwise there would be no need for sociologists who, as professional classifiers, are able to make these implicit principles of classification explicit. A whole tradition of American ethnomethodology – which has developed in different directions – is devoted to studying the unconscious principles of classification that different populations use to classify plants, illnesses, animals, and so on;[19] the work of the sociologist in the social world consists in objectifying, that is to say transferring a system of classification from its practical, incorporated state – where it is embodied in the person who practises it – to an objectified state consigned to paper in the shape of schemas, diagrams or formulae. And it is a professional task. But if the professional is unaware of the implications of his professional mission, he will expect an unprofessional person to undertake this professional task – in which case, neither of them achieves anything useful at all.

Secondly, practical classification mobilizes practical schemas (high/ low, distinguished/vulgar, intelligent/uninteresting, etc.), based on simple oppositions which may not reach linguistic consciousness – although they are often formulated in terms of pairs of adjectives – but nevertheless work on a practical level. This kind of classification is always subordinate to practical functions: we never classify just for the sake of classifying, but rather to manage our daily lives in the real world. Whereas, with theoretical classification, the theoretician has the luxury of taking the problem of classification as his object. In the first instance, the task he sets himself is how to choose the best system of classification: he can take his time, he can multiply the criteria and adopt more than one viewpoint. One of our strategies in everyday life consists in manipulating classifications; in situations where we need to limit conflict as far as possible, we will seek out in the universe of properties of the alter ego facing us the properties closest to our own: we adjust the classifications so that we can recreate the same person as someone that we met on national service, or danced with at a party, for instance. The scholar does not proceed in this way at all: he takes a whole set of criteria and proceeds to examine the links between them and assess their relative importance.

The fact that practical classifications are designed for practical purposes explains on the one hand why they draw on practical schemas and on the other hand why they are not very consistent. They are, as their name indicates, practical; and in order to be practical, they are better, as you might say of clothes, if they are a loose fit. If they are too tightly tailored, we cannot make any adjustments. The schemas we use are in some ways identical with the logic of myth – I refer you to my studies of Kabyle society.[20]

To show you how the system works, I might have taken the case of politics and a questionnaire that we used in this field, which is interesting because it is situated halfway between practical and theoretical classifications: here we have the most fully conscious and verbalized of the classifications that we practise in everyday life. A demonstration of the different ways of reacting to a problem of political classification is very interesting because, in this enquiry situation, which is artificial, but can be adapted according to circumstances, we see how the strategy of social agents consists in constantly varying the angles of their response to the classification. They may move from a cognitive approach (classifying political parties along a left-to-right axis, for example) to a much deeper level.[21] As I shall not have time to finish this argument today, I shall leave you to reflect on the following example of an experimental micro-situation that we devised, inspired by the techniques of componential analysis used by ethnologists in order to try to elicit the principles of classification used implicitly by the natives of a given society to classify plants and animals, and so on.[22] We had a packet of thirty-six cards bearing names of professions that we asked people to classify. One man in his sixties, a non-union building worker, divided them into five separate piles. The interviewer, who was on familiar terms with him, chatted away in order to change the situation (one of the experimental variations that you can try in an enquiry consists in varying the enquiry effect, which is one of the most elusive variables of any enquiry). Turning to leave, he made as if to say goodbye, and asked him: 'Is there anyone's job that you wouldn't like to have?' 'Yes, a coalminer . . . a travelling salesman, or a TV presenter.' 'Why?' 'Because I don't have the gift of the gab, and they are jobs for people who have peculiar habits, most of them are queers.' He looked through his piles again. 'The queers start with the secretaries, the office workers and the civil servants [*laughter*]. With the workmen and the farmers, you do get it, but not so much. It might happen by accident with them, but not with the others.' The respondent takes the 'travelling salesman' card, puts it into a different pile and says, 'It starts halfway through, you get to the middle, and from there on, they're all a bunch of queers.'

Here we see how an entirely implicit criterion, the sexual one, can intervene. How many of those of us who inquire into people's political sensibilities would have thought of this criterion for classifying social classes – dominant meaning effeminate? The respondent had this criterion in mind, but was using it only in practical terms. By carefully manipulating the interview situation, the interviewer was able to break down its artificial character enough to allow a deep, latent, practical criterion to come to the surface. And as soon as this criterion, which had been implicit and was at first expressed as an occasional term of

abuse, had been formulated and objectified, although almost by accident, it became a rule: we can classify, and so, for instance, we can
change the ranking of the travelling salesman. So, whereas a scholarly
classification is a critical classification that is based on several criteria and organizes a whole population in terms of consistent criteria,
avoiding overlaps, a practical classification functions piecemeal, and
can accommodate contradictions. If we take the example of political
classification, you must have all found that you can be more right-wing
or more left-wing than your usual self, depending on whether you are
talking to someone who is more right-wing or more left-wing than you
are.

Next time I shall conclude the first stage of my argument. Having
described subjective, objective and practical classifications, I shall
proceed to show how a truly scientific classification must make the
scholarly mind aware of the fact that scholarly knowledge is not
the same thing as practical understanding, and vice versa, and that
classification is a subject of conflict. This has consequences on the
methodological and theoretical level: the reintroduction of the notion
of classification as conflictual into the theory of the construction of
classification itself has very significant consequences.

Lecture of 26 May 1982

Moving beyond the alternatives – Reality and representations of reality – The autonomy of the social and the problem of self-awareness – The law, a special case of theory effect – Words as common sense

I have suggested that a strictly rigorous science of social classifications should endeavour to integrate a rigorous theory of objective classification as well as a theory of the practical classification that social agents use in their everyday activities. It should go beyond the limits of those over-familiar alternatives in sociological thinking: 'physicalism' or semiology, objectivity or subjectivity, realism or nominalism.[1] For instance, it would be easy to show that the principal theories of social class are divided between these alternatives, one camp claiming to find their classes rooted in the real world, the others reducing them to subjective or at least nominal constructions produced by the researcher.

Moving beyond the alternatives

In concrete terms, moving beyond these alternatives would require us to integrate objective classification with the conflict over classifications, instead of simply juxtaposing the two. In the case of social class, we cannot avoid the encounter with Marx, and we cannot help thinking that he himself achieved this merger, because it was he who gave us both an objectivist notion of social class and a theory of the class struggle. Yet it seems to me that this integration is superficial, and I fear that the weakness of Marx's thought lies in the fact that he did not integrate a scientific theory aiming to describe the social classes according to their objective properties with a theory of the struggle between different classificatory systems that might transform or modify this objective structure.[2] It seems to me that he failed to achieve this integration and that he allowed Marxist theory to oscillate successively or simultaneously between, on the one hand, a physicalist, mechanistic and determinist kind of theory – with, for example, the theory of the final catastrophe which was much discussed in the interwar period – and, on the other hand, a theory of revolution as a kind of engine where compression leads to explosion. The theory of self-awareness or class consciousness does aim to reconcile this physicalism with the spontaneity of the will, but in my opinion it does not succeed very well.

Since the problem of the integration of the two poles of the alternative was neither stated nor resolved, the Marxist position, it seems to me, was led to internalize a kind of dualism, which we find at both the level of theory and that of practice. I would like to get to the heart of this failure to integrate. We are confronted with a sort of social physics, which describes social relationships and social classes as quasi-mechanical power relationships, that are objective and independent of individual will and consciousness, according to Marx, and which may be measured by criteria analogous to those employed in physics and the natural sciences in general; social classes become social groupings based on their almost automatically defined position in relations of production, which are a sort of defiantly intractable and recalcitrant reality that nobody can modify, and that a rigorous science must duly study and bring to light. Then a strictly scientific study of these objective power relations would enable us to elaborate a theory providing an understanding of objectively grounded groups, knowledge that would be both theoretical and practical, and thus able to act as a guide for political action.

This distinctly physicalist, objectivist and realist tendency (we might give each tendency a separate title) is opposed to a more or less spontaneist tendency, that would prefer to define social class in terms of will. I am thinking for example of E. P. Thompson,[3] a Marxist historian, loosely speaking, who describes class as an event, a 'happening', an 'eruption', or, obviously, of Sartre's reading of Marx.[4] According to this spontaneist tendency, class is no longer a kind of reality inscribed in the very structure of the social world, but a sort of collective will, more or less produced by the sum of individual wills. Since these theories are often quasi-mythological, I cannot really formulate them clearly. I can only suggest that you refer to the kind of justifications we find offered for the 'fused class' or the 'inspired class' (there is a sort of Bergsonian Marxism). As I do not appreciate the arguments, I cannot discuss them objectively. But I think that the Marxist tradition is bound to oscillate between these two poles (this oscillation exists within the minds of people who think of themselves as Marxists), and we might write a social history of Marxist thought that would reveal its pendular swing from one pole to the other. What I am saying here is far too brief and caricatural, but my aim is less to describe these two ways of envisaging the social world than to try to discover why Marx was led into this kind of double bind, which, I believe, he thought he had found a way out of. In this field, as in many others, Marx broke with the common representation of the world, but was unable – perhaps because no one person could do both things at once – to integrate into his theory of the social world the recalcitrant forms from which he had to wrest this theory.

We might be able to see this in the case of the Marxist theory of labour.[5] The scientific endeavour requires a refusal to accept the data presented by the given world, along with their phenomenal appearances, such as the idea of work as a vocation, which Marx often discusses. The scientist aims to destroy and deconstruct common representations in order to construct an objective truth in opposition to them, and reconstruct labour as a producer of surplus value (or to construct objective classifications as multicriterial rather than monocriterial, as I did for my own construction of the economics of taste).[6] But it is understandable that the person who managed to break away from these surface appearances found it difficult to reintroduce into his construction the recalcitrant given forms that he had to reject in order to construct it. Having broken with the version of reality imposed by ideology (in this particular case, the intuitive theory of classification), the person making the break forgets to integrate into his model the forms that he had to reject in order to make this break, and whose social power is apparent in the very effort needed to make the break. If the objectivist break constantly needs to be repeated, it is precisely because it constantly conflicts with all our normal social experience.

My own work has in fact, on more than one occasion, consisted in trying to achieve a break, and then to go beyond this break by reintegrating the lived or practical experience which it had to overcome. In the case of labour, if we reduce the whole truth of labour, that is, both its objective and subjective aspects, to its objective truth according to the Marxist tradition, that is to a producer of surplus value, we forget that failure to recognize the objective truth of labour as producer of surplus value is part of the objective truth of labour. If Marx had discovered the whole truth about labour, everyone would be a Marxist and there would be no need for political analysis or argument. This is why the opposition between objectivism and spontaneism that I set out to describe is most often an opposition between the scholarly and the militant. For there is also a division of labour in the tradition of the labour movement: the theorists and the militants often have different social roots and different cultural experience. The theorists are commonly of a scientistic, objectivist, determinist and mechanistic persuasion whereas the militants actually involved in work tend to follow a spontaneist, voluntarist and activist path, one that favours a class in the making rather than a class to be found already composed in reality. I think that this distinctly fatal alternative is based on a logical error. We can understand why the person who did the most to destroy lyrical visions of labour or the social world was particularly vulnerable to this error, since the effort of breaking away does not incline you to understand and reintegrate what you have had to destroy.

Reality and representations of reality

The basic idea that I have in mind is this: the way that social subjects represent the social world is part of the objective truth of the social world. The social world is not simply the objective reality that the scholar constructs through statistical work and the accumulation of different criteria. For although the social agents engaged in the objective practices of action suffer a sort of blindness – they are condemned to individual, partial views, and do not know the objective truth of the social world – this fact is itself a part of the objective truth of the social world. The scholar who forgets that not every social subject experiences the social world as he describes it in his research is guilty of ethnocentrism; and one of the most difficult aspects of scientific work is managing to integrate into the scientific account the primary experience that scientific study leads us to forget. For instance, although it is so tedious and awkward that we don't want to take on this additional burden, we ought to make the effort to constantly record our manner of representing the object that we are studying. In fact the researcher himself is constantly remodelling his representation of the object, which means that he finds it very difficult to rediscover the initial experience that he had of his object; and when he delivers his final representations and conclusions he is likely to make this mistake of perspective. Thus for instance, once a scholar has characterized the realm of thought as a field, and decides to describe the intellectual field or the university field as a space in which agents face specific challenges and deploy specific strategies to pursue their interests, there is no text – from a biography of Monet to an interview with Sartre or a debate between Brunschvicg and Nizan[7] – that will not reveal an objective strategy: every document, every letter, every style of writing starts to speak with the logic of this strategy. There are even ways of reading a document that objectify it: for example, I could read out aloud the famous text that Sartre wrote on the death of Merleau-Ponty,[8] and, simply by emphasizing here and editing there, make you feel what strategies of recuperation lie behind the humble and respectful homily. As soon as you have captured this objective vision, you find it difficult to reproduce your original naive reading. Luckily, certain philosophical texts have remained in my mind just as I found them when I first read them at the age of twenty or so. I can relive the naive experience that I had when I read Heidegger's 'das Man',[9] and manage to experience the overlap of the two experiences, one naive, and one, shall we say, disenchanted. But from the moment when you have seen in 'das Man' ('they', or 'the people') the opposition between the crowd and the distinguished individual, the text takes on the guise of a gestalt figure: once you have grasped its structure, you can see nothing else and *a fortiori* you find it almost impossible to communicate it.[10] I often dream of a language of exposition which, like a musical language, would deliver at once the naive experience (what the faithful read in a Heidegger text), and what you can read between the lines. It ought to be possible to express both at once, but the difficulty also lies in the fact that the cost of discovering what you should read between the lines, and the reward of feeling an ironic disenchantment, are so considerable that the scholar hardly wants to forego these benefits; it is much more agreeable to adopt a supercilious tone and make mock of the object. However, this leads to considerable errors of perspective, if only because the social world would not function at all if it resembled the researcher's objectivist description. Even if it is a reductive example, we can take the case of Sartre: if Sartre's eulogy to Merleau-Ponty had really been cynical and calculating, the eulogy would not have functioned as a eulogy, either in his eyes or those of his readers. There had to be a touch of innocence and naivety even in his strategy of posthumous recuperation and settling of accounts. This is true on every occasion that society follows the path of belief (which is very often and even almost always the case); for objectification, by simply presenting as an ensemble things that are not usually recognized as a cohesive whole, does bring to light a hidden aspect of things, but it also destroys something constitutive of objectivity itself, which is the fact that things do not actually happen like that, and if they did happen like that, society would not function at all.

    To return to the problem that I am analysing, which is a special case of the wider issue of the objectivist relation to the object, and the nature of ordinary experience in the social world, it seems to me that the objectivist theory of classifications and the objectivist vision of the social world as it is, ignore the fact that it is not entirely objective. For example, if I constructed a space of teachers of French in higher education, which I could draw on the board as a diagram with measurable distances, we can be sure that the work involved in bringing this reality to light would change the nature of our thinking – I even think that, to survive and above all to succeed in that space, you need a practical mastery of the structure that I can draw on the board, although the structure depicted does not exist in anyone's conscious mind; and it is certainly not explicitly controlled by any of the agents. The difference between belief and cynicism is a very important social fact, and it depends precisely on the fact that we know not what we do, and that we can make people believe we are doing something other than what we are actually doing.

If social agents were constantly obliged to attain conscious mastery of their practice, even supposing that they were not paralysed by the excess of information and depressed by the sense of doom that it inspired in them, their experience of the social world would not correspond to what the social world and, in particular, its cultural universes require, that is, belief, innocence, naivety and so on. If artists were conscious of what they are doing when they do what they do, they would not be able to do it at all. These are things that people like intellectuals and artists, who claim to be individual, unique, and distinguished, very often oppose to sociology. For years I saw this as an ideological posture, a sort of defence of the human individual, a spiritual *point d'honneur*. But the fact that this discourse is ideological and defensive, that it is linked to what Marx called the 'spiritual *point d'honneur*'[11] of intellectuals and artists, does not mean that it does not contain its share of the truth. I think that, like any effective ideology, it has a foundation in reality, and that the objectivist approach really mutilates reality; ordinary experience does not include a complete knowledge of itself and the space in which it operates. To summarize all this in a single sentence, I would say that the partial, fictitious and mystified representation that agents make of the social world is part of the objective reality of the social world. Which immediately implies that the 'theories' – I shall return to this word – which provide representations of the social world, whether religious, scientific or political, are themselves part of the social world. The paradox is that the theory of the social world which above all others has had the most powerful theory effect did not include the theory of that effect: if there is a theory that has become reality, revealed the world to us and made us believe its explanation of the world, it is certainly Marxist theory; yet this theory, especially at its scientistic and mechanistic extreme, leaves no place for the fact that reality is constituted by representation. This is what I would like to reintegrate into a more inclusive analysis.

The autonomy of the social and the problem of self-awareness

I am somewhat embarrassed by the direction my argument has taken. It is not that I am embarrassed to disagree with Marx, but I worry about disagreeing with Marx in the presence of people who might wonder what is implied by this disagreement. It is such a sacred realm, and I do not wish to commit sacrilege. But what I am saying is serious, and absolutely relevant to the problem I am discussing. I believe that a true science of classification should integrate and define itself as a science of the relationship between practical classification and the objective classification constructed by the scholar through the accumulation of diverse criteria. The objective classification that allows us for instance to place social agents and their properties in a three- or four-dimensional space is more real (in the sense that it is more predictive of reality) than a practical classification: in this sense, it is a more natural classification, as a zoologist would say. This is what we often say when we credit a thinker with the capacity to reveal differences that we did not see before, that we sensed but did not know how to express. The academic classification, which reveals structures and relationships that go beyond partial appearances and perceptions, is closer to reality, but at the same time it is quite unreal in the sense that it is not socially manageable; it is not practical in real life, you cannot use it to act, because it is too complex. It is not functional, there is nothing we can do with it, it is born of a 'disinterested' relationship with the social world . . .

If we make the effort to integrate the two, we shall have to reject subjectivism and admit that the objective classification, the one that the scholar constructs with multiple criteria, is the basis for practical classifications; the practical classification of the social agents will match their objective position in the objective classification. The objective classification is the basis of the practical classifications: it defines internalized, incorporated divisions in terms of permanent dispositions and classificatory schemas; it defines their objective boundaries, that is the material conditions of existence within which the practical strategies of classification will operate. The objective, or latent, classification determines the form that the conflict over classification will take. I could take the example of regionalism, where the classificatory stances adopted reflect the classifiers' own positions in the classifications, according to their propensity to use a particular type of classification, whether incorporated or objectified.[12] The forms and uses of classification depend on the criteria used by the classifier. The prime example is that of taste, that incorporated system of classification, which serves to classify, but which classifies the classifier. We should then replace subjectivism with a model where practical classification is subordinate to objective classification and objectivism – this is more or less what I was saying about Marx, whom I had reduced to his objectivist aspect. The standpoint adopted is relatively independent of the position held: their relation is not automatic. A position in the objective social space does not correspond automatically to a particular political, religious or aesthetic stance. The social space that we might characterize as political enjoys a relative autonomy from objective classifications.

Is this autonomy the autonomy of awakening consciousness? This, I think, is the key issue, even if I shall not insist on it today: the awakening of consciousness is one of the means which may help agents move away from their social position, but I think that it has taken an entirely disproportionate place in the Marxist tradition. It seems to me that in everyday life the relations between people's positions and the stances they adopt are negotiated not through acts of consciousness, but through what I call the *habitus*, that is the unconscious dispositions that are the result of incorporating structures and positional properties, and lead to practices reformulating their position in terms of their own particular logic, without becoming explicitly conscious. You might raise the objection that others often put to me, which is that, if the only possible relationship between positions held and stances adopted is fashioned by the mechanisms of the habitus – which is in its turn largely the product of positions held – no autonomy is possible. Yet what I would like to show is that autonomy is possible, if not in the area of consciousness: the objective classifications define the conditions within which all the classes – whether present as name, representation or will – can operate, and have a chance of coming to fruition; but it remains the case that certain procedures – which we might call theoretical in the widest sense (I shall return to this) – endowed with their own logic, produce representations that are independent of the positions held. What is the nature of this symbolic autonomy? Where do we locate the source of this disparity between what people actually are socially and their representations of the social world?

The objective positions define the limits within which the representations may vary, but, within those limits, there is room for manoeuvre, which – I would like to emphasize – is precisely what characterizes symbolic power. In fact, symbolic power is the power to exploit this leeway between positions and dispositions, and we can find the same dispositions translated by different stances. I would like to take a very simple example: I do not believe that a certain position in production relations (to use strictly objectivist language) defining the proletarian in rigorously theoretical terms must automatically elicit the alternatives of remaining unconscious or consciously awakening to a dazzling revelation of the objective truth of the worker's condition. It relates rather to dispositions that are the incorporated product of a certain experience of the social world, defined precisely in terms of holding a certain position in production relations, and which – whether rightly or wrongly, I leave you to judge – can be reflected in very different explicit representations of the social world.

In other words, dispositions enjoy a certain fluidity in their relationship to discourse, and the passage from a practical disposition to a discourse claiming to express it is a qualitative leap of such radical discontinuity that, in fact, diverse explanatory discourses can account for the same disposition, or, inversely, some dispositions can be plausibly located in quite different explanatory discourses, although each claims to represent the sole truth of the practice. I have often described these phenomena of *allodoxia*,[13] and I think that the move into politics occurs when we leave the *doxa*, that is, that sort of purely dispositional experience of the pre-explicit, pre-thetic, subconscious and sub-lingual world that guides the majority of our everyday actions, and move to an orthodox or heterodox experience – the orthodox experience being the belief in a just and righteous belief, in a dominant faith. It is in this passage from the *doxa* to an orthodoxy or a heterodoxy that there is room for manoeuvre. Ultimately if each and every disposition implied the disposition to produce its own legitimate explanation, there would be no place for politics, no place for all those who manipulate and exploit this discrepancy, that is, not only the politicians but all professional commentators. These professional commentators make a living from this discrepancy and their lives depend on the possibility of *allodoxia*, on the fact that people can think different things.

Let me go into more detail. In so far as science discovers that there are both objectively well-grounded classifications, and also classifying acts that, despite being closely linked to objective positions in the classifications, are relatively autonomous in relation to these positions, sociologists are faced with an alternative: they can take as their aim either to champion their own objective classification against all the other systems of classification competing for the legitimate representation of the social world (this is the temptation of objectivism, which always claims that its classifications are superior to those of its rivals), or declare that reality is constituted by the most powerful competing classifications, which means that it is ultimately the dominant ideology that constitutes reality. The dominant representation of the social world is part of reality and, in this light, 'the law' would become the social science par excellence.

(As I said in passing one day: from its very beginnings, this science has had to affirm itself and constitute itself against the law. If Marx, Durkheim and Weber all see the confrontation with the law as capital, it is because the juridical discourse on the social world has a form of validity. To a certain extent, when conservative sociologists believe they can describe the world as it is, or as the dominant representation says that it is almost legally bound to be, they have some justification; they are so difficult to attack because in a way they have social reality on their side. Most often, the people who are content to repeat the dominant account of reality have social reality on their side, and in this way have every likelihood of finding their representation confirmed.)

One possible mission of sociology then might be to register the most powerful classifications, that is, the most predictive, and establish certain nomenclatures – the word 'nomenclature' is an important word in some societies – which are reality, which become reality itself. We can well conceive of a scientific-juridical theory, sufficiently founded scientifically to be validated in general terms and at the same time founded in law, that is able to provide its own verification because it would bring into existence what it declares to exist. This would be the supreme challenge for the social sciences. In fact, the societies that experience this situation hardly have any social sciences at all. So I think that social science is an absolute challenge, we have to choose between social order or social science.

The argument that I am developing here is particularly difficult; I am reaching the limits of what I can think. It raises the question of what precisely we mean by scientific thought. It seems to me that the first conclusions to be drawn from the reflections that I have pursued so far are as follows: the conflict over classification is part of the objective truth of classification, although it enjoys a relative autonomy from the classifications themselves. In the second part of my argument, I now hope to determine what constitutes the specific logic of the conflict over classification, to say what forms the basis of its autonomy and, therefore, the source of its symbolic power, seen as a power relatively autonomous from other forms of power like economic power or the power of purely physical violence. What is at stake in the battle over classification is the production and imposition of the legitimate mode of representation of the social world, of the mode of representation of the social world able to impose its authority and thereby to guarantee its own verification. As I said just now when speaking of the law, a legal discourse may ultimately become a performative discourse; it may be false from a scientific point of view but may still have the ability to verify itself. If I am powerful enough and I say: 'Tomorrow the entire French working class will rise up and demand a 35-hour working week', I can make this proposition come true, even if, from the point of view of a rigorous scientific account of social structures and power relationships, my declaration might appear to be fraudulent.

Does this mean that such a power to mobilize reality has no limit? In fact, how far it can operate beyond objective limits is prescribed by objective reality. For it to succeed, however, there must be an objective basis, although this does not mean that everything has to be present in the objective conditions. The struggle over classification is a struggle for what I call the constitutive power, that is, the essentially political power to bring into being what is declared to exist. It is a struggle for the imposition of an accredited and universally recognized classification. The success of this certified classification will not depend merely on the fact that politicians, for example, will agree to acknowledge it, or scientists to say that it is official, but also on its ability to constitute reality; it will take on the force of law, in so far as people will really be classified according to this system, with all the consequences resulting: they will or will not have identity papers, they will be well considered or looked down on, properly or badly paid, etc. The struggle for accredited classification is therefore more than an ideological struggle, in the usual sense of a struggle which would take effect only in the realm of ideas or representations. The struggle to impose a dominant representation is at one and the same time a struggle to make that dominant representation become real, operate in the real world and constitute reality. For this, it must be convincingly compatible with reality, which does not mean that it has to be inscribed in reality in advance.

The law, a special case of theory effect

I will try to illustrate the nature of this struggle with a simple example concerning the problem of law. We live within the law without thinking about it; and the power to say what is just and right (i.e. the right as opposed to the left, the straight versus the crooked, the masculine in relation to the feminine, the dominant and the legitimate rather than the dominated and the illegitimate, the religious and the official, instead of the magical, the unofficial and the hidden, and so on) depends on being able to wield precisely the symbolic power that is able to impose a common set of points of view. It is the power to impose a consensual view of the meaning of the world, to impose universal principles that direct this vision and the actions and representations that it entails. Finally, this power is what I will call in the broadest sense the power to exercise a 'theory effect',[14] taking the word 'theory' in its etymological sense: theory is a commonplace concept in the epistemological tradition; it is what makes us see things that we would not otherwise have seen. The epistemological tradition has provided many examples of the theory effect: when a theory is constituted, phenomena that were not previously perceived and realities that were confused become distinct. In other words, we see only what we devised the theory to look for. The law is a special case of the theory effect, just as political action is, for through the exercise of legitimate nomination someone who holds symbolic authority can force social subjects to abandon their doubts about the meaning of the world.

To understand the power of the theory effect, we need to realize that it is not at all easy to acquire a clear vision of the world, and especially of the social world. What has often been said of the natural world, namely, that it is ambiguous and indeterminate, and that social subjects can only discover an order to it by applying structuring systems, is almost *a fortiori* true for the social world itself. Max Weber spoke of *Vielseitigkeit* ('many-sidedness'), that is to say the multiple facets of the social world, where social realities are only ever revealed as outlines or fragments.[15] These realities are never entirely grasped as a whole, which leaves the social subject more or less disarmed when facing the present condition of the social world, let alone its future. It is no coincidence that fore-casting or pre-diction are one of the central problems in political life, because one of the factors affecting the uncertainty of meaning of the present is precisely the future that it is pregnant with. We cannot tell what is making it uncertain. This is a classic trope of the philosophy of history. The power of prediction of those who have a theory that will enable us to see the relevant connections is effective because the meaning of the social world is not given and finite, but open and provisional. Weber's theory of prophecy says just this:[16] the prophecy effect, which is one of the archetypal forms of the theory effect, consists in providing systematic answers to the urgent questions asked by social agents in their greatest need, ranging from the questions of life and death that all prophecies have to answer, to the most banal questions of everyday life: should we wear a hat, or not? Should we place our hand on our heart when we salute the flag? The purpose of prophetic discourse is to relieve believers completely of any anxiety about the meaning of the world.

Words as common sense

What I would like to show is that even the most ordinary language that we use to express our world functions in this way. A saying or a proverb is a prophecy in miniature. An American philosopher, Kenneth Burke, has written an analysis of proverbs and slang, showing that they are not neutral formulae at all, but a kind of action plan that targets a specific person and at the same time indicates how to deal with them or what to do to them.[17] They are not impartial commentaries at all; they are incitements to act in a certain way. The most ordinary sayings define an attitude that is approved and authorized by the whole group. Proverbs are common sense, and having common sense on our side gives us strength, because their every word is ethically loaded. If you are an ordinary individual engaged in the social world, it is very reassuring to have common sense on your side. You only have to think of slogans, which I shall return to later. Proverbs are always slogans. The pleasure and gratification that we derive from repeating sayings that have been pronounced a hundred times in circumstances socially devised to elicit them – I could think of countless examples – is due to the fact that we live our lives as if we had the backing of the whole social order, with its fashions, its morals and its orthodox thinking and behaviour. The cleavage dividing righteous and lawful thinking from left-leaning thinking, seen as clumsy, shameful, clandestine, unofficial and unwilling to speak its name out loud, clearly echoes the whole opposition between religion and magic analysed in the sociological tradition. We can ascribe to the realm of magic all the things that we have never been able to express. One of the most powerful effects that the social world exerts, the effect of formalization, relies purely and simply on this magic. It doesn't actually change anything in reality. People who have lived together for twenty years go to the town hall and they come back married. We are often satisfied to say that this is just a social convention, but in fact it concerns things that are not consciously analysed: the fact of getting married in full public view, leaving the unofficial, the clandestine, the shameful, the unmentionable and the hidden, in order to pass over to the official, is a radical change, and I think that one of the most powerful political effects is the publication effect, *Öffentlichkeit*, which is the act of making open, patent, or public, the act of publishing or displaying.[18] The people who follow the straight and narrow, who are in the right and on the right, are those who can expose themselves and what they are with no shame, since they have the whole social order completely on their side.

I think that this logic of making public is a significant example of the theory effect: when a theory becomes orthodox and dominant, it becomes a collective vision of the world and this collective vision of the world becomes the world itself – it is only an artifice of the materialist tradition that has accustomed us to distinguish between the social world and our vision of the social world. A vision of the social world, when it is consensual, is the social world, it creates the social world. And, with the whole social world to support me, there is no longer any discrepancy between what I think and what exists. The whole point of the struggle for symbolic domination is to impose this immersion in orthodoxy. In a way, the prize fought for in all the struggles between intellectuals, administrators, and, more generally, between all those who have the power to define the social world with authority, is the right to impose a consensual vision of the world that can not only describe the world, but bring it into being. In *Dictionary of Indo-European Concepts and Society*, Benveniste remarks that all the words which designate the law in Indo-European languages are related to the root 'to say', 'to speak';[19] as if to speak was always to say what is right, to say what exists, and in what form. As soon as you are allowed to speak publicly, without concealment, you are backed by a whole group that delegates to you the power to say with them and on their behalf what exists, and since you are supported by a whole group, you draw on the power that it has to constitute and impose reality. This is precisely the logic of the performative. It goes without saying that the goal of the struggle for symbolic power is to gain the authority that allows one to pronounce performative statements that carry positive sanction.

In conclusion, I return to the conditions that make this performance effect possible. There are, of course – as I shall consider later – conditions that must be met by an individual agent in order to be able to speak on behalf of a group, that is, the conditions for acquiring authority. But there are also conditions that concern the social world as object of this authority, properties which make the operation of the theory effect possible. I have already underlined the ambiguity of the social world, and, contrary to the realist theory that is often accepted consciously or unconsciously by sociologists, I think that our representation of the social world is not a reflection. It is neither a direct insight nor a mechanical reflection, but a construction that is nearly always collective and relies in particular on language. I think that if, like Benveniste, we can use a purely linguistic analysis to derive a theory of the social world, it is because we use language to construct the social world. If there is an area where the Sapir-Whorf hypothesis (the hypothesis according to which language is constitutive of reality) and the Humboldt-Cassirer tradition, which is independent of the preceding one but is also neo-Kantian (language constructs reality, and provides the structures that inform the social world), are true, it is the realm of the social world. The objective indeterminacy of the social world allows us to apply to it that elementary instrument of thought, the word, the ordinary word. For example, I think that one of the most interesting objects of study in the field of the moral code of a class could be the use of interjections and exclamations: we can find a whole social philosophy and representation of the world contained in this kind of exclamation, which is a bodily and verbal way of reacting to the world and one that has been acquired in a completely unconscious way by associating with and imitating people faced with the same situations. It is through the use of ordinary language, proverbs and set phrases that a group assimilates and acquires its moral code.

Of course, the social conditions affecting the production and mode of operation of the diverse proverbs or political slogans are many and various: in one case, they may have a common, unanimous sense, given in the language; in another, they may depend on individual agents whom we can locate in a specific position in the social space. But in terms of the effect exerted on our perception of the social world, the logic is exactly the same. For example, although the social world is a place of continuity, the symbolic power of the classifiers consists in introducing discontinuity (imposing a right and a left, a masculine and a feminine, and so on). I am thinking, for example, of the work of a statistician who has tried to show how statisticians in our societies are constantly dividing up continuums and classifying things that escape classification or are absolutely unclassifiable.[20] When the people of INSEE classify as 'student' a student who earns their living as a waiter in a restaurant they introduce an arbitrary separation into a dual or even multiple reality. They introduce discontinuity into the continuum, as do the primitive classifications described by Lévi-Strauss when they say: there is hot and cold, wet and dry, sunshine and moonlight. This discontinuity strikes true immediately when it is backed by the social order, because it can be published, declared, and openly displayed and illustrated, which leads to the predictions formulated by this classification being confirmed, at least by the other members of the group. A world view is a system of predictive schemas that, being shared by all, become true and validated. The system of prediction that you are using may seem crazy seen from the viewpoint of a different forecasting system, but, within a universe where everyone else shares the same system, you are in the right. Thus, in a society where the dominant classificatory principle was religion, behaviour which now seems incoherent to us was seen as coherent, and its coherence was constantly reinforced, since it found confirmation of its own validity in other people's behaviour, orchestrated in accordance with the same structures.

Lecture of 2 June 1982

The act of consecration – The symbolic struggle over classification – Symbolic capital – The manipulation of boundaries between groups – Defending one's capital.

Today I propose to examine what is specific to the symbolic struggle. I described last time what I called the 'theory effect', the effect of nomination whereby drawing conclusions about the social world tends to impose a representation of this world. I could just as easily have called this theory effect any one of the following: 'nomination effect', 'institution effect', 'constitution effect', 'consecration effect' or 'legitimation effect'. It is part of my method to deliberately offer a series of partially interchangeable names. In fact I have often found in the course of my work that the mere fact of exchanging one word for another creates considerable opportunities for progress in research. For example, the theory effect that I analysed in my last lecture was similar to a subclass of the institution effect that I had analysed elsewhere, and the mere fact of comparing two analyses conducted each according to the different logic of its own particular theoretical space, and on different occasions, provided new clarity and insight. By giving different names to an identical operation or institution, a number of obstacles to systematic thinking caused by the fact that each word operates in a separate semantic field can be eliminated; substituting one word for another is an important research technique that often leads to progress. To speak of a 'theory effect' is to insist that this designation or nomination gives us a new way of seeing things.

The act of consecration

What I have said of science is also valid, I think, for political discourse, which makes us perceive things that previously went unnoticed, because they were self-evident. For example, the Russian formalists' whole theory of poetry underlines the fact that the essential feature of poetic discourse is to produce an effect of 'estrangement' which makes us perceive things that we routinely consign to the 'that's obvious' category.[1] It is no accident that there is a link between poetry and the issues that I am discussing, and that one of the exemplary cases of discursive imposition – institutional discourse, or the theory effect – is poetic discourse, in the form that we witness in primitive societies. In these so-called 'archaic' societies,[2] this role of nomination, and constitution of the social world through such nomination, falls to the poet, who does not produce for himself or herself or their fellow producers, as happens in societies where there is a field of relatively autonomous intellectual production, but is invested with a social mandate and the mission of naming the world in the moments when it becomes unnameable, that is to say in the difficult, tragic circumstances which leave the common man struggling for words.

This is also the role played by the prophet. In my last lecture I recalled Max Weber's definition of prophecy as a discourse that typically emerges in times of crisis: when there is nothing more to say when confronted with a world so enigmatic that it leaves us speechless, it is the prophet who speaks out and says: 'This is what you should see.' This effect of theory or constitution (the word 'constitution' being taken in both senses, the philosophical sense and that of political science) is also an effect of legitimation and consecration. The word 'consecration' is important, I think, in helping us to see another aspect of the effect I want to describe. This word is extremely rich and powerful sociologically; it designates a most peculiar act, since in consecrating something we are using language to reduplicate something that already exists. The act of consecration is in a way redundant; it is superfluous to reality; we could quote Mallarmé: 'The world takes place, there is nothing we can add.'[3] It is easy enough to deride the act of consecration, because we can only consecrate a difference that already exists, so why should we consecrate it if it already exists? In a way we could denounce the symbolic power of consecration precisely by saying that it is entirely symbolic (in the sense that we might say: 'He made a purely symbolic gift', that is to say, a gift of nothing at all). It is this very paradox of the symbolic that is echoed in the word 'consecration' – and I think it is important to reflect on this word: consecration duplicates something that already exists, by the use of language. But, in a way, this duplication changes everything: what was merely a difference becomes a distinction, something legitimate and sacred, a sacred boundary.

In fact, for the existence of a group, with its social distinctions, structures and divisions, the act of consecration is fundamental, since it is typically one of those symbolic interventions that would have no effect, or at least very little, if they did not rely on differences that already exist, and which at the same time are all-powerful, because they transform purely material differences into meaningful differences and differences before the law. The various differences (gender, age, region, class, etc.) that I have had at the back of my mind throughout my research must pre-exist in order to be symbolically constituted, but they are profoundly transformed by their nomination, by their institution – and the word 'institution' that I have already used must be taken in the strong sense of the term. In the legal tradition, the word 'institution' had an active meaning: as used in the case of the institution of an heir, that is to say, the act by which the father of a family instituted one or other of his sons before the law as his legal inheritor, that is, designated him through a symbolic act as entitled to inherit, designated as it were by socially constituted properties to inherit (he was the elder, the strongest, the most handsome or brave, etc.).

The act of institution or constitution is one of those apparently useless and insignificant acts that is nonetheless charged with the specific and fundamental symbolic effectiveness of transforming the factual into the legal – transforming the absurd *brutum datum* of the 'that's it' and the 'that's how it is', into a 'this is how it must be'. This operation of constitution, institution and consecration, this power of nomination or legitimation is possible, of course, because the differences exist, but also because these differences are never completely constituted, never completely indisputable. In my last lecture I insisted on the objective foundations of the symbolic action of institution or constitution, namely the objective polysemy of the social world, with its relative indeterminacy, which is due on the one hand, as Max Weber said, to the multiplicity of its aspects, and, on the other hand, to the fact that the future of the world is always open, which means that we are never sure what is going to happen. Hence the fact that the act of constitution almost always takes the form of a prediction even if it passes itself off as an observation – 'the new school term is a success' means: 'we must make sure that it is a success'. Political language is full of such propositions, which appear to be constative, but are in fact performative. The act of constitution therefore presupposes the existence of differences which are not absolutely indisputable, which allow a difference of opinion. It is in the relations linking this symbolic power of constitution and institution to the ambiguity of the real world that there arises what I want to describe, namely the struggle for the monopoly of symbolic power, which is the struggle for the power to legitimately enunciate the truth of the world.[4] This struggle for truth, for the power to say what exists – since the power to state what does exist is always a way of saying what must necessarily exist – this struggle for the monopoly of performativity is the political struggle properly speaking (or the religious struggle, which is one of the subdivisions of the political struggle). It is a struggle for recognition, that is, for the imposition of a form of knowledge of the social world that people have to acknowledge. The struggle for symbolic power is therefore a struggle for the imposition of a principle of perception of the world, a principle of classification, division, diacritics, criticism and judgement, that should be acknowledged to be legitimate. This principle is grounded in the *consensus omnium*, and in return derives from this very consensus a form of objectivity.

This leads to a crucial problem that seems to me to be at the heart of any reflection on the status of the social sciences and the specific role of scientific discourse in the social sciences. I will not develop the argument today, but I will at least refer to it: like any discourse claiming to be scientific, a discourse on the social world can ground its existence in validation through facts and objects, and it can claim to be founded by these very things themselves. But it can also claim to be grounded in the consensus of a group. There are therefore two ways of justifying a discourse on the social world. It may be said to be true because the laws which it establishes make it possible to make predictions that are verified in the real world; but we can also say that it is true because a whole group, or all those who dominate the group, say that it is true, and since they are able to establish the truth for this group, they possess the power of verification. I shall return to this central point,[5] because, if we fail to distinguish between these two principles of validation of the discourse on the social world, we are trapped in an endless debate over the scientific status of the social sciences.

The symbolic struggle over classification

However, I intend to save this problem until the end of my lecture course, because I believe that it is the most difficult. Today, I would like to define the logic and the aim of this symbolic struggle over classification. The aim of this struggle is to establish the existence of the group, and even people's social identities, in so far as the identity assigned to particular individuals depends on the group to which they are allocated and the identity assigned to this group. Raising the question of classification therefore inevitably raises the question of the nature of the group: What is a group? What makes a group? Who has the right to say, 'This is a group'? Which groups have the right to say, 'We are a group'? To whom do groups delegate the right to say, 'This is a group'?

To give you concrete matter for reflection, rather than indulge in thematics that you might find too abstract, I propose to take a specific example, the conflict over the nation or the region. Nationalist, regionalist, feminist or class struggles challenge the existence or non-existence of groups, the boundaries of these groups and, by the same token, the identity of the populations defined by these boundaries. In a text that I will not rehearse here, I analysed what is at stake in regionalist struggles, and what the struggle to impose the existence of a region means,[6] and I pointed out the insight that etymology provides in this case. As Benveniste notes in his *Dictionary of Indo-European Concepts and Society*[7] (which I quote frequently, to prompt you to read it as a matter of urgency), the word 'region', *regio*, comes from the term *regere*, with two key formulae: *regere fines*, which means 'to erect borders', and *regere sacra*, which means 'to institute or constitute sacred things'. These are in fact the same thing twice over, in so far as, according to Durkheim's definition, *sacer* or *sacra* is what is constituted by a division, generated by a border. As soon as you draw a line, there is a good and a bad side of the line. This constitutes the sacred. Which is more or less what Durkheim says.[8] To institute a limit is to put oneself in a position to *regere*, which is the act of a *rex*, a king (the word *rex* belongs to the *regere* family). The boundary marker dons the mantle of the archaic *rex*, who took a plough and traced a boundary around the city, which delineated the city and its sacred space. The *rex* institutes a group. He assumes, or usurps – and whether this usurpation is legitimate or illegitimate is the crucial question – the right to divide up the social world, to draw up borders in a social world which, as I said earlier, appears always to furnish only blurred, crossed or intermittent lines. His role is to institute divisions where before there was only a continuum.

We can thus transpose onto the social space what I said previously of the symbolic struggle (I said that there is a theory effect which is possible because there is ambiguity): as soon as we analyse the social world statistically, for example, it appears as a sort of interwoven skein of intermittent, overlapping yet heterogeneous dotted lines. The division into castes thus differs from division into classes through the insertion of clear-cut divisions into these fuzzy, overlapping zones, so that each individual knows on which side of the line they are placed. I take the metaphor, often used by statisticians, of the cloud or the forest: in a cloud, there is a fuzzy zone where we pass insensibly from the place where it is still a cloud to the place where it is no longer a cloud. Similarly, at the edge of the forest, the trees start to thin out and it is very difficult to say exactly where the forest ends and where the prairie begins. We should bear this problem in mind when we think about what a border is. Anyone who has crossed the border from France to Switzerland will have noticed that a border is something very arbitrary, that there is no geographical transformation of place. Geographers and politicians, of course, always try to make social, that is arbitrary, boundaries coincide with a natural boundary, and they are deeply satisfied when the truth coincides with a natural boundary ('Truth lies on this side of the Pyrenees'),[9] because the boundary can then be naturalized. But there are artificial boundaries that are acknowledged as such. In these cases, the legal act of separation displays its arbitrary nature and reveals its truth as a discontinuous cut in a continuous tissue. The logic of competitive academic entrance examinations shows that my analysis is neither formal nor abstract; indeed, some of the reflections I am sharing with you arose from my taking a serious look at the sort of question that we have all pondered: why is the twenty-ninth candidate admitted to be a Polytechnique student, while the thirtieth is not? It is well known that there is only about half a mark's difference, and that the statistics are not accurate enough to guarantee the validity of this difference. Here we have an archetypal authoritarian action, a division carved out by a social *rex*, with the education system acting on behalf of some obscure force (the role played by the representative is a vital issue). A social decision or decree will introduce a clear division into a continuous tissue. On the one hand, there will be consecrated people who, throughout their lives, will be consecrated as such, whatever may become of them. Even if they suffer brain damage, they will continue to have their skills and competence acknowledged – in spite of any accidents or natural impediments, they are socially gifted for eternity with a mandate to be intelligent, professors, and the like. On the other side of the line, half a mark lower down, people will be thrown into utter darkness by cuts that resemble the last judgement – to use a familiar metaphor – with their brutal divide between the elect and the excluded. This process of discrimination, of *diacrisis*, this definitive separation and limitation, does in its way typify the social process, which must disguise its arbitrary nature in order to function socially.

What I have said about natural frontiers might be said of all kinds of social frontiers: they are divisions which, in order to function socially, must not be recognized as arbitrary divisions but must be assumed to be natural. In order to achieve their objective – for a fundamental difficulty of sociological analysis is that attempt to distinguish, for example, between the technical effects and the social effects of the education system – these divisions created by consecration, in the sense that I have set out, must as far as possible be superimposed on pre-existing divisions, or must at least be socially effective enough, in cases where there is no difference *ex ante*, to produce *ex post* the differences that they are supposed to sanction. This is the consecration effect, the 'noblesse oblige' effect that I have described elsewhere, and so shall not reiterate here.[10]

To continue considering the logic of the border, I shall return briefly to the regionalist struggle. For Corsica to be both a goal and an instrument in a regionalist struggle, there must be some objective basis: it is best to have an island, and one with another language, and so on; but even if a regional group possesses all the features by which we recognize a region, it does not necessarily generate an independence movement and, conversely, a group that has none of the features by which we recognize a region (language, natural boundary, indigenous production, etc.) can have a very powerful regionalist movement, which gives an idea of how autonomous the power of the symbolic can be. That having been said – and this raises the whole problem of how these struggles relate to the representation of their objective chances of success that a knowledge of the objective truth provides – it seems to me that the struggle to control classifications and representations is all the more likely to succeed, the more it is rooted in the objective classifications. I think we can safely say as much. Nonetheless, these struggles enjoy a relative autonomy, especially in so far as they may be fought with symbolic weapons. Terrorism is one such weapon, acting as much through its symbolic impact as through its technical efficiency. There are all sorts of techniques, such as the demonstration (I shall come back to the word 'demonstration'), which make it possible to constitute and institute a difference that already existed, albeit on another plane, the realm of 'that's how things are'.

For instance, the Occitans survived until the twentieth century without knowing that they were Occitans – and the term still makes them laugh: they are not yet fully aware of being Occitans. Someone who addresses the Occitans – because of a vested interest, because of a personal interest in being Occitan, etc. – and says: 'You have a right to know that you are Occitans', relies on objective foundations for his opinion, but they are often not the ones he thinks. That was the drift of my article:[11] I think that there are no very objective grounds for the Occitan movement, except for the fact that the Occitans are stigmatized. Throughout history, many groups have been formed without any deeper grounding than the stigmatizing effects of a previous symbolic struggle.

Symbolic capital

Having suggested this set of examples – I believe that the case of feminism would be even clearer, but at the same time perhaps too facile and superficial – let us consider what will be the logic behind the specifically symbolic struggle. The goal of this struggle will be the acquisition of a specific type of capital that I call a symbolic capital, that I shall summarily call a recognition capital (which I shall explain later). In short, it was implicit in everything I have said so far that to exist socially is in the first instance to exist in the mode of 'that's how things are': there is an Occitan region that does not recognize itself as such, an existing, given Occitania, as there is an existing, given working class, and so on. When a researcher applies objective criteria, his theories reveal that groups exist on paper, but in fact these groups exist on paper because they exist in reality, without necessarily existing symbolically or objectively in the conscious representations made by the individuals concerned. Social existence is therefore an *esse*, a being, but also a *percipi* (I use Latin because it draws on tradition, it is self-explanatory, it is easier to follow for those who are in the know, and it makes no difference for those who aren't [*laughter*] . . . No, it is important, because if I deprive myself of these thinking aids, there are a lot of things that I cannot think anymore). One level of social existence, then, is a *percipi*, a being perceived, and symbolic capital is a form of perceived being which implies that those who do the perceiving acknowledge recognition of those whom they perceive. We might say that one of the goals of the symbolic struggle is to change the mode of actual being by changing the way being is perceived, since perceived being is indeed a part of the whole truth of our being in the social world. This is what I concluded in my previous lectures: we cannot completely understand social reality if we do not accommodate the fact that this reality is not simply what exists, for it also includes the representation that social agents make of this reality.

The example of regionalism illustrates perfectly how one can change ways of being by changing the perception of being. The mode of existence of the Occitans is no longer the same as soon as Occitania becomes an issue and people begin to write 'OCC [for Occitania]' on road signs. This is clearly important, as we can see in a situation of decolonization: to take an archetypical example, as soon as a minister from independent Algeria speaks on the radio, people say: 'Doesn't he speak good French!' Whereas when he was a colonized Algerian, they said: 'Hasn't he got an awful accent!' This is a very important social change, and I think it could be the same for Occitania: if you went to Aix-sur-l'Adour, you would find that people there speak French with a charming accent. It is just a detail, but it can change quite considerably the way people perceive themselves and the way we perceive them. These examples are in themselves rather trivial, but I believe that if we were to develop the argument further, we would reach some important conclusions.

The goal of the symbolic struggle then is to change groups and the relations between them, to change their boundaries and hierarchies by changing the way that members of groups perceive their own and other groups. The challenge, then, is to change the principles of vision and division, since there is no vision that does not divide: as soon as I propose a class, I imply a complementary class; if I sketch a form, I imply a basic underlying structure. This is one of the reasons why representations are almost naturally dualist: the logic of symbolism is almost automatically dualist. This is one of the flaws in our thinking, especially on the social world, and social studies are saturated with such dualist typologies. If you take my advice to heart, you will be suspicious in the future: it is normal for discourse on the social world to be spontaneously dualist, since this echoes the logic of our spontaneous knowledge of society, but this does not mean that social science must sublimate this kind of knowledge into a seemingly learned discourse, as sociologists often do – they might, in fact, do better to take this knowledge as their object. The symbolic struggle is a struggle to impose the legitimate vision of divisions, to impose the right perspective on, and view of, the social world. The relationship between this struggle and what I call 'symbolic power' or 'symbolic capital' is very simple.

We can state this in a formula that I will comment on later. Authority or symbolic power, as implied by a performative statement whose very utterance contains the conditions of its own fulfilment, is a *percipi* which enables one to impose a *percipere*: someone perceived is authorized to impose a mode of perception. In other words, symbolic capital is a social status, a way of being social, of being in the social world, of being for others. The person who is recognized as authorized to say: 'You see, there are two classes', is a social being. This follows the pure logic of perceived being having the ability to impose perception. Anyone can say anything they like – it is even the very nature of language to say anything and everything – but in order to be able to say, with some chance of success, 'there are two classes' (or, perhaps: 'You may not have noticed, but there is a new petite bourgeoisie and an old petite bourgeoisie', or even perhaps: 'Here we see some upwardly mobile petit bourgeois, but others on the way down, and this difference in status will determine which newspapers they read'), certain conditions are necessary, and one of the conditions is precisely that the person who performs, pronounces and predicts should be perceived as authorized to do so. But this is obviously a circular argument – we want to know how this symbolic capital is acquired. I do not use the term 'symbolic capital' to distinguish myself, but because I think there are scientific advantages in doing so rather than talking about 'prestige', 'reputation' or 'honour'. It is worth analysing the differences between these very important words. The word 'honour' refers to a capital in certain societies lacking economic capital; it is the power that one wields when one is recognized as worthy of wielding power. There is a sentence by Hobbes that goes like this: 'To be considered as having power is already having power'.[12] Strategies based on bluff are social strategies whereby social individuals or groups allow themselves to take some liberties with their objective circumstances. By making people believe that we have power, and making ourselves believe it, we achieve autonomy from our objective position. This is a typical characteristic of the petite bourgeoisie, whose claim to possess more than they actually own generates a kind of surplus above and beyond an objective definition of their condition.[13] Their claims can be contradicted, but this perceived surplus allows them a certain autonomy from their position as defined in strictly economic terms.

In many societies symbolic capital consists essentially of a surname, and it is no coincidence that even now in modern society family names, and especially noble names, are a form of symbolic capital, a capital of recognition, which has its own logic of accumulation, conservation, transmission and also conversion into other species of capital. We can interpret the marriages that were practised in the nineteenth century between the members of the declining aristocracy and wealthy American men or women as a form of exchange of one kind of capital for another. In the literary world, symbolic capital can be exchanged for literary notoriety, with the symbolic capital consisting of a name, a distinctive surname; and there are universes where the accumulation of capital consists in making a name for oneself, that is, creating a distinctive self-image.

What I am saying here could be the starting point for a whole host of analyses for you to follow up. Some you might find satisfying, others not – I am simply sketching out a few themes briefly, before I return to my basic argument. In societies governed by the logic of honour, the family name is therefore the principal capital: there can be struggles for the inheritance of a name. In societies which use the surname and first name (as in 'Eric, Ericsson'), the children will fight for the right to inherit the first name. For example, in a patriarchal lineage where the prestigious head of the family has a prestigious first name to transmit, there can be a struggle between three brothers who each have a first-born son to decide which grandson will inherit the grandfather's first name and, with it, a form of capital that benefits from the kind of magical identification practised by all groups. When we say, 'This man is the son of a *polytechnicien*,' we follow the logic of participation described by Lévy-Bruhl,[14] as if, by giving the name of the grandfather to the grandson, we hand something down to him. Neither case is more magical than the other, but I shall return to this.

The name is thus one of the properties that are central to the constitution of symbolic capital, because all the other representations turn on it. It is not the name in itself that is at stake, but the name in so far as it is the basis of a whole historical series of representations. So-and-so is the son of so-and-so, who is the son of so-and-so, who was a leading pioneer in some domain or other, or a charismatic guru, or a name in *Who's Who*. The brand names that help to make a product prestigious have different functions in different companies, but they obey the same logic. This kind of representation accumulates credit imperceptibly, it is a capital of credit ('credit' also implies 'credence', or belief) which accumulates very slowly and collectively. All the members of the group share in it, but it can be destroyed by a single individual. Hence the sometimes tragic solidarity of societies of honour: the error of one can destroy the capital of all. The same is true for the *numerus clausus* in our grandes écoles, for example: if there is a completely unconscious and uncalculated defence of what their graduate title-holders see as their standards, it is because they know very well that a fault committed by any one of them threatens the patrimony of the entire lineage. In archaic societies, it was through woman that misfortune struck; in our societies, it is failure by the son of a *polytechnicien* that ruins the symbolic capital of the whole lineage. There would be an opportunity here for a complete scholarly study of the transhistorical strategies by which groups try to control and increase their capital of reputation, for example by the rational management of co-optation: when co-optation is good, symbolic capital and credit increase; when it is bad, they diminish. So many of the social reactions that strike us as psychological are in fact a rational management of symbolic capital. I shall not develop this point further.

The manipulation of boundaries between groups

This struggle for symbolic capital always revolves around acts of nomination, and if the official title or the popular name of a group, clan or tribe is the peg on which the properties of reputation and representation are hung, it is because behind any accumulation of symbolic capital there lies an arbitrary act of nomination which constitutes the group. I would like now to try to clarify the strategies that the symbolic struggle will proceed to exploit. One strategy is the manipulation of boundaries between groups. I have already drawn attention to the universal logic of the *numerus clausus* that emerges in situations of fierce competition where the operations of discreet exclusion have to obey the letter of the law. Victor Karady has shown, for example, that the racist laws introduced in the interwar years in many countries of Central Europe intervened at times when social mechanisms of discreet elimination were no longer sufficient.[15] As long as the borders are shrouded in mist, there is no problem: there are just enough successful outsiders to support the argument that anyone can succeed, but there are not enough of these new arrivals to pose a threat to the happy few. Basically, it works the same way for a school system in a phase of expansion: there are enough children from the dominated classes to allow us to say that everyone has a chance, but there are not enough to threaten the successful reproduction of the dominant classes. However, when the statistical laws of elimination no longer work, it is necessary to invoke the law. The *numerus clausus* intervenes as an urgent measure in a situation of defeat; it is a consequence of a failure of those mechanisms that are all the more effective for being more unconscious – the best frontiers are those that do not have to be publicized. One way to wage symbolic warfare is to manipulate the perception of divisions and the definition of groups, to manipulate the boundaries of groups, say, for example: 'Is So-and-so really an X [*polytechnicien*], and son of an X? Is he a loyal graduate? Does he really have all the necessary qualities?' In other words, do all the individual members of the class conform to the legitimate definition of the class? Obviously, the debate becomes all the more complex with the more refined classes, which are those that have no definition, and are in fact indefinable.

Since this is a point that I shall not return to, let me say immediately that it is the most elite and elusive groups which define themselves as indefinable. It is an impregnable position, since there are no rules defining access; you have to be inside the group to say what it is you need in order to be there. It is a simple law of all aristocracies never to say what an aristocracy is. And it is typical of the upwardly mobile classes to demand a definition of the indefinable; that is the reason why – as Max Weber puts it so well[16] – they have the law and a certain rationalism on their side: 'We would like to know what makes a good pupil, what defines intellectual brilliance.' But if we have to ask about such things, it is because they are not self-evident. An example that I like to take is Plato's dialogue, which people do not always read as I do, because they tend to translate *arété* as 'virtue', whereas Plato is talking of 'excellence': 'to come first, to be the best', from *aristos* 'the one that surpasses all others'): Can excellence be defined? How can we define excellence? The older generation and the traditionalists say that it does not need to be defined, that it is indefinable, that it cannot be passed on, that Themistocles was very strong and a fine horseman, while his son was hopeless. But our own sophists, that is our teachers, say that it can be taught and therefore defined.[17]

There is therefore a struggle that is an ideal-typical form of the conflict between a rising class that wants to know where they are headed, and a privileged class who, unconsciously but in the name of an entirely rational strategy, refuse to define the very principle of their election, because if they did define it, that would give access to it, as well as provide a standard of measurement that would show how they fail to conform to the public image they display. What I have just described is a perfect example of the struggle for classification, the fight between rival views of where to draw the lines and between the conflicting principles cited in order to draw up a hierarchy of groups. Raising the entrance fee, making the cost of access more onerous, in the economic field as in all the other social fields, is a classic strategy of all dominant groups. The *numerus clausus* is the brutal solution, but there are much milder forms, one of which involves creating an artificial penury of opportunities.

The other strategy may be to discredit or disqualify. The fundamental schema of the symbolic struggle in all fields where the stake is symbolic (whether religious, intellectual or literary) is a struggle between the holders of the consecrated symbolic capital and their challengers. The most classic strategy of the challengers is a return to the roots. This was the strategy of the Reformation in the religious field. It consists in telling the dominant that they no longer conform to the values in whose name they rule, and that we must return to the roots, the letter of the Gospel, the straight and narrow, the Cathar line.[18] The principles on which the dominant base their domination are thus turned against them in order to discredit them and undermine the foundations of their capital. Similarly, in the intellectual field, the struggle classically opposes the young and the old, with the newcomers reproaching their elders with becoming bourgeois, old-fashioned, pedantic, dreary, pompous, self-important and formal. And they go about it in the same way that their predecessors had done in order to constitute their own capital, that is, by claiming the moral high ground: 'We reject everything given, to return to the original tradition.'

This is the case within specific fields of symbolic manipulation (religious, intellectual, literary, artistic, and so on) but, more broadly, in the social field as a whole we find a similar strategy in the fight to accredit or discredit, using gossip, calumny and all forms of symbolic action capable of destroying a reputation or an image. For example, when I was studying the question of Kabyle honour – an inexhaustible subject – the Kabyle waxed eloquent with cautionary tales on the subject of suspicion and the suspect person.[19] Just as with Caesar's wife, it is enough just to attract suspicion.[20] In fact, the whole theatre of the Spanish Golden Age turns on this theme. A novella by Cervantes, *The Curious Impertinent*, shows clearly that the mere fact that someone thinks badly of me will threaten my representation, that is to say my self-representation, but also the representation that others have of me. This means that the man of honour is a sort of permanent warrior in the symbolic struggle. The old Kabyle say that the man of honour is always on his guard; he looks to the right, to the left, to the front, to either side; he is always on the alert to nip in the bud any attempt to discredit him. And with every challenge that he foils, he accumulates capital. I think of this sentence: 'The family with a good reputation is the one whose women can cross the market place with crowns of gold on their heads without anyone passing a remark.'[21] In other words, they are people so endowed with symbolic capital that they nip in the bud the slightest attempt to discredit, dishonour, or destroy their reputation.

Defending one's capital

The deeper logic underpinning these struggles, that I have described at the phenomenal level, obeys a perfectly simple law: each of the combatants seeks to impose the principle of division and perception most suited to his properties, the one that will give the best return to his properties. This principle is at the heart of any definition of ideology (although in recent years there have been more and more new definitions, often rather academic). Ideology is born of this kind of fundamental strategy, whereby every social subject endeavours not only to project a positive image of himself, but to impose as universal the principle of classification that awards him the highest rank. In the academic space, which I have mentioned several times, there is the clash between scientists and men of letters, which is partly fuelled by each camp's attempts to make its principles of intelligence and culture dominant, each unconsciously taking as its principle the universalization of its interests. You see the most naive and blatant effects of this conflict every day, it is really surprising. Confronted with these intellectual debates, we are struck by the extent to which intellectuals are unaware of the degree to which they are manipulated by this principle: the greater part of what people say of literature, art and philosophy is based on their interest in being literary, artistic or philosophical if they are teachers of literature, art or philosophy. In other words, most of these panegyrics have no principle other than to plead the cause of the universalization, not only of a way of being, but also of the principle which establishes this way of being as the most excellent way of being.

Similarly, the debate between the major academic institutions (the École des Hautes Études en Sciences Sociales, the Sorbonne, the Collège de France, etc.) can only be understood in the logic of the following oppositions: research v. teaching, priority of teaching v. training for research and research into education, etc. A considerable number of the papers published in the *Bulletin des études grecques*[22] are motivated by this kind of principle, seeking to impose a discriminatory principle particularly favourable to the person seeking to impose it. This means that the conflict will be fuelled by a strategy aiming to overturn the scale of values, and will lead from symbolic revolution to symbolic revolution, since those dominated within a symbolic space have an interest in upsetting the criteria regulating the hierarchy, and therefore in adopting an unconscious strategy of overturning the hierarchy of power. From the start of this lecture I have been concerned to underline the fact that the criteria taken by objectivist science to be value judgements are in fact instruments of domination: when, as a researcher, I use 'has a degree in Latin' as a code – a precise criterion that allows me to distinguish Latinists from non-Latinists – I should realize that in practice it is no longer a criterion, it is an instrument of power. In 1968 for example, Classicists were mocked and their teaching trashed by the supporters of Boris Vian,[23] and were therefore concerned to defend this criterion in order to protect their values and the market that guarantees the reproduction of their values. When academic struggles, with all their pathos (and even tragedy, in 1968), take a dramatic turn, they are very similar to a clash of civilizations. In our sentimental society we typically bewail the fate of peoples living in the depths of the Amazon who are losing their culture, yet there are people in Europe who are ready to die for Latin and Greek. We have less sympathy for them, because we see them before our very eyes, and we see that they still rule the roost, but the logic is exactly the same – we just have to know how to universalize in the other direction. They are people who, in order to defend their values – that is to say their very being – without even consciously resorting to a strategy, feel obliged to defend the whole universe which their being relies on for its reproduction. I take a simple example: if, overnight, Latin and Greek ceased to be taught in high schools, all those people whose capital is the knowledge of Latin and Greek, who have invested their time and therefore money in it, would be like the holders of pre-revolutionary Russian bonds. Seen in this light, we can easily understand why they are defending the market. Sometimes my arguments may seem too abstract or too self-indulgent, but now you see that they do have something serious to say.

Another example that follows the same logic is the linguistic struggle. When they want to insist on the importance of linguistic struggles in Canada, Belgium, or Ireland, which are suspected of not being 'real struggles', people argue that economic issues are at stake. But defending one's language is in fact itself an economic issue of the first order. A language opens the way to careers and status, and so to income and opportunities for profit. From the day when free Quebec became a little freer, a lot of people who had been dominated were appointed to positions in radio and television. So there are very serious issues at stake. A revolution in the structure and the hierarchy of criteria amounts to a revolution in the hierarchy of powers.

In his *Dictionary of Indo-European Concepts and Society*, Benveniste says that words meaning 'to say' (*dico*) and those meaning 'justice' (*dikè*) share a common root.[24] In my interpretation, all the words that are related to saying are performative; they play a part in a struggle for the symbolic power to say what exists, and thereby to make it exist. To say authoritatively: 'Occitania exists' is to contribute to the Occitan struggle, whereas if I use my combined authority as sociologist and militant to say: 'Occitania does not exist', I can strike a terrible blow to the Occitan struggle. Even if I say it jokingly, the joke can be deadly serious. To say with authority that something exists is to help to bring it into being. When I speak of 'being recognized as having authority', this is a tautology. And yet, who is authorized to speak with authority? And how can we determine who has authorized them to speak with authority? It is no accident that we find ourselves in one of Wittgenstein's vicious circles that I have mentioned several times before. The only way out is through metaphysics, and I can tell you in advance that I do not think I can find my way out of it as a sociologist. The best we can do is to say that this vicious circle exists, which would still represent some considerable progress, because sociologists have been caught in this circular argument for generations, revolving around idealism and realism, and constantly starting all over again.

Who has the authority to speak with authority? In many situations, it is the social universe that designates the person who has authority to speak with authority. Here at the Collège de France the pointers are a microphone, a table, and so on. Benveniste points out that the Greek orator was given a *skeptron*,[25] a staff which became our sceptre, and as long as he held the staff, he was the legitimate speaker, he was justified in speaking. Who now is granted the legitimate authority to deliver the special kind of discourse that comments on the social world – which is a subclass of symbolic discourse, but one that is nonetheless at the heart of the symbolic struggle – and what are the socially recognized foundations that authorize them to classify the social world? Roughly speaking, there are two major classes of authorization.

The first category concerns classifications that commit no one but their author. The insult or abuse, which I discussed at the beginning of these lectures, is typically an *idios*, a singular classification. The opposition between the *idios logos*, the singular discourse, and the *koïnon kaï theïon*, which is communal and divine, is absolutely central to my argument: a person who puts himself in a position to classify, without being classified as able and authorized to classify, always leaves himself open to being judged unworthy of classification, to being rejected as an idiot or a madman. I'll come back to that. Society treats as madness any claim to classify that has no chance of not being rejected. I think someone might undertake a whole study of the social psychology of the mid-life crisis. You may not see the connection, but the mid-life crisis illustrates the problem of the discrepancy between the *idios* classification and the *koïnos* classification: there comes a time when 'you lose touch'. You see that we can all sociologize . . . There are classifications that commit only their author, but are still authorized. If you remember, 'authority' comes from *auctor*, and the *auctor* provides the link between legitimacy and the magic blessing: Benveniste, to quote him once again, relates the word *auctor* to the root *anacréo*, which means 'to grow', in the sense of 'to encourage growth',[26] which is a property of charisma, as described by Weber. According to Weber, the charismatic leader brings prosperity to his people, mainly through warfare and adventure, but also by ensuring bounteous harvests and fruitful labour.[27] The charisma depends on the capacity of the *auctor* to be his own guarantor; he has no guarantor other than himself, his gift, his person. He is the medicine man as opposed to the doctor. There is another category of people who commit no one but themselves, it is that of the idiot. He commits no one but himself, and he fails. He is the sorcerer whose magic fails, the insulter who is insulted in his turn.

The second category concerns those who represent the group, that is, those classifiers authorized by the group to classify. The group endows them with the power to form a group, to define the proper divisions between groups, to create groups, using this kind of Mephistophelian power. We find here what I call the theory effect, which consists in making people see and believe, in saying: 'Look, here we have a petit bourgeois, and there a bourgeois.' This theory effect becomes what I call an institution effect when the person who exercises it is given authority to do so by a group, is empowered to validate his own judgement, and has at least some of the trappings of normative, legal power.

We could make a double-entry table, articulated around two axes – one for the degree of institutionalization, the other for the degree of positivity.

		Institutionalization	
		−	+
Positivity	−	Abuse (3)	Life sentence (2)
	+	Flattery (4)	Official nomination (1)

The official nomination (1) – someone appointed by the President of the Republic or by the Prime Minister – is both positive (a person in a noble position) and highly institutionalized. A life sentence (2) (or a death sentence) is a negative judgement by the group, and strongly institutionalized. Abuse (3) is a weakly institutionalized and negative judgement; flattery (4) a positive but weakly institutionalized judgement (these tend to be individual exchanges, avoiding witnesses). There is now a circle of legitimacy: an authority will be all the more powerful as the group that authorizes it is more powerful, holds more authority itself and counts more members. The official public nomination, by the government or the President of the Republic – which raises the whole issue of the role of the state[28] – is a direct opposite of the private appointment, that of the father who flouts the civil law by deciding which one of his sons is to be his heir – which still happens in rural communities.

The degree of legitimation will depend on the extent of the group mobilized by the act of classification operated. An act of classification that involves the state has the force of law, and becomes real. The three orders, as described by Duby,[29] thus become the royal reality of the social world in France. Duby's book matches my analysis perfectly: the goal of the struggle between the knights (*bellatores*) and the bishops (*oratores*) – the *laboratores* are not players in the game, they are merely prizes to be won in the power struggle – is to proclaim the predominant principle of domination, and according to the law that I have just formulated, each camp claims that the predominant principle of domination is the principle of domination where it is predominant. This makes it easy to understand the internal struggles of the bourgeoisie (artists versus bourgeois), it explains a lot. I am simplifying (and I'm glad that Duby isn't here, you really would do better to read his book), but *grosso modo* the regal or state power institutes this struggle and proclaims that three orders coexist: *bellatores*, *oratores*, and *laboratores*. The king himself surveys these three orders from on high, placed vertically over the orthogonal structure of these three orders, and he reigns over these three constituted orders as from a divine point of view. The objectivist sociologist adopts this perspective – he puts himself in the place of the king.

So the problem is how to accumulate as much symbolic power as possible in these conflicts. You must be the king. In situations of perfectly matched rivalry, it will be the insult: I say that you are an idiot, you say as much of me; so it is a performative failure, a performative with no support. At the other extreme there is the absolute monopoly of the king, who says: 'You are a knight, you will attend the court in due order, you will assume your rank, you will have the right to attend the *petit lever* or the *grand lever* – the private or public audience – according to your station', etc. These situations of absolute monopoly or perfectly balanced rivalry are in fact very rare, which is why I wanted to frame my analysis initially with the striking extremes of the insult and the king – most situations are somewhere between. There are situations in which relatively established groups with fairly large social bases fight to extend their bases: everyone would like to be in the king's position, in order to be able to say: 'I am legitimate, because I am the one who says so.' This is the mistake made by Napoleon at his coronation, when he took the crown from the hands of the pope, and crowned himself.

One of the principles of legitimization is that it is better for two people to work together to consecrate each other. When you read *Le Nouvel Observateur*, you are struck by how short the circuits of consecration are; they are so short that they sometimes become so obvious that they lose their effect. For consecration to work, it must be recognized, that is, in fact, misrecognized. For that to happen, the circuits must be long.[30] Napoleon is a very short circuit: he crowns himself. This is like someone who calls himself 'the greatest living writer,' which frequently happens in literary circles.

Sociologically speaking, the interesting situations (which I shall try to describe next time) are those where we find a process which lies somewhere between monopoly and perfectly balanced rivalry, where some concentration has started but the process has not been successfully completed (as with the grandes écoles, for example, in the intellectual field). This causes uncertainty as to what is their true *ranking* in the field. This atmosphere is expressed very well, for example, in what Proust says about the salons in *Remembrance of Things Past*: for those who live entirely in the aristocratic universe, there is no doubt about the hierarchy of salons, but as soon as we take a step outside, we may fail to distinguish between the salons of the Duchesse de Guermantes and Madame Verdurin. One of the problems of institutionalization to be studied is how hierarchies come to be established in a floating world.

The intellectual field is very interesting in this respect, because it closely resembles those precapitalist worlds where each individual fights for their honour, completely alone, disconsolate and isolated, constantly looking over their shoulder. This kind of universe shows the process in its purest form. There is then an unofficial classification (of the grand families, the great intellectuals, etc.) whose configuration depends in each case on the position of the classifier himself in the rankings: the higher you rate in this unspoken classification, the more likely you are to know your true rank. This is most upsetting for those who are at the highest level, because as soon as they leave the universe of the few who know the true hierarchy, they are in danger of being confused with any passing stranger. The appearance of Francis Ponge[31] on television provides a remarkable sociological testimony – for the chosen few, there is no doubt that Francis Ponge is a very great poet, but how do you explain this to the world at large? So many people in the broadcast said: 'He is a great poet.' This universal, institutional classification transcends all groups, it is recognized by everyone. It is a populist rating, based on the *consensus omnium* and not only on the consensus of the best, *primus inter pares*; it is

a classification that transcends the group. How then does this classification function, what is the process that constitutes this capital of
authority that grants the authority to say how we should see the social
world?

Lecture of 9 June 1982

The accumulation of symbolic capital – Names and titles as forms of objectification – Making public – The institutionalization of symbolic capital – The two bodies – Consensual imaginaries

I want to deal today with the logic of the accumulation of symbolic capital. I tried to show in my last lecture how symbolic action, that is, action which can be considered magical in so far as someone acts on society through language, supposes the possession of what I call a symbolic capital, that is to say, an authority acknowledged by all, or by the whole of a group. I intend to analyse the kind of social magic, designated by the notion of the performative, that enables certain social agents to use words, orders or slogans to change the real social world. I refer here to Auguste Comte's celebrated distinction between the bourgeois and the proletarian, the former acting on the world at a distance through a quasi-magical action, that is, using words, and the latter acting directly on the world and possessing a 'positive spirit'.[1] I think that Comte's analysis, if we ignore its somewhat metaphysical connotations, is compatible with my argument. In order to account for this magical activity, I must analyse the conditions that combine to constitute this charismatic authority or symbolic power. In other words, we must in the first instance briefly describe the logic of the accumulation of symbolic capital. That is what I intend to do today.

The accumulation of symbolic capital

To put the question simply and directly: what is the difference between the lunatic who thinks he is Napoleon, and Napoleon himself? The individual subject intends to act upon the world through insult, abuse, or peremptory command. I think of an example given by Benveniste: if I personally shout 'I decree a general mobilization', I will be treated as a lunatic.[2] It would be an abortive performative, lacking the necessary 'conditions of felicity', and bound to fail. How can we give orders that are satisfactory? We need to reflect on terms like 'satisfactory', which can be taken both in their objective and in their subjective sense; I think that subjective satisfaction presupposes an objective satisfaction, that is to say, a match between the conditions of objective satisfaction and the actions themselves, which must necessarily include some of the conditions required to succeed. Napoleon's performative, or the administrative performative, like that of the judge who opens a hearing, the head of state who declares a general mobilization, or the gendarme who says: 'I arrest you', obeys certain conventions that require the person who performs these utterances, these 'speech acts', to be mandated to do so.[3] In fact, I would like to reflect on the notion of the mandate or delegation, which, strangely, has attracted very little attention since Rousseau.[4] (The history of philosophy remains an extremely important discipline in so far as it can provide a reservoir of questions that arose in a past age, but have been forgotten since.) I think that this notion, which was debated by Rousseau but which has since been completely abandoned, should be resurrected. This is what I propose to do with the help of the historians who, since Kantorowicz and Post,[5] have tried to show what institutional action or acts of institution were.

If this problem has not been discussed, at least in relation to the question of the existence of classes as I have formulated it here, I believe this is because, as is often the case, the issue has been clouded by various false leads, in this instance the problematics of awakening consciousness. I have referred to this question on several occasions, and the various indications I have given should be enough to allow me not to elaborate at length on this point. In general, the problem of symbolic power, or the theory effect as a particular instance of symbolic power, has been couched in terms of a question of awakening consciousness. Can we find a theoretical discourse, grounded in reality, capable of giving the group access to its own truth and thereby allow it to constitute itself as a group? – the group concerned by this theory obviously being the proletariat. I would like to show that this problematic is an intellectualist type of questioning, which bears the hallmark of the classic illusion of the intellectual, namely, the ethnocentrism which presents the problems of society in the way that they are perceived by intellectuals. I would like to show how this problem can be set aside in favour of the one that I propose, which consists in asking ourselves how the serial group, from being a set of individuals aggregated *partes extra partes*, like objects, becomes a constituted group able to act as one man. Instead of making awakening consciousness the condition of the constitution of the dynamic of the group, I shall therefore try to show how it is the mechanisms of delegation that are the condition of these phenomena of collective, or apparently collective, action.

We might describe a series of stages, from the struggle of each against all, the symbolic struggle that I mentioned previously in the context of conflicts of honour, to the action exerted by a person explicitly mandated to act on behalf of a group, that is to say, a person appointed by the state, or at least an agent of the state. At one extreme, we have the individual action of the person defending their honour, prestige or symbolic value, in the intellectual field, for example. They can rely only on their own strength, that is to say, an authority of a charismatic, personal kind. At the other extreme we find the mandated representative, described very well by Max Weber (since Rousseau there has of course been important work by Max Weber, and I shall be developing Weber's argument in what I am going to say). The ideal mandated representative, as Weber describes him, is the official who acts within the terms of reference of his official function. In the opposition between the priest and the prophet that I referred to last time, there is obviously a reference to the notion of the official and his official function, the function being precisely one of those mandates which the group confers on an individual and which allows that individual, endowed with a professional name denoting their function, to act on behalf of the group as if they were the group in whose name they act.

The generative process that I am going to suggest is obviously a theoretical model – things do not happen like that in reality – and I will show later that we must not see this process of objectification as a kind of evolutionism in which we would start off with symbolic capital incorporated in a single individual and end up with symbolic capital instituted in a state. In societies that have developed a state, there are sectors that are still never completely institutionalized, and, in societies that lack a state, there are the beginnings of institutionalization. It is therefore not a linear process or a kind of organic development. What I am going to describe as evolution is actually a process that is born of struggle and is always an issue in the struggle itself.

Names and titles as forms of objectification

I mentioned in my last lecture an elementary form of objectification affecting the proper name, the family name. I have found a text by

Montesquieu that illustrates my argument very well: 'Names, which give men the idea of a thing that seemingly should not perish, are very appropriate for inspiring in each family the desire to extend its duration'.[6] In this way, Montesquieu points out that the name, which transcends individuals, not only in the present moment but also and especially in the long term, is likely to induce the bearers of this name to transcend themselves in order to perpetuate the name. In fact, those who justify natalist policies often argue that it is a question of perpetuating or defending the family name. There is a kind of social reality in things nominal – this is the core of what I have been arguing: the nominal is as real as the real; words, being social things, are real things; words are things and do things. Names such as the family name are the beginnings of institutionalization, of objectification, that is, something that transcends individual actions and the individuals who bear the name. They transcend individuals and lead them to transcend themselves: it is well known that the 'noblesse oblige' I have referred to[7] is inspired by the need to preserve the capital inscribed in a name. We might think of the whole tradition of the theatre of the Golden Age, or the struggle for glory in a Corneille tragedy. We could characterize this logic as inspired by a concern to defend something very real, the nominal value of a group, in so far as it is the group name that makes the group and, of course, in so far as the name gains its value from what the group is worth: it is a reciprocal, dialectical relationship.

Another example of elementary objectivation is the acronym or logo. A group begins to exist when it has an acronym or logo. It is not by chance that there are struggles for the ownership of titles, although these are only words. People fight for the right to claim a name. For example, in fights over an intellectual legacy, the struggle to inherit a name is extremely important. To take possession of the title of a review, or the legacy of the Durkheimian sociologists, is a very important issue, because these founding fathers of the intellectual field play a part in our societies that corresponds to the role of the ancestors in precapitalist societies, and if the *Revue française de sociologie* devotes 60 per cent of its pages to discussing Durkheimian sociologists, it is of course because it is interesting to deal with them, but also and especially because theirs is an important legacy and the person who inherits this legacy acquires the rights, for example, to the social definition of the legitimate way of practising sociology. Names and acronyms – and I will come back to the acronyms – are very important, in so far as the holder of the name and of the monopoly of the acronym has very important rights over the group. It is like the right of signature, to which I shall return.

Another example which is of capital importance is the title: titles of nobility, academic qualifications, and titles of ownership. The title is the performative par excellence, it is a way of saying that the bearer of this title is not just anyone, that is to say, he *must* be *someone*. The titles always speak in the indicative, but in the affirmative mode that we use when we say: 'This man is a man', that is to say, a real man. The language of the title is always performative, and a Portuguese sociologist told me that in Portuguese, to declare that someone has passed their bachelor's degree, they say that he has been 'created a bachelor'. This is the language of creation: it is our perceptions of the social world that turn the thing named into reality; they do not merely describe a pre-existing reality, they produce it. Academic qualifications, like titles of nobility, say to the bearer: 'You must be worthy of the title you bear.' They have this function in the eyes of others, and they enjoin the title holder to behave in the eyes of others in accordance with their description of what he is. We could expand upon this. These titles are evidently objectifications. They exist in the form of paper certificates; they can be framed and hung on the wall, because they are visible objects. They are official and have the force of law, that is to say they involve guarantees, they give entitlement to posts, benefits, and privileges. They are sometimes transmissible under certain conditions (there we would have to make a comparative analysis of the properties of the different types of titles); they are subject to devaluation, in the case of inflation for example, as they depend on people's confidence in their value. The most basic form of objectification is the constitution of named classes, but its ultimate form comes in the shape of an institutional guarantee. In fact, it is actually the state that introduces a perfectly guaranteed form of institutionalization.

I ought really to elaborate on what I have called 'rites of institution' in the light of this logic, but I shall not do so today because I do not have enough time. I refer you to the latest issue of *Actes de la recherche en sciences sociales* where I have tried to develop this notion.[8] I shall simply give you the outline of my argument here. What appears to happen is that this institution that we call the 'state' (without knowing what it is – I always hesitate over using this word, and I often say that we must never write sentences which start with 'the state does something', but if we really have something to say we are obliged to write such phrases),[9] is entitled to say, in well-defined circumstances that I call 'rites of institution', that a person is 'this' or 'that'. These are the acts of nomination, in the banal, legal sense this time, by which the person named becomes both mandated and licensed, that is to say both authorized and summoned, to do something. It is through this process that acts of nomination, which presuppose an institution that mandates and guarantees its delegates, treat individuals as holders of a function which transcends, precedes and survives them. This is the formula of the canon law, *dignitas non moritur* ('the function is eternal'); for the characteristic of the social within the structures of a state society is precisely the ability to perform the miracle of producing eternal social functions, positions and roles, so that their temporary holder participates in a moment of this eternity. I shall return to this when I discuss Kantorowicz's famous theory of the king's two bodies.

Making public

What is the process of objectification, whose two poles I have indicated – at one extremity, the struggle of every man for himself, the symbolic struggle in which each individual seeks to maximize his or her symbolic profit by crediting and discrediting others, and at the other end of the scale, state power? What does this process of objectification comprise? How does it produce its effects? I think that all these acts, which consist in pinning stripes onto someone's sleeve or stripping them off, have at their heart one of the fundamental properties of the social: our communal knowledge. It is not by chance that the rites of institution are always rites that are called official or public. One of the most important actions that a group can accomplish is one that affects its own nature, that is, to publish, publicize, ostentatiously display and render official their rite of passage.

The opposition between the official and the unofficial has provoked very little discussion. Everyone knows what an *eminence grise* is, but very few people reflect on the actual notion of making public, on what, for example, is meant by publishing wedding banns. These are very interesting things that everyone knows but no one stops to think about. A very important word that was analysed by Heidegger (who always went for the key words), is the notion of *Öffentlichkeit*,[10] the condition of being open, or patent. Things named 'official' by society are placed out in the open, accessible to all, as opposed to being hidden, secluded or sheltered within small, clandestine groups. Here we find the opposition that the Durkheim school made between religion and magic.[11] Magic is clandestine; it is the forest, the night, the feminine, the left hand, and so on. The official is something public, something that can be shown to everyone; it is the masculine, something that can be declared publicly, without shame. One of the magical operations performed by society, enabling groups to adjust and structure their form and constitution, to classify themselves in advance as they lie in wait for the sociologist who comes to classify them, consists precisely in bringing into view things that were hidden, or, on the contrary, censoring ('censorship' is a word that would merit further reflection), repressing and burying the hidden things that attempt to emerge into daylight. This dialectic of publication and censorship is one of the most powerful processes that can be generated from within the group, and it is through this action that groups create a symbolic world. In the opposition I have already mentioned, between the informal hierarchy (such as the hierarchy of salons described by Proust, which is known only to the initiates, the insiders) and the public hierarchy (which is displayed in gazettes and newspapers, etc.), publication has a decisive effect, in so far as the hierarchy ceases to be known only to the initiated and becomes known to everyone, including the layperson.

Popularization is a good example of the logic I have just described, and if we consider the word 'popularization' in the light of my analysis of 'publication', it is clear that popularization must be a major issue for a scientific community. If researchers have a very ambivalent and contradictory relationship with popularization – I refer to the work of Luc Boltanski and Pascale Maldidier, who presented the results of a survey of scientists on this problem[12] – it is precisely because it represents the passage from the internal hierarchy for initiates, which must always be questionable even if it is in fact uncontested, to a common public hierarchy based on the *consensus omnium*. To underline the importance of this issue, I will simply quote a statement by Schopenhauer, who said – I'm not sure where, but I remember reading it in my youth – that one of the most devious strategies that a specialist discussing with another specialist in the presence of an uninformed third party can use, is to ask a question so difficult that his interlocutor cannot answer it without becoming unintelligible to their uneducated audience.[13] This is important for understanding debates in the social sciences and the role played by journalists in arbitrating between specialists, which, unfortunately, is typical of the state of social relations within the intellectual field.

Schopenhauer's paradigm is very important for understanding the challenge of integrating a hierarchy that must be undisputed, so that it can be declared in public, and thus, through this same public declaration, become undisputed. Publication can be a force in its own right, as for instance when a newspaper publishes a hierarchy of French intellectuals[14] – to give you a very concrete example (I say that, because I hope that you have understood that in sociology the more abstract calls forth the more concrete: there is nothing worse than the half-concrete

or the semi-abstract which contribute neither anything real nor anything theoretical). When a review publishes a hierarchy of French intellectuals, in a show of *force majeure*, there is no escaping the fact that
this is a major coup, and anyone who wants to contest this hierarchy
becomes open to challenge by this very hierarchy (they will say that he
protests only because he has been wrongly ranked), and there is no end
or solution to the dispute. I am not going to expand on this, but I think
that it has always been an obsession haunting the scholarly community. For example, Kant's *Conflict of the Faculties* constantly returns to
this problem, concerning the relationship between pure science and the
applied sciences.[15] If the scholarly community has always reflected on
this problem, quite hypocritically, it has to be said, it is because what
open publication threatens is the autonomy of the scientific field.

The passage from the unofficial to the official is an operation that
looks inoffensive, yet it is the supreme example of social manipulation. It is a marriage as opposed to an affair, or something that can be
said aloud, and therefore known and acknowledged by all, as opposed
to something shameful and clandestine. In fact, if publication has
such an important social effect, it is because publication as such has a
legitimating effect: if something can be said in public, it must be good.
(I am stating this in crude and peremptory terms, but I shall want to
make subtler distinctions later.) When we say pejoratively of people
who flaunt some illicit action that they are 'showing off', we mean that
they are transgressing the unwritten law, which according to Weber is
one of the most fundamental social laws, that people who transgress
legitimacy must hide in order to do so: the plainest evidence of the
acknowledgement of legitimacy is the fact that the thief hides himself
in order to steal.[16] Where a naive definition of legitimacy would see the
thief as an exception to legitimacy, he does in fact provide the supreme
proof of legitimacy. Similarly, cultural shame illustrates the clearest
acknowledgement of cultural legitimacy.

So we see how making something public procures legitimacy, even
if the claim itself may be based on bluff. One of the common strategies of the rising strata consists in overthrowing the censorship that
only existed, however, in so far as they recognized it as such. The
fact of uttering words that were taboo – just think of the language of
sexuality, which is quite typical – is an entirely self-legitimizing transgression. This inevitably involves the struggle for symbolic power, for
the author of this transgression of censorship risks being condemned
and discredited as a coiner of barbarisms, in order to discredit him,
but he may also prevail, if he manages to have his transgression recognized as legitimate because it exists, and if he manages to find a

group to acknowledge him. To be recognized by a group is simply to be heard, to gain a hearing. Obviously if he starts influencing people to talk like him, he has won, but the simple fact of finding an audience ready to lend him an ear, so to speak, is already a victory, because this means that he is recognized by a group. The subversive charisma of the prophet makes itself manifest precisely by making things previously unspoken become audible to a group that was just waiting to be allowed to think them, and whose act of recognition introduces people to a new way of thinking and being in the world. Legitimizing, objectifying, verbalizing and making explicit (through signs, gestures or acts) are already sufficient to imply validation. They convey an affirmation of the right to stand up and be counted. We should add into this logic the role of ritual, especially rites of passage.

The institutionalization of symbolic capital

There is a third mechanism. Objectification in institutions, titles, acronyms, logos or slogans leads to the establishment of a kind of mechanism whereby accumulated symbolic capital becomes self-reproducing. This differs from the struggles for honour, where a person's symbolic capital is at stake at every moment. The Kabyle say, 'Honour is like a turnip seed': it is round, it rolls and you cannot catch it.[17] In other words, it is extremely volatile, you can lose it for the slightest reason, and you can be dishonoured without knowing why. Honour is highly insecure, as is intellectual fame, whose credit and discredit are equally insecure. With institutionalized names or titles, it is less vulnerable. We saw it in what Montesquieu said. One can lose one's mind and remain a teacher. Institutionalization provides a guarantee over a certain period of time; it guarantees duration and creates objective mechanisms capable of ensuring their own reproduction.

This is another argument that I cannot develop here, but I may take the example of the intellectual field: as long as the struggle remains in an anarchic state, it is a case of every man for himself; it is extremely difficult to concentrate symbolic capital. We might say that there are states of the intellectual field in which the struggle of each against all reminds us of aristocratic society under Henri IV, as described by Elias in *The Court Society*, where the great man must be ready at any moment to take up his sword and fight a duel, to defend his honour by himself.[18] When symbolic capital starts to accumulate, as soon as there are institutions, academies, and schools which reproduce the academies, as soon as there are clubs and institutions in the political field,

such as parties with structured administration, regional and central sec-
retariats, membership cells, that is, as soon as an institution comes into
being, with the language and legislation to dictate its operations, with
rules of conduct and conventions of social intercourse, and its ability
to use them to manage all kinds of affairs, then the reproduction of
symbolic capital can be assured by the simple control of the institutions
– there is no longer any need to draw your sword. And just as Louis
XIV no longer needs to fight a duel on every occasion, but needs only
to regulate the ceremonies of the *petit lever* and the *grand lever* (private
and public audiences), so the member of the central committee can concentrate on ensuring the reproduction of the central committee, which
is no easy matter, but is still easier than having to ensure the reproduction of your prestige by appearing on chat shows, writing masterpieces,
telling everyone what they should think of society, avoiding all error,
and bringing happiness to the people, at the very least. As soon as
symbolic capital becomes concentrated, objectified and accumulated in
procedures and institutions ensuring its reproduction, the management
of this capital assumes a completely different form.

Now, having described this in general terms, I should very briefly
point out the conditions under which this accumulation occurs. As I
said earlier, this is not a linear process. This pattern of linear evolution
from the struggle of every man for himself to the state monopoly with
delegation, is one of those hand-me-down patterns which we all have
rooted in our minds, but which a psychoanalysis of the scientific mind
must destroy. For there is in fact a never-ending struggle, with retreats,
setbacks, and fresh departures. The concentration is never completely
accomplished; there are always some rebel areas, which can spread to
infect the centre, and so on. Which underlines what I said earlier: that
there is a struggle for the institutionalization and objectification of
the capital already objectified, and the monopoly over it. Moreover,
the struggle for symbolic capital in an advanced state of objectification is a struggle to control access to the instruments of production
and reproduction of this already objectified symbolic capital. I refer
you to my description in the first part of *The Logic of Practice* of
the contrast between societies where power depends on the personal
capital of individuals, and societies where it depends on the control of
objective procedures.[19] So it is the opposite of a linear model, it obeys
the logic of a struggle for the conservation and increase of objectified
capital, by controlling the institutions in which it is already embodied.
It is through a kind of social magic that groups construct themselves,
and their own representations of themselves. (The word 'representation', I must insist, should be taken in all senses of the term: as mental

imagery, as theatrical spectacle, and as delegation, when we speak of the representatives of the people.) What does this process consist of, and how does it emerge? The question I really need to answer is: how do groups come to constitute themselves? I do not mean by this that the groups are masters and manipulators of their own identity, that they can by pure decree decide to exist however they wish. I have said clearly enough in my previous lectures that these magical strategies succeed only within certain limits. That having been said, within these limits, groups do perform a kind of magical action on themselves, and on the other groups as well.

The two bodies

To describe the logic of this magic, I shall refer to two important authors, Kantorowicz and Post. These two historians share a common interest in studying an argument that has been pursued since the Middle Ages. The subtitle of Gaines Post's book is *Public Law and the State, 1100–1322*.[20] Post considered essentially canon law, and canonical commentaries on the law, whereas Kantorowicz analysed the work of the English jurists, in a later period. What they have in common is to take as an object of sociological study, or, more precisely, to consider in terms of a sociological discourse on the social world, something that had long been read only as a simple theological argument. This is not by chance. For example, Kantorowicz says that in this literature of the English jurists there is a kind of equation which constantly recurs, a kind of equivalence between *mysterium* and *ministerium*, to such an extent that it seems almost like a misprint.[21] This is very interesting for several reasons. If we read a treatise on canon law in an innocent way, we gain the impression, even if we have no particular anti-clerical prejudice, that it is all about theology, using language that is quite unreal and unrealistic, discussing the hereafter and having nothing to do with the things of this world. But in fact, once we go beyond these surface appearances, we discover, for example, that when the canonists say that 'the church is the body of Christ', 'the bishops are the church', or 'the church is the bishops', and so on, they are not formulating theological equations, but sociological equations, in so far as sociology is a theology, and the social world contains its share of magic. I was unfair just now when I said that the notion of delegation had not been debated since Rousseau: Max Weber is the person who has reflected most profoundly on this mystery of the incarnation of the state in a person, since the official is someone whose biological body incorporates a transcendent moral being. But although Max Weber reflected on this mystery of the incarnation of collective entities, he remained a prisoner of the rationalist illusion, since he described this process as a process of rationalization. In Max Weber's classic analyses of the sociology of law, or power, among others, he always takes us through three stages: a traditional, routine stage, a charismatic stage and then a rational or bureaucratic stage. He makes everything proceed as if the magic, present in the charismatic stage, for instance, disappeared in the bureaucratic stage.[22] Whereas, if you have followed my argument so far, you will see that what I have been suggesting all the time is that there is magic at the heart of the rational state. Grading university students, for example, is a magical act exactly like the actions described by Lévi-Strauss in 'The sorcerer and his magic.'[23] This undermines the notion of an evolutionary pattern, which I have indeed already refuted several times by now. The division of ethnology and sociology into separate disciplines has helped prevent us from seeing that the two processes are the same. Kantorowicz cites a sentence quoted by Francis Bacon summarizing the entire tradition of English lawyers under the reign of Queen Elizabeth: '*Corpus corporatum in corpore naturali, et corpus naturale in corpore corporato*' – 'A body corporate in a body natural, and a body natural in a body corporate'.[24] There is another English phrase: 'the king as King was "incorporated with his subjects, and they with him"'.[25] The interesting words are obviously the words for 'body' and 'corporate'. The sociologists who study the major administrative corps of the state and their recruitment have never made the connection between these administrative bodies and the physical body. The merit of this phrase is to say: the body *corpore* is the constituted, corporate body. This is the definition of the king, but it can also refer to the President of the Republic, the professor, or the priest, etc. In fact, it is the official in the broadest sense of the term: it is the person who is mandated to perform an *ex officio* function and not *motu proprio*, on his own behalf. As for the second quotation ('the king in his political body is incorporated with his subjects and his subjects with him'), there is a similar saying by a medieval saint who said: 'The Church is the bishops; the bishops are the Church.'[26] This amounts to positing a simple equation: the constituted corporate body, the *collegium* for example, is the same thing as the biological body which we have described as being mandated by a rite of institution to represent the constituted corporate body: 'You are officially mandated from now on to be the *collegium*, the *communitas*, etc.'

Rites of institution (the examining of doctoral theses, for example) produce a sort of transubstantiation in a manner quite analogous to what happens with the Eucharist: 'This is my body, this is my blood'; they may appear to be bread and wine, seemingly offered by an ordinary mortal, but in reality, it is the group, and the *king* is no longer a mortal body. There is a splendid phrase saying that the body is always vulnerable to an attack of *imbecilitas* (it is weak, it is mortal) but that it bears another body within.[27] The title of Kantorowicz's book is *The King's Two Bodies*, and the metaphysical problem that his theologians posed was to know how these two bodies could live in concord. They say, of course, that the juridical body is the superior body, it is the body constituted as collective will, it is the king coextensive with his subjects, it is de Gaulle saying, 'I am France.' I began by raising the question of the difference between Napoleon and the lunatic who thinks he is Napoleon. If someone walking down the street were to say: 'I decree a general mobilization, I am France', we might wonder if he was in his right senses, but if the head of state says 'I speak in the name of France . . .' it can be effective in certain circumstances, and will thus become a particularly successful realization of the *corpus corporatum*. The fundamental question that faces any society is this: how to make transcendental realities, things that cannot be named, or rather that are only a word, exist in a permanent and stable condition. I think that Durkheim did sense this problem, and you will recognize this theme of the group transcending the individual. However, I think that while he designated the problem, he neutralized it with all his theories of collective consciousness.[28] He found metaphysical answers, and the difficulty of social science is to speak scientifically of things metaphysical and not metaphysically about things that we take to be real. Metaphysics exists in the social world; the sociologist has not invented it. I believe that the sociologist has to deal with metaphysical, that is magical, realities. Society is constantly making magic, and the great difficulty for the sociologist, as a scientist wanting to reflect on these magical matters, is being obliged to rely on a science that is hostile to magic, and destroys it. That is why the danger we face with this kind of issue is to believe too soon that we have understood it.

I return now to *mysterium, ministerium*. The word 'ministry' is an astonishing word that specifically refers to delegation. The government minister is a vicar of . . . something not entirely clear. Just as the priest is a Vicar of Christ, the cabinet minister is an agent of, shall we say, the state, that is of all the citizens. I shall now try to summarize Post's argument.[29] He tries to describe the theory by which the canonists claim to explain what kind of ministry the constituted corporate body is. The constituted corporate body they are thinking of is the church: What is the church? Who has the right to speak in the name of the church, to execute performative acts, to say, 'the church is unfavourable to contraception'? According to the in-house theories of the canonists reported by Post, the existence of constituted corporate bodies is linked to the right of representation, the word 'representation' being taken in all three senses: it is the right to speak and act on behalf of the group, to stand before my group and other groups with the aim to incarnate my group, and to make everything I say appear to be said by and for the group. The spokesman is not even a person who speaks on behalf of the group: he is the group. There is clearly a kind of fetishism here. The spokesman, especially in 'democratic' applications of this logic of delegation, tries to indicate or to imply that he has not forgotten that he is not the group, but the logic of social fetishism is such that the group is inclined to 'forget' the delegation that gives the spokesman priority. And the characteristic of social fetishism, which is inscribed in the logic of delegation, is that the delegate 'forgets' that he is a delegate and, at the same time, forgets that he is the source of the power that controls him.

How does the representative declare himself, how is he recognized as a legitimate representative? I quote: 'The representative, whether he be king or bishop, personifies the group as *procurator*,'[30] that is, the person who is charged with the power of attorney, or proxy. This is a Heideggerian theme. Although Heidegger attacked the social security system, which he saw as using the type of delegation by which the masses were alienated, treated as dumb beasts, and robbed of their responsibility for their own destiny,[31] the fact remains that he did at the same time consider an extremely important issue: the process of delegation whereby groups abdicate their own freedom for the benefit of the state. The representative personifies the group as a substitute or proxy authorized to monopolize their collective expression and actions; this monopoly is symbolized by the monopoly of the *sigillum authenticum*; the *sigillum* is the seal and the *sigillum authenticum* is what authenticates the official seal, which may be engraved with, for example, the symbols, effigy, arms or motto of a sovereign, a bishop or a community. The two communities to which lawyers have given much thought are, on the one hand, the university community, *universitas*, *collegium*, and, on the other, the ecclesiastical community. When does a group have the right to exist as a group? It has the right to exist when it has been granted the *sigillum*, that is to say, the mysterious social gift that allows the seal holder to authenticate all his acts and words as collective acts, and thereby make the group exist as a single man, which is extremely important.

I said earlier that I had dismissed the problem of awakening consciousness. But if you think back to Sartre's *Critique of Dialectical Reason*, you will see that the problem I am discussing is, I believe, the one that Sartre wanted to tackle when he described a kind of transcendental genesis of the group:[32] We start with the individual and how to escape individuality, and then we move on to the oath and the fused group, etc. Unfortunately, the group as such is nowhere to be found within Sartre's logic. Why? Because there is a wild, and possibly mortal leap from the group that exists *partes extra partes* as a collection of individuals to the group that, by dint of the *sigillum authenticum*, has already delegated to a person or group of persons the plenipotentiary power to act, think and speak on its behalf. From that moment on, the representative becomes a substitute for reality, a sort of material substitute for the universal, and if he is the substitute for the universal, that is to say, the state, or the *consensus omnium*, he is the universal made flesh, and his word has force of law. His word is therefore automatically self-verifying. If he says, 'I nominate you professor', you become a professor. I could have cited another author, Schramm, who follows the same logic as Kantorowicz in order to reflect on the symbols of royalty and the notion of the crown (in both senses of the word: the crown as an object, but also in the sense of the 'laws of the Crown' and the conventions of regal succession).[33] He offers a fine example, describing the crown as objectification: as soon as there is an objectified crown, one can stage a *coup d'état* by seizing the crown, whereas as long as there is no objectification, there can be no *coup d'état*. Among the Kabyle, there can be no *coup d'état*, any more than there can be in our own intellectual field. For there to be a *coup d'état*, there must be a state, that is to say, symbolic power must be concentrated in institutions that one man can appropriate, in order to govern as one man on their behalf.

Consensual imaginaries

So far, this seems relatively simple, but what does this kind of transubstantiation consist of, this transition from a simple *corpus naturale*, or biological body, to a social corporate body? The canonists call it a *fictio juris*, a legal fiction – we must take the word *fictio* in the strong sense of deriving from *fingere*, that is, as 'imagination'. Again, I do not have time to develop it, but I think that the best analysis of this imaginary production of the group by itself would still be found in Pascal, with his notion of imagination and the power of the imagination, where the whole function of the symbolism of power is to be the power itself.[34] Naive theorists of ideology still think that it would be enough to remove the wig and the gown from the judge. In fact, the wig and the gown are power personified, as is the language of the law. The obscurity of legal discourse is the very essence of the language of the law, just as the philosopher's language of self-important significance is the essence of philosophy.[35] If these attributes were removed, along with the conditions that allow them to be reproduced even when they are removed, there would no possibility of social magic.

Social functions are fictions,[36] but not at all in the sense of being simply an imaginary reality, capable of being destroyed by a simple statement of reality, as something imagined dissolves when confronted with what is actually perceived; they are productions of the collective imaginary, which endows them with an entirely objective truth; they are collectively accredited and constantly self-verifying imaginations, in so far as they are able to impose their own verification and to show that they are somehow more true than the truth. Remember Pascal's 'Cause and effects', where he says that power is imaginary, but at the same time quite real: "I am supposed not to bow to a man in brocade clothing followed by seven or eight lackeys? And if I do not, he will have me thrashed.'[37] This calls for more detailed analysis, but I have given you the outline, and you can take it further yourselves.

It would be a useful exercise to use the notion of the imaginary and the fictitious to show how the group, by manipulating its own image, manipulates the fundamental structures of the imaginary. I hardly dare say it in public (there are reflections that are perhaps true but which are so private they are sometimes difficult for me to express), but I think that one of the properties and strengths of this fetishist logic is that it acts on the biological body, and that by incarnating the transcendental, legal, social body in a biological body it produces biological effects. In the end, it all comes down to the social world manipulating the deep structures of the imaginary, so that, for example, when we say 'the state', we evoke the image of the father. If the social world makes such a great use of magic to found the seemingly most rational structures, it is because it can only persuade the bodies that it transcends to turn into mystical, that is to say social, bodies by plucking the deepest heartstrings of the body and the most deep-seated representations of the imaginary. That is where sociology and psychoanalysis might for once come together in a non-fictitious way.

To briefly sketch out the practical consequences of this logic: although it is true in a way that groups can only exist as constituted groups, as constituted bodies, through the alchemy of transubstantiation, nonetheless, any constitution of a group as a group runs the risk of the possibility, or even the probability, of usurpation. If what I have said is true, any group, particularly a more subordinate one, is faced with the following alternative: either no longer to exist as a group and be reduced to the fragmentary state of existing only *partes extra partes*, as a series of individuals in chaotic competition, or exist as one man through delegation, and then become vulnerable to the delegate's inherent tendency to usurp. I will return to this argument next time. My hope was to reach a point where I might have said with a flourish: I have said enough, go away now and do it yourselves, apply all this to the social classes. I cannot do it myself, because I am not at all sure that I could see it through to the end; but I think I have said enough for you to do the exercise yourselves. Next week, I will try to bring this problem of mystery and ministry to a firm conclusion.

Lecture of 16 June 1982

Acting 'in the name of . . .' – On delegation – The state and perspectivism – The problem of the truth of the social world – Validation by consensus or objective evidence

What is a group, or, to put the same question in different terms, who are the creators of a group? The answer is that groups create themselves by creating people who create the group. I think that there is no point in trying to escape this vicious circle by tracing some kind of false genesis, although for the purposes of exposition we need to adopt a linear language to provide an explanatory structure. So, groups are created by creating people who create groups, that is, by attracting a concentration of symbolic capital. The logic of this accumulation lies in the mystery of the ministry, best expressed as a direct equation: *ministerium = mysterium*. The group is thus created by the mystery of the ministry, that is, by the mystery of the power of procuration, or proxy.

Acting 'in the name of . . .'

It is worth analysing the etymology of the word 'procuration', or 'proxy'. The 'procurator' is the person who acts on behalf of, or in the name of, a group – the expression 'in the name of . . .' is crucial here – and in so doing they make the group exist by acting or speaking in its name. Here, we might recall, albeit in a different perspectival logic, Heidegger's famous analyses of concern (*Fürsorge*) and the power of proxy. A whole tradition of right-wing conservative thought has emphasized this phenomenon of proxy and delegation, imputing to it the sort of self-surrender that they see as a key feature of the welfare state – taking the word *Fürsorge* to mean 'social security'. I refer those

interested to the article I wrote a few years ago in which I tried to
show the crucial part that these notions play in the construction of
Heidegger's ontology.[1]

The logic of this delegation consists essentially of two entities. It
consists in materializing the group in bodies or other things. Whether
it is a trade union, a party, a state or a family, the group exists when it
is objectified either in things or their equivalent – such as names, acronyms or logos, seals, signatures and, obviously, the law – or in bodies:
the body of the spokesperson who incarnates the group, the person
who can say that he or she is the group, and who in a way gives bodily
form to the group by lending their body to the group. It would be
worth making a full study of the rites of institution, rites conducted by
a group in order to establish an individual as its accredited representative. The predominant function of these rites is as it were to welcome
the body of the appointed representative, and it is no accident that
these rites (usually called 'rites of passage', but which I have renamed
– more appositely, I believe – 'rites of institution')[2] do in fact 'institute'
or establish a person as the holder of the relevant social authority.
Whether nominating an heir to an aristocratic estate, appointing a
professor, or electing the President of the Republic, the rites establishing a character in a social role affect the body of the representative
profoundly. It is impossible for the rite of institution to be performed
by a proxy, and unthinkable for anyone to be represented by someone
else at the very rite by which he is to be instituted. It is essential for the
person to deliver himself up, body and soul, to be there in person with
his body – as someone once said: 'I have given my body to France.' The
person designated and recognized by a group delivers up their whole
self, body included, and the mutilations and physical trials that most
societies impose on initiates in the rites of passage take on their full
meaning in the light of this logic.

The rites of institution are therefore the rites by which groups are
constituted as institutions. The 'institution', a word which is as old as
sociology, and frequently used by Durkheim and his school,[3] seems
to me to warrant more reflection. This notion has gradually become
weakened by its various social applications, and one of the objects of
my reflection this year is precisely to try to revive this rather moribund
notion (in the social sciences, we can try to create new words or, using a
different approach, revive old words, although we run the risk of seeing
them revert to a limited personal usage, or even return to the dormant
state from which we tried to resuscitate them). You could argue that an
institution exists in a twofold form, in the form of those characteristics
acquired by the socialized body that I call the 'habitus', but also in

things that may be material objects. The church, for example, exists in churches in terms of visible objects and all the apparel (in the Pascalian sense) of religion: surplices, chasubles, ciboria, missals and catechisms; all sorts of objects in which a whole history is objectified, but it also exists in the bodies of all the clerics, who are socialized beings who assign value to these objects as being part of the church. If there were no Christians to use it in a Christian service, a ciborium would obviously become merely a decorative object. Thus our museums are filled with religious objects which no longer function as religious objects, but have become the object of a new cult, the cult of aesthetics.[4] An institution like the church – and you could say the same of the state, or the legal system, among others – presupposes at one and the same time not only those things which are a form of incarnation of the institution, but also the socialized bodies that will recognize them as things of the church, or the legal system. What generates the life, the evolution and the very existence of institutions is the encounter between these two states in the same historical moment, the incorporated state and the objectified state. What makes it possible to say a mass, that is, to accomplish an act that can be designated as Catholic, is the combination of a clerical habitus and the practice of using institutional objects according to the rules that constitute the institution. The same can be said for a university lecture or for any social event: there has to be a convergence of the right habitus with the right objects.

Does this analysis allow us to break free from the vicious circle I described earlier? In studying the phenomenon of the institution, we encounter a major difficulty, beyond which no analysis of the social world may be able to penetrate, namely, that the mystery of the institution lies in the fact that it is the group itself, as it comes to constitute itself as a group, which founds the institution that constitutes the group. In other words, the group does not know and recognize itself as a group, does not exist for itself and for other groups, until it is incarnated in this twofold formation: it must take on bodily form and reify itself in a person, a representative or an acronym (the CGT, Mr X or Y, etc.), but at the same time this incarnation owes its authority and its existence as an authorized institution to the group which lies behind it. There is a sort of circular causality, or vicious circle, linking the representative – the proxy or delegate – with the state, the church, the college or other group that finds expression through him, in a reciprocal relationship. It is then the same *fictio juris*, the same social magic – as I have argued from the start of this lecture course: we are constantly dealing with the logic of magic – the same social fiction that creates the group and creates the representative who creates the group.

As I said at the outset: groups come into being by creating creators of groups. If I keep returning to this circle, it is because I see it as a vital key to understanding the fetishistic relationships that groups maintain with their own materialization in people or things. It is clear that the representative, the spokesperson or delegate is the substitute for a group which exists through this representation, or rather, exists only through this representation. In the article by Post that I referred to last time there is another quotation taken from the canonists: *Quod faciunt magistratus videtur ipsa universitas facere*[5] – 'What the masters do seems to be done by the university' [the *universitas* is the group]. This is the equation formulated by another canonist, *status est magistratus:*[6] social status or rank clothes the person who occupies the position: the post is a function in action. This is what the gendarme means when you try to touch him by saying: 'I have three children, etc.', and he replies: 'I have to go by the rules', that is to say: 'Do not try to touch the person in me, I am my function.' The official is a victim of the function. This fundamental equation between the function and the person reminds us that the group recognizes itself as a group only through the representation given to it by its representatives. It recognizes itself as a group through its representatives (we must take the expression 'to recognize oneself' in the strongest sense of the term) and it can even experience this as a feeling of euphoria: 'He expresses us well.' This logic can help us analyse, for example, the relationship that viewers may feel as they identify with one of the parties in a televised debate, seeing them as their spokesperson.

At the heart of this circular relationship of delegation we detect the principle of fetishism. As I said the other day, social functions (posts, professions, social status) are social fictions, they are products of a collective belief that generates the very pomp and circumstance whose effects the collectivity experiences. This is the very logic of fetishism. The *magistratus* can take himself to be a *status*. If the President of the Republic can take himself for the President of the Republic, it is because other people take him for the President of the Republic, and even for the Republic – which not only authorizes this kind of megalo-maniacal madness, but summons him to take himself for the state and accomplish this transcendence of his individual bodily limits in order to be equal to his position. It is becoming more and more common for a President of the Republic to say: 'The state has decided', 'France has decided'. The formula seems to me dangerous from a strictly norma-tive point of view, but I am trying here to analyse its logic. If the mag-istrates can take themselves for the magistracy, and if this legitimate usurpation – referred to by Austin defining the performative[7] – is not recognized as usurpation but recognized as legitimate, if it is possible and has social, that is, magical effects on the social subjects who make it possible, it is because the relation of delegation is occluded by the circular effect: the social subjects end up revering, adoring or respecting the product of their own reverence. In other words, the group, forgetting the logic of delegation, worships itself in its own personification. In a way, the logic of acclamation, whose meaning I shall explore in a moment, is a sort of cult where the group adores itself in effigy, in an imaginary realization of itself as its own personification.

On delegation

I think the very process that makes the group exist as a group generates the risk that the group may be dispossessed of itself. This is perhaps the main idea I would like to offer you: groups only exist as such through the logic of delegation and objectification by incorporation, and from the outset this logic entails the risk of misappropriation by delegation.[8] The logic of acclamation, whereby the group in unison acclaims the words of its spokesperson, is one of the social fictions by which groups conceal social fiction and its consequences. When they applaud their delegate's speeches, they are actually avoiding facing the reality of delegation. They are publishing the belief, and do themselves believe, that the group itself is the author of the speech.

   I have shown elsewhere the form taken by this logic of delegation in the case of the dominated classes. I do not wish to develop this analysis too far here, since it is too long. But although you may find a simplified version rather dubious, I think it is important and, as I have had it at the back of my mind throughout these lectures, I would be dishonest if I did not set it out before you. In a text called 'Questions de politique' I analysed the relationship which the less educated have with political issues.[9] From an analysis of the blank returns or 'don't knows' to the questions posed by the polling organizations, I tried to show that the lower one descends in the social hierarchy and in the hierarchy of levels of education, to put it simply, the more it appears that the individuals interviewed, especially on political issues, feel out of their depth and take refuge in refusing to reply, in abstention or delegation. They rely, as it were, on spokespersons.

   This is what theologians of the Middle Ages called *fides implicita* (they also called it 'blind faith': they said that the believers who were not able to arrive at the *fides explicita* (that is to say to a faith capable of expressing itself, of explaining its rationale, of founding itself in reason and in discourse) were doomed to an 'intuitive faith'. The theologians did not despise this faith, which, although unaware of its own rationale, is a trustworthy and important kind of faith: I have written somewhere a little maliciously that the clergy have always adored intuitive faith because it grants them free speech, that is to say, the monopoly of speech. When we are dealing with structural phenomena of this kind, comparisons are not superficial analogies at all, but structural homologies between different situations: between the discourse of theologians speaking of blind faith and the discourse of politicians speaking of the great mass of the people, there is an obvious analogy which corresponds to homologies of structure and therefore of interests. If we liken this *fides implicita*, this blind delegation, to the logic of delegation that alone enables groups, especially dominated groups, to exist – through the process I have described, with all its inbuilt risk of misappropriation – we can draw important conclusions for understanding the relations between the party and the masses, which have often been described in an idealist or rather an intellectualist logic, through the theory of awakening consciousness. Basically, one of the results of my analyses so far has been to provide a different model of the relationship between delegates and those who appoint them in what we call popular movements.

I mentioned earlier the phenomenon of concentration as one of the effects of the power of proxy: where the group was constituted as a *collectio personarum plurium* (in the words of the canonists), as an accumulation of individuals – or, as Sartre would have said, in a serial state where the group existed *partes extra partes* in a logic of discontinuity – the institution of a mandated delegate or group of delegates introduces a concentration. It enables a representation of the unit and its unity: the delegates can represent the group, and give as it were a theatrical presentation of the unity of the group.

Finally, in so far as institutions are materialized in bodies and above all perhaps in things, and in mechanisms capable of reproducing the functioning of bodies and things, they assure the group of a permanence that it does not have on its own. This is the problem that Sartre addressed in the *Critique of Dialectical Reason*: Sartre could not imagine the group existing in any form other than that of the mobilized group that demonstrates in the streets, or mobilizes to storm the Bastille, to take the example that he regularly uses.[10] If the group exists as group only in this kind of circumstances, it may not exist more than once every hundred years. Yet the problem for a group is to exist every day, in order to respond to interviews or attacks, and so on; whether the working class is militant or not, whether or not there is a long downturn in the price of gold or an increase in the price of bread. It is institutionalization as I have described it that allows the group to exist permanently, with a permanent staff, and offices permanently manned, and so on.

Before mentioning the risk of misappropriation, I should have mentioned permanence, a property inherent in delegation: concentrating the power to act in one person instead of the group obviously already offers opportunities for misappropriation, but if in addition we include this property of permanence, as opposed to the dispersal and discontinuity of the groups represented, we can see that the risk is inherent in the very logic of things. For the paradox of delegation means that the group using delegation and institutionalization to break away from serialization and discontinuity finds itself in a serial and discontinuous state in the face of its delegates. This is clear to see when members of a group sign a petition – the petition being the archetype of serial logic – against their own delegates. The petition is 1 + 1 + 1, and so on, and they try to make the numbers add up to the highest possible total sum, in order to try to snatch back a little of the power delegated to the delegate. So I believe that this logic of serial isolation in the face of the strength of the body of the permanent delegates is an integral part of any consideration of the nature of the institution. It goes without saying that we cannot make this kind of commentary in a vacuum, ignoring our own historical circumstances.[11] We should never ignore the debt that our apparently formal analyses may owe to situations where the problem arises in a particularly acute form: 'The owl of Minerva spreads its wings only with the falling of dusk.'[12]

The state and perspectivism

Another conclusion I wanted to draw is that this logic of delegation takes a very special form in the case of delegation by the state because, rightly or wrongly, the representative of the state appears to be a universal representative. His authority or the truth of his actions is grounded in the *consensus omnium*: he is as it were the repository of common sense. For example, when nominating someone (I keep repeating this in a somewhat obsessive manner, because I think it is an important example helping to connect the different arguments I have been formulating), the representative casts the nominee in a perspective that is not seen from an individual viewpoint which might seem questionable from a different point of view, but from a viewpoint that claims to be universal. When the state representative says formally,

'You are a teacher,' unlike someone who says informally, 'You're just a teacher', he bestows on the person nominated a title that has a value in every market, for the truly universal appellation in our society is, I believe, the academic qualification. It is a kind of currency which has value in all social markets (with variable exchange rates: it has its highest price in the strictly academic market, and obviously a much lower price in the social market, although the gap is more or less wide in different periods and different social circles). Roughly speaking, the academic title is one of those appellations that can claim, with a reasonable chance of success, as Weber says,[13] to retain its value in all the markets and submarkets that can be found in a particular social space. It is therefore a designation for all, as opposed to a singular designation, such as the insult. In other words, the state could be defined in Leibniz's words, as the established 'geometral', the geometric point of convergence of all perspectives.[14] And, being this geometric point of convergence of all perspectives, the state holds the monopoly of the legitimate viewpoint over its social subjects.

(I am not going to dwell on the word 'legitimate', which may be misunderstood by some, but which, in the technical language of sociology, means 'what is recognized as legitimate', 'something that, simply because its arbitrary nature is not recognized, is acknowledged as worthy to exist in its given form'. This is not a value judgement at all, I am merely saying that people recognize legitimacy without even having to take it upon themselves to make a declaration of allegiance or recognition, they merely have to accept the nomination, call 'Professor' the people who are appointed professor, respect those people to whom respect is due.)

What the state says of its social subjects, through agents or institutions embodying it, speaks of its claim to universal recognition. And just as Max Weber said that the state is defined by its 'monopoly of legitimate violence',[15] I would say that the state is defined by the monopoly of legitimate *symbolic* violence, and that those acts of symbolic violence – such as insult or abuse – which we use at any moment to impose our point of view on others, and with it our vision of the world, tend, when they come from the state, to be recognized as universal by all. And we can see the success of this claim to monopoly in the very struggle that opposes some social agents to this monopoly.[16] I think that it is this logic that can help explain the relation that intellectuals have with certain forms of consecration, such as the Legion of Honour, where the arbitrariness of legitimate symbolic violence is particularly apparent: the intellectuals' attitude to some of the more ostentatious and therefore derisory forms of consecration can be understood as a rejection of the monopoly of legitimate violence. By refusing external consecrations of this kind, on the grounds that they alone are entitled to consecrate themselves as intellectuals – this serves their strategic interests, and they would be far better defended if they always reacted consistently in this way – intellectuals affirm that they hold the monopoly of the consecration of things intellectual. But the fact that they have to reject worldly titles and honours so ostentatiously tends to prove that there are some intellectuals who do agree to recognize themselves in these tokens of recognition. I shall not pursue this analysis further, because it could become embarrassing for all of us.

The state can claim the monopoly of legitimate symbolic violence, but, of course, this monopoly is never complete and absolute. It is possible to find tentative or exaggerated passages in official statements that can call everything into question. And any challenge to the state's discursive monopoly is a challenge to the state itself, for this symbolic monopoly is a prize fought for by those who would aim to lay hands on the power of the state, but is also an issue within society as a whole. That having been said, I think that the monopoly of legitimate state violence, on the cultural plane for example, is hardly disputed. It is through the school system that the monopoly of the legitimate violence of the state is exercised, and even if we encounter half-hearted challenges to academic qualifications, it is clear that in everyday practice the academic diploma attracts disproportionate respect, and that any kind of protest against its monopoly of symbolic violence is utterly derisory.

In a way, the state thus prises social subjects away from their individual perspectivism (here, by perspectivism, I refer to the theory developed by Nietzsche in *The Gay Science*: in the struggle of each against all for knowledge, where each individual tries to impose the perspective most advantageous to his or her interests,[17] and in fact one aspect of what I have been arguing here could be expressed in Nietzsche's terms: insult or abuse presuppose a perspectival philosophy, where each individual tries to impose his or her own perspective on the social world). The state in a way is therefore a kind of neutral place that provides an authorized, socially recognized perspective on all social agents. I shall not develop this theme here, because I have done it often in the past. I prefer to refer to Spitzer's analysis of *Don Quixote* in his essays on sociology and literary history, which is entirely in keeping with what I have been arguing all this year.[18] Spitzer notes that in *Don Quixote*, Cervantes constantly changes the names of his characters. Even for Don Quixote himself, he uses different names, as if he were leaving it to the reader to make their own choice. Spitzer remarks that this is a generalized procedure that tends to create a social universe in which no one person has the last word on the others. It is not by chance that this kind of unstable designation is found in a novel whose hero is an *idios*, that is to say, someone who claims to be in the right against the social world, and so falls victim to the logic of the lone insult, taking the risk of challenging common sense (I should add that it is the state that is common sense). We could reconsider Dostoyevsky's *The Idiot* in the same light. But I use these literary references merely to underline the implications of my argument, which is not as straightforward as it may sound. By giving you several different systems of reference, I hope that each one of you will be able to find a personal way to construe the mechanisms of the system.

The problem of the truth of the social world

These reflections on the logic of the institution and its delegation, together with the latent misappropriation that they harbour, lead us to consider the problem of the truth of the social world. I hesitate to broach it in twenty minutes, but I do need to say a few words none-theless. Behind what I have been saying throughout these lectures has been this question: What does telling the truth about the social world mean? Who does reveal the truth of the social world? I have invoked Wittgenstein several times in connection with this circle: who can measure the Parisian standard metre and pass judgement on its length, who can say which sociologist is right about social class, capital or the class struggle? The scientific community avoids this question, almost as if on grounds of health and safety, because it is so difficult to live with, it seems to me. Sociologists, historians and ethnologists have developed a sort of provisional positivism, and act as if they had an answer to the question of the truth about truth, to the question of the truth of propositions on the social world. If what I have tried to show has some truth-value, it seems to me that this will have a number of consequences for evaluating the truth criteria used by the social sciences.

To some extent, as far as the social world is concerned, some degree of perspectivism as defined by Nietzsche is inevitable: everyone has their own truth, the truth of their own interests. We are not used to thinking this way, since this kind of relativism is discredited by a whole tradition that treats as an 'error' the rationalized expression of the interests of others. In fact, if we were to attempt a strict definition of awakening consciousness, we would say that it is what leads to the

expression of an interest properly understood: from the point of view
of the dominated, we would say that their best interest is to become
conscious of their subordination, to denounce it and overthrow it;
from the point of view of the dominant, their interest lies in becoming conscious of their dominance and discovering its foundations in
order to perpetuate it. We could then put Marx and Pareto[19] in the
same boat, whereas people usually take delight in contrasting them,
saying, for instance, that Pareto turned Marx upside down. At least
both agree, I think, to implicitly accept this perspectival theory of the
truth. Pareto, for example, when he describes what he calls the 'wither-
ing away of the elites', invokes precisely the fact that the elites, that is
to say the dominant, fall into decline through a sort of false consciousness of their own dominance which prevents them from accepting
themselves as dominant and leads them to accept the view of them held
by those they dominate. Consequently, if the social world is an arena
for the confrontation of social groups which become aware of themselves by constituting themselves as groups and making explicit what
it is that constitutes them as groups, that is to say, a set of common
interests – whether defending their capital or fighting to abolish capital
– it follows inevitably that radical perspectivism is a key initial stage in
the social struggle. The truth of the social world is necessarily a bone
of contention between antagonistic social groups.

I may be repeating this rather obsessively, but it is a helpful and
striking formula: that is, if there is a truth, it is that the truth is a controversial issue. This follows from the proposition that each group
has an interest in its own truth, and that a group accepting as its own
the truth of a hostile group is committing suicide as a group. In other
words, truth is not one, it is multiple, and there is really no universally agreed evaluation of the social world. I refer you to a number
of arguments that I advanced in *Distinction*, particularly with regard
to the problem of lifestyle – it is one example among thousands: what
the dominated classes see as easy-going, open-hearted, uninhibited
behaviour, the dominant classes see as culpable negligence and lack of
common decency. This is why writing sociology is extremely difficult,
because words are constantly cleft – and I refer you to a very fine analysis by Bakhtin, one of the great post-revolutionary Russian linguists,
who said that in periods of revolution there are hardly any words free
of double meaning, hardly any words that can be pronounced with the
same meaning by two characters situated in the two opposing camps;[20]
in other words, the consensus on a language that reflects the state and
its universal linguistic order is a consensus that is shown to be fictitious
the minute that the truth of social relations is revealed, as happens in

periods of revolution. In a sense, since truth is an object of conflict, it is the task of social science, not to decide where the truth lies, but to acknowledge that there are two irreconcilable truths confronting each other which both refuse to die – 'truth' being understood, I repeat, in the Nietzschean sense of a perspective grounded in vital interests.

Having said that, can social science be satisfied with merely taking note of these unavoidable but insoluble and irreconcilable truths? It can, in fact, assess the social force of different truths, in so far as the social force of a social truth depends on the material and symbolic power relations between those who recognize themselves in these truths and those who reject them. A social truth endowed with great social strength is capable of imposing itself universally, of achieving a *consensus omnium*; this is a convenient way of defining what we call a dominant ideology. When a partial and partisan truth succeeds in being recognized as universal, if only from a misrecognition of its particular foundations, it becomes a dominant truth, that is to say, a truth based on what logicians recognize as a truth criterion, namely consensual validation. We may call on linguistic analysis again here: the genesis of the French language as an institution is parallel to the genesis of the state.[21] As soon as a language imposes itself as the only legitimate language even for those who are speechless because unable to use it, people forget that it is only a partial truth. There are silences which signal total compliance with legitimacy: in the same way, in places where people are invited to speak, silence is never randomly distributed, but varies quite predictably according to education, gender and age, and offers a passive, and often unconscious, recognition of legitimacy.

I am offering a series of different definitions of truth, which I hope are not contradictory. This social truth based on consensus is the truth associated with the legitimate perspective, that is, the perspective that is dominant but not recognized as such, and thus acknowledged to be universal. I could return here to the problem of social classification that I raised at the outset; one of the issues at stake in the symbolic struggle over the social world is establishing what is the legitimate classification. For example, one could say that classification by INSEE is as basic to the problem of classification as speech acts are to the problem of language, in so far as it is a sort of state classification, which manages to pass itself off as legitimate. It is a basis for collective bargaining, the trade unions discuss it and haggle over its terms – INSEE and the trade unions have just negotiated an agreement on a new classification[22] – and thus we arrive at a kind of classification recognized by all and sundry, based on a sort of collective bargaining:

its perspectival representations cease to be perceived as a perspective once they have received a conceptual validation. Will this dominant truth, grounded in conceptual validation, acquire the force of law and perform efficiently? Will this sort of 'reason of state' take control of social practices? I think it will, and to a much greater extent than we are led to believe. Earlier I took the example of the imposition of a hierarchy of human excellence that is based on academic qualifications but recognized beyond educational circles, which makes academic qualifications the measure of humanity in many universes: the legitimate perspective, the one that is dominant but not recognized as such, and is thus implicitly acknowledged, imposes its rule far beyond what we would expect when we think of the law of the land (in fact, if we think of the law in terms of specific legislation, it is easier to detect its links with the interests of a class, or a category of people in power). This enables the legitimate truth based on consensus to work with a force that is precisely that of the performative.

I would like here to allude briefly to an argument that might shed more light on what I have been saying about the performative throughout these lectures. This is Kant's distinction between different types of divine understanding – I believe this is a valid comparison. He differentiates between two types of intuition that may be attributed to God: an *intuitus originarius* and an *intuitus derivatus*. The *intuitus originarius* is a perception or intuition that creates the thing it sees, or makes it emerge (*origo*): God creates what he sees and sees what he creates. We could use the same logic to say that there are performative words, words that make what they say emerge into existence, words (such as slogans) that create groups, or words (such as orders) that do things by proxy: these are words that are creative, that have a real effectiveness. The *intuitus originarius* (original intuition) is the monopoly of God for Kant, while man is doomed to the *intuitus derivatus* (derived intuition),[23] that is to say, an intuition which cannot appropriate the object, make it exist, produce it or bring it out into the light of day, an intuition that can only register a pre-existing reality.

This distinction seems to correspond exactly to Austin's distinction between performative and constative.[24] Social science is constative, it tries to state what exists, but among the actions that it does connote, many are performative. The sociologist is a classifier, someone who has to say how people are really classified, to understand how they act and where they are situated, to predict what their attitudes and opinions towards the present system of distribution in society are likely to be, and how they may influence or react to different distributions in the future. But at the same time the sociologist is also someone who spends time observing people who spend their time in symbolic reaction to these divisions, saying, 'This is not right', 'Things have to change', 'Some people here have too much, and some not enough', 'We should make the rich pay, we should make the poor pay', 'We must give to the poor and make the rich pay', and so on.

Validation by consensus or objective evidence

Sociologists can solve this difficulty, as I indicated at the outset, by pretending that the problem of truth does not arise. They can construct their classification and base their claim that it is the right one on a whole gamut of criteria, contrasting it with the rather monocriterial indigenous classifications, and say: 'There is one classification and only one, which is the one I have to offer. I have a resolutely constative point of view, I state what is there, I do not engage in the conflict over what we should state and how we should state it.' I think that this attitude is a mystification for two reasons. Firstly, those who engage in the game of classification have to face the constant effort by those classified to change the classification, among other things by performative actions aimed at imposing the right classification, the proper viewpoint, the legitimate perspective. Secondly, the sociologist betrays scientific truth by failing to include in the assessment any account of the performative struggle to change the terms of the assessment. They fail to include in their model, which claims to be the truth, the fact that the definition of truth is itself a contentious issue within this very truth that they claim to describe truthfully. And they omit something crucial, that in a way there are always necessarily two truths, which in some cases may claim to coincide, but which correspond to two antagonistic definitions of the truth. There is the truth which they claim to be grounded in the thing itself: they produce it, and then claim to find it verified by matching it with reality. For example, they will establish a set of divisions that they claim will show that all the differences and distributions have been taken into account, including those they have not taken into account in the specific system at issue. Or they may say that their classification is true because it is grounded in reality.

But they may find their version of the truth challenged by a different definition of the truth, truth based on the *consensus omnium*, which is a possible definition of objectivity, and in whose name we may say: 'There is a kind of state truth, and the state is an institution that, by definition, has the means to make its truth come true' – since the state as I have defined it can achieve a consensus on its official representation of the social world. A very simple example can illustrate what I am saying: imagine that as a sociologist I would like to seek public endorsement of the truth of what I have been able to establish on the educational system, namely, the existence of a very strong statistical link between social origins and academic achievement. It would be a lost cause, because I can guess the results of an inquiry asking people if they think that academic success depends on social origins.

There are then two forms of validation of a social truth: validation by consensus and validation by objective evidence. And when consensual verification gives its backing to an agency that, like the state, has the performative power, not only to tell the truth, but to make it exist by telling it, scientific truth is quite disarmed and helpless. There is then, to put it quite simply, a fundamental antagonism between science and the state, and this antagonism is all the more inevitable, almost tragically so, because this consensual truth has only to adopt the appearance of a science to find consecration ready and waiting for it.

What is the attitude of science towards the problem of social classification, for example? (I do not have time to develop this point as I would have liked.) Science, involved in this struggle for truth, says that there is a struggle for truth. It describes the opposing camps arrayed in battle formation (*tagma*; *tagmata*), waging war over the *taxis*,[25] fighting to devise and impose the best way to classify. Science may describe the positions of the various camps and the logic of their combat, but, try as it might, its research will implicate it in the struggle. This means that, unlike positivism, it cannot take one particular state of the struggle and proclaim that it is the alpha and omega of the struggle. Positivism is the philosophy of all scientists who do not want to be disturbed in their science, who want peace and quiet. All researchers are positivists at certain times (research is so tiring . . .). They say: 'I describe things as they are; I apply the criteria, and this is where the social classes stand today, that's how things are, this is the distribution at a given time t, and, take my word for it, you can predict from my schema which people at any particular point in the social space will be more likely to read one newspaper rather than another, to be believers or not, to vote on the left rather than on the right, and so on.' This is what sociologists do when they remain at the positivist level and want to believe that their version of the truth of the social world is the alpha and the omega. But if they admit that they are themselves involved in the struggle for truth, despite all their efforts, and accept the fact that the objects of their study are fighting to establish their own truth and discredit the sociologist's version, among other things – there are people who have an interest in discrediting what the sociologist says

– they cannot avoid inserting their own truth-seeking model of classification within a meta-model of the struggle for truth which implies a possible falsification of their own truth, which will become merely a plausible hypothesis. I believe that this can be sociologically established and that the truest scientific proposals are socially the weakest. I could develop this argument at length, but I think that I have already said both too much and not enough, and it is too late for amendments or corrections.

What I would like to offer you finally is a sentence by Bachelard which I came across quite by chance: 'Everything easy to teach is inaccurate.'[26] In which case, given the subjective and, probably, objective difficulty of my teaching, I can hope to have achieved some degree of accuracy.

Situating the Course on General Sociology in the work of Pierre Bourdieu

Patrick Champagne and Julien Duval

In the early 1980s, Pierre Bourdieu was a little over fifty years old. He had just published two very important books, *Distinction*, which is a kind of synthesis of the research he had devoted to cultural capital and social class in the 1960s and 1970s, and *The Logic of Practice*, which sets out his theory of practice, and is based essentially on the investigations he had conducted in Algeria at the very beginning of his career, in the late 1950s. He had also just been elected professor at the Collège de France, a prestigious French university institution that dates back to the sixteenth century and brings together a small number of eminent researchers from the various fields of knowledge. It was in April 1982 that he began his teaching in this very special institution, which does not issue any degrees and where the lectures are open to all, and are attended less by students strictly speaking than by researchers and a cultured public of all ages. About fifty professors make up the faculty of this institution. They must, each year, give a series of one-hour lectures concentrating on their research in progress, with the only constraint being to give a new series each year.

Bourdieu went on to teach at the Collège de France until his retirement in 2001. Over this period, he gave a series of lecture courses on relatively specialized subjects (the state, the economy, domination, the fields of cultural production, the symbolic revolution operated by Manet, the scientific field . . .),[1] but for the first five years of his teaching, that is to say between 1982 and 1986, he chose to offer a course of lectures on 'General Sociology'. As he said at the very beginning of the first session, he wished to present the 'fundamental lineaments' of his research work, that is, the outlines of the sociological theory he had been developing for more than twenty years, and the state of his reflection on a discipline, sociology, which he intended to refound.

The purpose of this introduction is to give an overview of the whole of this lecture course and to provide some information concerning the place and circumstances in which it was delivered, as well as its situation in Bourdieu's work. These elements of contextualization can help in understanding why Bourdieu had set himself this rather surprising semi-pedagogical, semi-theoretical goal, which he strove to achieve without major concessions, using it to develop aspects of his thinking that were less apparent in his other writings.

Overview of the course

This course on general sociology forms a coherent whole which aims to give a general presentation of the sociological venture, starting with the concepts of habitus, field and capital which constitute the three fundamental concepts on which Bourdieu bases his sociology. The first year of his teaching, which was relatively short, focuses on the question of classification, the constitution of groups and 'social classes'. It forms a sort of preamble to the 'theorizing work' announced and provides a kind of prologue to the whole course on general sociology. During the second year, Bourdieu explains how he conceives the object of sociology, develops reflections on knowledge and practice, then begins a systematic presentation of the major concepts of his sociological approach, explaining their presuppositions and the sociological function he assigns to them in the general economy of his theory. He explains how his work has led him to elaborate these concepts, as well as the traditions in philosophy and the social sciences with (or against) which he has forged them. Without ever losing sight of the 'articulation between the fundamental concepts and the structure of the relations that unite the concepts', he begins with the habitus, the concept which takes into account the fact that the subject of sociology, unlike the subject of philosophy, is a socialized subject, that is, invested by social forces. After showing how this concept makes it possible to escape the alternatives of mechanicism and finalism, he deals with the concept of field, presenting it at first from what he calls a 'physicalist' approach, that is to say an approach which considers the fields as fields of forces that impinge upon the social subjects. He returns in a later stage of the course to an analysis of the dynamics of the fields, considering them as fields of struggles aiming to modify the field of forces, in so far as individuals are not inert particles subject to the forces of the fields, but act on them through the particular social representations that they implement.

The third year focuses on the concept of capital. Bourdieu recalls the link he established between the different specifications of the concept and the plurality of fields. The coding and objectification of capital are also the subject of particular attention as they constitute one of the mainsprings of a certain continuity of the social world and are in principle what separates precapitalist societies from our pluralist societies. The fourth year addresses the concept of field as a field of struggle, since it is the object of perceptions by social agents and these perceptions are generated by the relationship between habitus and capital. In this fourth year, Bourdieu develops the project of a sociology of social perception, which he conceives as an inseparably cognitive and political activity on the part of social agents struggling to define the *nomos*, the legitimate vision of the social world. The fifth year extends these analyses, but, as he prepares to conclude his course, Bourdieu also seeks to bring together the two aspects of the concept of field (the field as a field of forces, and as a field of struggle) by the simultaneous mobilization of the three major concepts. Symbolic struggles aim to transform the fields of forces. To understand them we need to introduce the notion of symbolic power, symbolic capital or the symbolic capital effect, which is a product of the relation of 'illusio' that operates between the habitus and the field. The year ends with questions about the position of the social sciences in the symbolic struggles to impose a certain representation of the social world, and with the idea that the social sciences must combine the structuralist and constructivist perspectives in order to study the social world.

One of the specific interests of the course is that it can be read as an introduction to Bourdieu's sociology and theory. Bourdieu continues the theoretical work presented in *Distinction* and *The Logic of Practice*, but goes further. On the one hand, he incorporates new concerns. On the other hand, he makes frequent connections between his 'ethnological' work on Algeria and his 'sociological' studies of cultural capital, questioning the division between anthropology and sociology, which he considers has no scientific basis in reality, in order to elaborate a social theory valid for precapitalist societies as well as for pluralist societies. This effort is particularly noticeable in 1984–5 and in 1985–6, where the question of the process leading precapitalist societies to become pluralist societies is discussed. The former are designated more than once as instruments for the analysis of the latter, because of the 'enhanced image' that they give of relations between the sexes or the symbolic struggle still at work in our societies. Bourdieu had never before tried such a broad synthesis, and he never repeated the attempt afterwards. The course is a unique experiment in his work that could be considered somewhat equivalent to Max Weber's *Economy and*

Society, published posthumously, although it should be recalled that Bourdieu had always been very wary of the temptation to offer 'general overviews' or definitive theoretical syntheses.[2]

It should be noted that what is published here is a course of lectures as they were delivered. The reader is thus to some extent projected into the lecture hall or the classroom, but is not in exactly the same situation as the audience of the time. This difference in situation has advantages. The reader can, for example, make a continuous reading of successive lectures, whereas the audience, assuming that they were able to attend all the sessions (Bourdieu emphasizes the 'intermittent' nature of his audience – 1 March 1984), had to wait between each lecture. For the reader, this facilitates the assimilation of 'a discourse whose coherence emerges over a period of several years' (1 March 1984).[3] In other words, the time spent reading the published lectures is not equivalent to that of their elaboration or even of their oral delivery; for the reader, reading acts as a sort of accelerator of the thought processes at work in the course. But to read the lectures as they were pronounced, rather than in the form that their author might have published them (Bourdieu always reworked his texts for publication), can also cause confusion, by drawing attention to the repetitions or sometimes creating an impression of disorder, since we do not bring to a written text the same expectations we do to the spoken word. For this reason, we should no doubt, in approaching these transcripts, pay particularly attention to Bourdieu's regular warnings to listeners who might misunderstand his apparent repetitions.[4]

The course, with its many sidetracks and byways, does not have the rigorous form of a theoretical treatise, but it must be said that the theoretical system presented does not lend itself to a linear exposition. In its apparent repetitions, as in its regular returns to points already discussed (but illuminated in new ways), the course shows very strongly how much the concepts of habitus, capital and field constitute 'systemic concepts ... whose use requires constant reference to the complete system of their interrelations'.[5] The articulation of these three key concepts is permanent, even in the second and third years, when they are presented successively, for the sake of clarity. The concept of capital is thus immediately introduced in relation to the concept of field, and the habitus reappears when the notion of 'informational capital' is introduced. The question of coding and institutionalization, as well as the notion of the field of power, discussed in the third and fifth years respectively, refer to the relations between capital and field; and the problem of perception, at the heart of the fourth year, involves the relation between habitus and field directly. The course is structured around a kind of theoretical space that may be negotiated through different pathways, as Bourdieu observes at the start of his fourth year of teaching, when he explicitly says he hesitated between several possible 'branches' (7 March 1985).

The form of the course is also the expression of a way of working that Bourdieu himself compared to a 'spiralling movement',[6] or an 'infinite rediscovery' of his research.[7] Very significant in this regard is the return in his last lectures, in June 1986, to 'this old problem of the social classes' which was at the centre of the first year (1982–3). This return to the starting point, probably unnoticed by most listeners, suggests in passing a way of reading the course. The first year, in the spring of 1982, presented itself as a reflection on classification and the social classes. In the second and third years, Bourdieu then presented his major concepts, and in the last two years proceeded to investigate the question of the symbolic struggle for the principles of perception of the social world, of which the division into classes is a kind of test case. Rivalry within the 'field of expertise', combined with the very particular power of the state in terms of appointment, which the problem of social classes makes it necessary to raise, are in general two major aspects of the symbolic struggle in our pluralist societies. Read in this way, the course does not follow a circular movement: far from returning to its starting point in a desire for closure, the final return to social class represents an opening and progression, combined with a form of generalization.

A 'performance'

The form and content of the course must first be related to the manner in which the lectures were delivered. On many occasions, Bourdieu complained about the conditions in which he had to teach. Since 1964, he had been teaching in places (the École des Hautes Études en Sciences Sociales (EHESS), first and foremost) where he gave not undergraduate lectures but research seminars for relatively small audiences composed of researchers and/or advanced students. At the Collège de France, the audience is more numerous and more disparate. It mixes researchers, students, Collège de France regulars, and simply curious listeners or observers. This situation makes it difficult to transmit knowledge, and fosters misunderstandings. The author of *The Inheritors* and *Reproduction*, who had been arguing since the 1960s for the institution of a rational pedagogy designed to fight educational inequality, was particularly aware of this far-from-rational situation.

He mentions it at the beginning of a lecture on several occasions, hoping without great expectations to neutralize the problem by analysing it sociologically and raising awareness on the part of the audience.

While many courses of lectures delivered at the Collège de France, because of their high level of scholarship or specialization, attract a very small audience, Bourdieu was immediately confronted with a large audience. The practice in this institution is that professors deliver a series of one-hour lectures for part of the academic year and, at another time and in a smaller room, a seminar of the same duration. From Bourdieu's very first lecture, the large amphitheatre of the college was 'packed to the roof'. The Collège de France had to open a second room for the courses to be broadcast on CCTV. As for the seminar, it turned out to be impossible to hold one, because of the numbers. It had to be dropped straight away. The following year Bourdieu made up the hours not given,[8] but opted for a series of two-hour lectures. From the third year, he chose to divide these two-hour sessions into two distinct parts: he devoted the first hour to 'theoretical analyses' (1 March 1984) and aimed, in the second, to 'give an idea of what a seminar would be, by showing how to construct a topic and elaborate its problematics, and above all how to implement these formulations and theoretical formulas in concrete operations' (1 March 1984). The 'tentative forays' or the 'impromptus' (26 April 1984 and 17 April 1986) that he offered in the second hour often echo the themes developed in the first hour, which presented a 'sustained ongoing argument, developing coherently over the long term' (26 April 1984). Thus, in the fourth year, the 'theoretical analyses' relate to perceptions of the social world and the second hour to a social category, the painters, who, with Manet, achieved a revolution of perception and vision (23 May 1985).

From his first year of teaching, Bourdieu was, like Foucault, or like Bergson before him, a 'star' of the Collège de France. A numerous audience – who made a point of 'applauding the artist' at the end of each lecture – came to attend lectures that were transformed into 'performances'. It is certain that Bourdieu dreaded these lectures. He suffered from not being able to give a real seminar, and from being in a situation very unfavourable to the intellectual exchange and transmission of skills that he sought to promote (a 'method' rather than knowledge as such – 28 April 1982). At the same time, he tried to use them for his benefit, taking the opportunity to test his arguments by exposing them publicly. He was also careful to maintain at least a minimal form of dialogue with the room, inviting his audience to hand him questions in the form of notes at the end of the lectures. Sometimes considerable parts of the lectures consisted in answering these questions. He resisted the style of lecturing that the place and the situation seemed to demand. All in all, those who had followed his seminars at the EHESS in the 1970s were not disoriented by the lectures he gave at the Collège, especially since he warned his audience from the outset that his approach was 'the only way that I can operate' (28 April 1982). They felt at home with this style of improvisation, which was based on copious notes, but which never made full use of them, amid all the parentheses, digressions, methodological precautions, changes of register and permanent reformulations of a thought that seeks itself and delivers not just the already-thought but also uses the teaching situation as an opportunity to keep thinking. And Bourdieu expressed right from the start his rejection of 'French-style teaching' which, aiming for 'elegance' and promoting the image of the orator, contradicts the logic of research, which cannot avoid being 'laborious', 'long-winded', 'hesitant', 'pedestrian' and 'tentative' on occasion. Far from the formal academic lecture that transmits predictable knowledge established according to a plan rigorously established and executed by the speaker, Bourdieu's lectures often overran the schedule and were in parts unpredictable because he strove to transmit a way of thinking that breaks with customary modes of thought rather than a body of established knowledge. This mixture of preparation and controlled improvisation produced a discourse which, although quite free, remained structured by a plan which Bourdieu quite regularly seemed to lose sight of, but always kept in mind and returned to, sometimes after the most unexpected digressions.

A sociologist at the Collège de France

For another reason, it must be emphasized that delivering a course of lectures on sociology at the Collège de France was not a neutral event. The election of Bourdieu to the Collège de France showed a certain personal recognition, which took place at the expense of the competitors of his generation (in particular Alain Touraine who was a candidate for the same chair and was quite a media personality in France),[9] but it also marked a form of recognition for the discipline. The Collège de France is unique in that the chairs, of which there are about fifty, are not allocated to particular disciplines. When a chair becomes vacant (that is, in practice, when a professor retires or dies), the other professors, before electing a new incumbent, are free to redefine the title of the available chair, which may belong to another discipline, allowing the institution to adapt to the evolution of knowledge. While the most established disciplines have one or more chairs at all times, this is not the case with sociology and Bourdieu did not fail to mention, in his 'inaugural lecture' (a ritual requiring the new professor to speak in front of a large audience and in the presence of his new colleagues),[10] the paradox of the presence of sociology in an institution like the Collège de France.

Indeed, it was one of the major failures of Émile Durkheim that he was unable, at the beginning of the twentieth century, to bring sociology to the Collège de France. In the 1930s and 1940s, his three most outstanding students, Marcel Mauss, François Simiand and Maurice Halbwachs, did so, but by quite devious routes and in contexts much less favourable to the promotion of the discipline. Moreover, their teachings were all interrupted in tragic circumstances, related to their premature deaths and/or to the historical circumstances of Nazism and Germany's occupation of France.[11] After the Second World War, sociology experienced an eclipse at the Collège de France. It is true that French sociology tended to be divided between theoreticians (mostly Marxists) and strict empiricists influenced by American sociology.[12] It lacked major scholars. In addition, the central position formerly occupied by sociology in the human sciences then came to be held by anthropology, represented by the figure of Claude Lévi-Strauss – who entered the Collège de France in 1959. In 1970 Raymond Aron was elected to a chair of 'Sociology of Modern Civilization', but although Aron played an important part in France in the institutionalization of sociology at the university (and in promoting Bourdieu's early career before the relations between the two men deteriorated considerably around 1968), he was not really a researcher, and he always strongly preferred the historical sociology of Max Weber – whom he helped to make known in France – to the Durkheim tradition. Moreover, during the years when he taught at the Collège de France, he engaged mostly in reflections on political science and came increasingly to play the part of the right-wing intellectual in the context of the liberal reaction that followed May '68.

The 'Course on General Sociology' delivered by Bourdieu was thus in a sense the first true teaching of this type delivered at the Collège de France. In accordance with the tradition of the establishment, Bourdieu offered a course based on his own work. But at the same time his teaching executed the programme announced by the title of the course. For example, Bourdieu continues to emphasize the ambition of his own sociology to integrate in a coherent way the different 'founding fathers' and the diverse currents of the discipline that we habitually distinguish and contrast. Likewise, he raises fundamental questions for the discipline. In the first year, he wonders about the particular form that operations of classification take in a science that deals explicitly with 'subjects who classify themselves'. In the second year, he confronts the problem of the proper object of sociology and devotes a session to the question of the position that sociology occupies in the space of academic disciplines, between science and literature.

A close reading of these lectures given from 1982 to 1986 shows a sociologist who is gradually finding a place for himself and for his discipline at the Collège de France. From 1984 to 1985, Bourdieu made references to conferences, seminars and colloquia that took place at the Collège de France, where he sometimes participated with colleagues representing different historical and literary disciplines (18 April 1985, 2 May 1985, 22 May and 19 June 1986). Although not mentioned in the lectures, he also played a central part in the preparation of a report on 'the teaching of the future' commissioned by the President of the Republic in February 1984 from teachers at the Collège de France, which they delivered in March 1985. As the education specialist, Bourdieu was the editor-in-chief, and even, to a large extent, the driving force.[13]

Similarly, the many dialogues in the lectures with linguistics, economics, philosophy, history, art history, and even zoology in 1982 are not unrelated to the desire for interdisciplinary exchange that the sociologist maintained throughout his teaching in this multidisciplinary institution.[14] He also makes reference throughout the course to the work of his colleagues (or recent predecessors) at the Collège de France: Georges Dumézil and Émile Benveniste are cited several times, as are some of the younger professors at the Collège de France, the historian Emmanuel Le Roy Ladurie (18 April 1985), the art historian Jacques Thuillier (2 May 1985) or the Indian studies scholar Gérard Fussman (28 March 1985). Three teachers deserve special mention. Claude Lévi-Strauss, whose work Bourdieu had continually engaged with, retired from the Collège de France when Bourdieu was appointed, but a conference that Lévi-Strauss gave in 1983 represented a moment of tension between the two men, leaving its mark on one of the lectures of 1986 (5 June 1986). The course also includes several references to the medieval historian Georges Duby who was older than Bourdieu but was undoubtedly one of the colleagues he was closest to.[15] We must finally mention Michel Foucault, whose lectures at the Collège de France were very popular. Bourdieu spoke much later about what had attracted him to and what had separated him from Michel Foucault, whose first seminar he had attended while he himself was a student.[16] In the 1980s, Foucault and Bourdieu found themselves united in actions to support Polish trade unionists and appeal to the French government. Bourdieu's lectures show a mixture of esteem and distance: Bourdieu refers explicitly to Foucault's work, for example to the notion of *episteme*, but the fourth and fifth years contain an ongoing critique of the analyses of power developed by the philosopher. In 1984, when Foucault died, Bourdieu attended the ceremony preceding the funeral in Paris[17] and published two texts of tribute to 'a friend and colleague'.[18]

The place of the work in Bourdieu's corpus

The theoretical synthesis proposed by Bourdieu in the lectures on general sociology in the first half of the 1980s came at a specific moment in his work. In these first two years of teaching at least, Bourdieu returned only rarely to his work of the 1960s. He drew mainly on the books he had recently published (*Distinction*, *The Logic of Practice*) or that he was about to finish (*Ce que parler veut dire* in October 1982), and his current research. He often mentions his work on the professors of the University of Paris that he started in the middle of the 1960s and was then finishing off: the book *Homo academicus* was to appear in 1984. He also often takes examples from a management survey published in 1978,[19] and a research project into the episcopate published in November 1982.[20] He also draws on two research projects, one on the grandes écoles[21]and the other on the literary field, started in the late 1960s, which became the subject of two books a few years after the course: *The State Nobility* in 1989 and *The Rules of Art* in 1992.

Bourdieu rarely mobilized his previously published research without reworking it. The lectures on the notion of habitus, for example, far from being a simple repetition of *The Logic of Practice*, allow him to revise the concept, notably through a (re)reading of texts by Husserl. This progressive search for greater depth is also very visible in his return in the first year of the course to the issues of classification and social class. These problems, which were already at the centre of *Distinction*, are reformulated here in the light of his other ongoing studies (particularly in his publications on language and political delegation)[22] on 'authorized' discourse (that benefits from the authority and/or delegation of a group) and the performatives that, under certain conditions, bring into existence what they state (even when they relate to topics – like the 'working class' for example – that have become virtually metaphysical entities). Bourdieu had come to emphasize an aspect of the 'classes' that is not much dealt with in *Distinction*, namely the limited but never completely curtailed capacity left to scholarly and political discourse to engender a collective belief in the existence of a 'class'. In 1984, he published a summary of this analysis in an important article which is a kind of addendum to *Distinction*, 'Social space and the genesis of "classes"'.[23]

One of the changes that Bourdieu makes is to move from an analysis that, in *Distinction*, still gives pride of place to the notion of social class, to a theory that is organized around the notion of a social space (or field). The lectures in general sociology are part of an effort to develop the concept of the field. *The Logic of Practice* (1980) had taken up and developed the implications of the concept of habitus, partially formulated in 1972 in *Outline of a Theory of Practice*. *Distinction* (1979) had then summarized fifteen years of studies of cultural capital in its various forms, and the major role that it would now have in any theory of social class, in particular because of developments in the educational system; it now remained for Bourdieu to do the same work for the third concept of his social anthropology, namely the concept of field, which also tended more and more to appear to him as the leading player in his conceptual trio, the one that integrated the other two. While the course develops the distinction between field of forces and field of struggle, and above all the relations between the concept of field and the concepts of habitus and capital, Bourdieu, in the 1980s, increasingly investigated the issues of the field, especially the university field, the legal field,[24] and the literary and artistic field in the nineteenth century, whose emergence and structure he painstakingly studied, and all of these concerns have left their mark in the lectures. In the years following the lectures, Bourdieu would also be interested in the fields of the state, economics, journalism, philosophy and politics.[25] The lectures in general sociology, especially for the last year, allow us to follow the elaboration of the notion of the 'field of power' which was very little used in *Distinction*, but was to become central in 1989 in *The State Nobility*. The lectures at the Collège de France constitute one phase in a long-term enterprise that would no doubt have been completed in the book that Bourdieu was preparing at the end of his life, on the theory of the field.

The course was also an opportunity for Bourdieu to present a first state of the new work that he was launching into during this period. In 1984–5, almost half of his teaching was devoted to the research he had conducted with Marie-Claire Bourdieu into the field of painting, probably a few years earlier (14 March 1985). In the years immediately following the course, he went on to publish the first articles deriving from this research,[26] and at the end of the 1990s he dedicated two entire years of his teaching to it.[27] The lectures for 1985 show that the research was already well advanced, even if it still lacked, for example, the analysis of the works of Manet that he was to offer at the end of the 1990s. Moreover, the issue at the heart of his work was then closely linked to that of *The Rules of Art* which he was working on in parallel: Bourdieu presented it as 'a series of analyses of the relationship between the literary field and the artistic field' (7 March 1985) and emphasized, more than he did later towards the end of the 1990s, the fact that the process of autonomization is played out in the area of the artistic field as a whole and cannot be fully grasped in a research exercise devoted to a single sector (painting, literature, music, etc.).

The research he presented in the 'second hour' of the lectures, in 1983–4 and in 1985–6, came from more specific studies and gave rise to no more than two or three successive sessions. Among these works is the analysis, which Bourdieu says he 'found when sorting through my notes' (1 March 1984), of a 'hit parade' of intellectuals published in 1981 by a literary magazine (*Lire*), which had quite a wide readership. A first text appeared as an article a few months later, then as an appendix to *Homo Academicus* in November 1984.[28] He would later cite this analysis as a kind of 'master work', similar to those made by medieval artisans',[29] even if this work on the hit parade, far from being a simple exercise in method or style, was also an opportunity to reflect on the properties of the intellectual field, with its weak institutionalization and its vulnerability to any 'social action' driven by the press.

The lectures present several analyses based on literary texts, an approach that Bourdieu had not practised before, except in his analysis of Flaubert's *Sentimental Education*.[30] He deals with *The Trial* by Franz Kafka[31] (22 and 29 March 1984), *To the Lighthouse* by Virginia Woolf (15 and 22 May 1986) and, more briefly, *Waiting for Godot* by Samuel Beckett (19 April 1984) and Kafka's *Metamorphosis* (22 May 1986).[32] Bourdieu seems here to take a greater interest than previously in literary texts and their analysis, which may be related to the composition of *The Rules of Art*. In fact, *The Trial* provided Bourdieu with a form of allegory, but also an opportunity to practise the 'science of works' whose principles he went on to expound in the 1992 book. He also experienced, as he admitted a few years later, a gradual change in his relation to literature: he repressed his literary education and tastes less than he did at the beginning, at a time when the scientific nature of sociology was not well established.[33] The 'Course on General Sociology' also invites his audience to reflect on their relationship to literature. In publicizing his reflections on the 'biographical illusion' which informs the work and the literary reflections of William

Faulkner and Alain Robbe-Grillet, Bourdieu emphasized the fact that the repression of the 'literary' (that is to say, of 'fine writing' as opposed to the laborious argumentation of philosophical writing) owes much to the position occupied by sociology in the space of disciplines, at least in France, and to the particular form taken by the opposition between literature and science in the nineteenth century (24 April 1986).

The lectures also show the emergence of concerns that were to become important in Bourdieu's later work. The sociologist was at a stage in his career when he was (re)reading Max Weber. He had drawn on Weber's economic sociology since his first work in Algeria, and a little later wrote a review of his *Sociology of Religion*, at a time when Weber was still very little known in France. In 1982, while French editions of Weber were still few and far between, Bourdieu published in *Libération*, a daily newspaper read by many intellectuals, a short text ironically entitled 'Who's afraid of Max Weber?!'[34] In the third year of his course he frequently drew on texts by Weber still unknown in France, and commented on the arguments in *Economy and Society* on coding, the notion of an 'academic discipline', and the sociology of law. Weber's observations on *Kadijustiz*, and on the justice of Sancho Panza or Solomon, began to recur frequently in the lectures. It was probably in the period when these lectures were given, and in particular through the reading of Weber, that Bourdieu developed a new interest in the sociology of law. The theme of the *vis formae* appeared during the year 1983–4. An article on the 'force of law' would be published in 1986,[35] that is, in the last year of the course on general sociology. This included references to research into the sociology of law (15 May 1986, 5 June 1986), and reflections on the legal field, which Bourdieu would return to in his teaching at the Collège de France in 1987–8.

Beyond the law, it was more generally the state that became a central object of study. The formula used by Bourdieu to enlarge upon Weber's definition of the state by speaking of a 'monopoly of legitimate symbolic violence' started to emerge in these lectures of the early 1980s. The theme had already underpinned the arguments developed in 1982 and 1983 on the issue of officialization or on the continuum that runs from the insult to the act of appointment executed and guaranteed by the state. His criticism in 1983–4 of linear interpretations of the process of rationalization heralded the reflections that he would develop a few years later when he discussed the genesis of the state. References to the state are very numerous in the last sessions of the fourth year when, dealing with social perceptions of society, Bourdieu speaks of the consensual or accredited viewpoint whose monopoly belongs to the state. His analysis of academic qualifications also implicates the state, defined as a 'field of agents competing for the control of social certification' (9 May 1985). This fourth year ends with the observation that a sociology of symbolic struggles must question the role of the state as 'the ultimate source of authority'. In short, the state became a major issue in Bourdieu's analyses. After completing his course on general sociology he went on to launch a new five-year cycle of lectures, explicitly devoted to the state.[36]

Other themes that occupied an important place in Bourdieu's work in the second half of the 1980s or in the 1990s are outlined in the course on general sociology. This is the case with 'scholastic bias' – although he did not yet use the term as such – but also with the question of 'male domination' which later gave rise to an article (1990), and then a book (1998).[37] In 1985–6, Bourdieu does in fact put forward several arguments on the political dimension of male supremacy, on the 'androcentric unconscious' of Mediterranean societies and, through his commentary on Virginia Woolf's *To the Lighthouse*, on the feminine vision of male control of social games. In some respects the work on the 'hit parade of intellectuals' announced Bourdieu's reflections in the 1990s on what he called the 'grip of journalism' on the intellectual field.[38] However, Bourdieu did not yet view the media from the perspective that became his ten years later, especially in the small polemical book on television and journalism published in late 1996 for a wider audience.[39] This is because the lectures on general sociology were given in the period just before the 'commercial turning point' experienced by the media in France, especially from 1986 when the most popular television channel, TF1, was privatized. In the early 1980s, the spirit of public service inherited from the beginnings of television remained quite powerful, and it still happened that Bourdieu occasionally participated in television shows or public discussions with prominent journalists, which he no longer did ten years later. He was persuaded by Georges Duby, his colleague at the Collège de France, to involve himself in an 'educational television' project that led indirectly to the birth of the Franco-German cultural channel, Arte.[40]

The intellectual field in the first half of the 1980s

The course bears the mark of the intellectual field of the time.[41] It contains regular references to great figures from previous decades, such as Jean-Paul Sartre and Jacques Lacan, who died respectively in 1980 and 1981, or Louis Althusser, who was interned in November 1980 following the murder of his wife. Bourdieu refers in one of his lectures to the current debate in the press over the search for a 'successor' to Sartre.[42] The dominant figures of the moment who accumulated intellectual recognition and celebrity with the educated public (and not only in France) are chiefly those 'fifty-somethings' like Bourdieu himself, along with Michel Foucault, Jacques Derrida and Gilles Deleuze. They made themselves known in the years before May '68 and share what Bourdieu calls an 'anti-establishment cast of mind' (2 May 1985). These 'consecrated heretics', according to another of his formulae,[43] had distanced themselves from the university and traditional philosophy. In the first half of the 1980s, they often found themselves signing the same appeals or petitions. Younger rivals, however, were already starting to refer them in the past tense: in autumn 1985, a highly publicized essay targeted the 'anti-humanist' thinkers of the May '68 generation that they allegedly epitomized.[44] Bourdieu refers to this book in one of his lectures (5 June 1986), and several times mentioned the themes of 'the return to Kant' and 'the return of the subject' that its authors represented.

Although he referred only allusively to the development of 'postmodernism', which dated from the second half of the 1970s, he made several references to the emergence, at roughly the same moment, of the 'new philosophers', a group of essayists who had written no significant works but managed to impose themselves chiefly through the circuits of the world of cultural journalism. The attitude to adopt towards this new breed of rivals, and more generally towards all the attacks threatening mainstream 'philosophy' at that time, became a contentious issue; several allusions in the lectures bear witness to Bourdieu's reservations or distance with respect to Gilles Deleuze's (in his opinion counterproductive) statements about the 'nullity' of the 'new philosophers', or the 'Estates General of Philosophy' organized by Jacques Derrida. His analysis of the 'hit parade', however, shows his awareness of the structural transformations that were accelerating at this time, and the threat they represented to the survival of the intellectual model that he embodied.[45]

In the early 1980s, his own status in the intellectual field changed, but not according to a single unequivocal logic. His election to the Collège de France, for example, or the success of *Distinction*, which very soon became a landmark, even for many outside the circle of specialists, increased the recognition of his work. However, at the same time, they set Bourdieu up as embodying a discipline and thought that many intellectual circles denounced as 'sociologism', as 'deterministic' or even 'totalitarian' thought.

The subspace of sociology in France

This ambiguity is found in the subspace of sociology. Bourdieu's work was already at a stage that allowed retrospective overviews. In his lectures he sometimes takes it upon himself to locate and formulate the general meaning of his research: he might insist on his efforts to emphasize the 'decisive role of the symbolic in social exchanges', in opposition to 'economic and economistic analyses' (22 March 1984); he may also argue that his 'historical contribution' has been to 'pursue his work as a sociologist to the very end, that is to include objectification of the professional objectifiers' (19 June 1986). At the same time he started to undertake a work of synthesis (which includes the course) and popularization. In parallel with his research work, Bourdieu started to publish books intended to give a more accessible overview of his work: in 1980, for the first time, he compiled a collection of oral interventions that he had delivered in various circumstances.[46] In 1983, one of his first students, Alain Accardo, published the first book that made the major concepts of his sociology available to an audience of students and activists.[47] His international celebrity was also growing. Thus, just before the start of his fifth year of teaching, he made a one-month trip to the United States, during which he gave fifteen seminars and conferences in American universities. In the years that followed, he travelled to other countries for similar trips.

This growing consecration did not grant him the status of a 'grand master'. In sociology, as in the entire intellectual field, Bourdieu's growing recognition in France seemed to generate increasingly fierce forms of rejection. In the first half of the 1980s, several associations attempted to describe his sociology as 'outdated', sometimes even mocking 'the actor making a comeback'. This was the case, in particular, with the 'methodological individualism' claiming to explain social phenomena using the devices of a desocialized 'homo sociologicus'. Its leader was Raymond Boudon who, after being in the 1960s one of the leading importers in France of Paul Lazarsfeld's 'methodology' (opposed by Bourdieu on epistemological grounds), went on in the 1970s to develop an analysis of educational inequality that claimed to compete with the vision imposed by *The Inheritors* and *Reproduction*.[48] If Bourdieu, in his lectures, repeats his criticisms of 'methodological individualism' on several occasions, or takes his distance from the vision that it tends to give of his work, it is because this school of thought was making inroads in the United States and had entered a particularly aggressive phase. In 1982 Presses Universitaires de France published a *Critical Dictionary of Sociology* under the direction of

Raymond Boudon and François Bourricaud, whose 'scrutiny of the imperfections, uncertainties and flaws of sociological theories, but also the reasons for their success' was aimed at sociology of Marxist or structuralist inspiration.

Bourdieu's remarks on the 'ultra-subjectivism' and the 'facile radicalism' that had developed in the sociology of science were a response in their turn to the publication in 1979 of the book *Laboratory Life*.[49] Based on the ethnographic study of a neuroendocrinology laboratory, this book intended to found an approach to the analyses of 'the scientific field and the social conditions of the progress of reason' different from the one that Bourdieu had been formulating since the mid-1970s.[50] For Bourdieu, this approach radicalized to the point of relativism the thesis according to which scientific facts are socially constructed. Its insistence on the search by scientists for credibility and their reliance on rhetoric, encourages us to ignore the fact that, in the scientific field, not all strategies are possible (28 March 1985 and 19 June 1986). Fifteen years later, when this 'new sociology of science' had developed considerably, Bourdieu would formulate these criticisms again.[51]

The lectures also mention the imports that occurred in sociology in France in the 1980s. The period is marked by a wave of translations of Georg Simmel, but also by the work of the Frankfurt School, as well as by the 'discovery' of interactionism and ethnomethodology, those 'heterodox' currents of American sociology dating back to the 1950s and 1960s. In one of his lectures, Bourdieu presents a critique of these imports (5 June 1986). Although he mocks the French provincialism that leads to the translation of works when they are out of fashion in their countries of origin, he is bound to be annoyed by these imports when they are explicitly opposed to his own sociology, especially in the case of authors he had been long familiar with, had helped to make known in France (most of Goffman's work had already been translated in the 1970s and 1980s in a series edited by Bourdieu) and, above all, had integrated into his approach.

Political 'news'

Beyond the intellectual world, the lecture course took place at a specific moment in time. In France, the political situation was marked by the election in May 1981 of François Mitterrand to the presidency of the Republic. In his lectures, Bourdieu says little or nothing about the experience of seeing the left return to power after its long, enforced absence, only to start adopting liberal policies in 1983 that would prove to be lasting. He contents himself with a few incidental allusions, for example in remarks critical of a Socialist Minister of National Education (12 June 1986) or a reflection on the problem of the attitude that intellectuals should adopt towards a left-wing government. Referring to the relationship between the field of intellectual production and external forces, he points out – 'to keep [his] audience up to date' – that the problem does not arise in exactly the same way when political power is wielded by the left rather than the right (11 January 1983). As an intellectual, however, Bourdieu was not totally inactive during this period, even if he was to become more militant in the 1990s.[52] One of the important stands that he made, with other intellectuals (including Michel Foucault), was in December 1981, when they challenged the new government, which, probably because it included some ministers from the French Communist Party, failed to condemn the state of siege decreed in Poland by the communist regime that the trade union Solidarność opposed. He also signed petitions on subjects such as the situation in prisons or, after the return of the right to power in 1986, the budgetary restrictions on research, and participated in political and communitarian initiatives which, from 1983, had decided to react to the rise of 'racism' towards immigrant populations (mainly from former French colonies in Africa).

If, at this time, the public interventions of Bourdieu were limited to subjects related to French politics, his lectures included some allusions to events occurring in foreign countries or at an international level. Bourdieu thus offered some elements of reflection on the Iranian revolution or the Irish conflict (26 April 1984 and 28 March 1985), but these were always grounded in his theoretical analyses and related to them. The course also reflects his interest in the ideological evolution and progression of neoliberalism, which became central to many of his political interventions of the 1990s and early 2000s. The early 1980s were marked by the rise to power of Margaret Thatcher in Britain and Ronald Reagan in the United States. Bourdieu refers several times to the economists of the 'Chicago School' which these leaders sometimes claimed allegiance to. He also mentions, when he discusses the difference between private charity and social security (9 and 23 May 1985), the criticism that the welfare state was increasingly subject to in the 1980s. The last lecture of the fourth year of his general sociology class (lecture of 30 May 1985) includes an argument on the tragedy that had occurred at the Heysel stadium in Brussels the day before. The relation that he sees between a riot provoked by hooligans, leaving 39 dead, and the policies of the 'Iron Lady' (Margaret Thatcher) heralds the theme of the 'law of the conservation of violence' that he would develop in opposition to neoliberal politics in the 1990s.[53]

Current affairs are quite present in the course but Bourdieu does not 'comment on the news' as such. With very few exceptions (such as the Heysel drama), current events are mentioned only to illustrate a sociological argument. The invocation of the events and personalities which, for a few weeks or a few months, are at the centre of the 'news' (or conversations in the intellectual or academic world) has the advantage of promoting communication with the audience. It shows Bourdieu's desire to deliver teaching that is not divorced from concrete realities but always goes hand in hand with a theoretical analysis. In this way the reference to a serious coach accident that had given rise to much debate in the French media is used only in order to show the complexity of the search for the causes of phenomena or behaviour, which is so often limited to finding the guilty party (9 November 1982). Similarly, when Bourdieu mentions unemployment figures (2 May 1985), it is because he finds an almost perfect example of his reflections on 'state science'. This indicator, the unemployment figures established by a public institute, was becoming a central issue in French political debates, with the rise of mass unemployment between the mid-1970s and the 1980s. The reformulation of the question of immigration that also occurred at this time (most dramatically figuring in the high electoral scores achieved by the far right in France from 1982) is invoked, because it provides a very clear illustration of one of the ideas that Bourdieu was developing: that the very principles informing our perspective on the social world (in this case, the question of whether a division between immigrants and non-immigrants should replace the sociologists' division between rich and poor) are contentious issues.

Because it was intended for immediate consumption, the course is, more than Bourdieu's books, marked by its context. If Bourdieu's analyses of the mode of existence of collective communities are so often illustrated with examples from 'the church' and 'the working class', especially during the first year of the course, it is because the French press and media of the time very often led with titles proclaiming the alleged statements, positions or intentions of these two 'collectives'. In France in the 1980s, the Catholic Church still remained an important social force and Marxism still wielded influence in political discourse as well as in intellectual circles. The French Communist Party had already begun to decline but still held a large number of local councils. Its candidate for the 1981 presidential elections took 15 per cent of the vote and its representatives still stood as spokespersons for the 'working class'.

If, to facilitate the reading of the course, it was necessary to recall these few elements of the context, notably that of France in the 1980s, it remains important to emphasize that these references to current affairs are only ever employed to illustrate a more general analysis. Confronted with these references that 'spoke' immediately to Bourdieu's audience, the contemporary reader, whether French or foreign, must adopt the posture recommended by Bourdieu when he mentions the relative antiquity of his enquiry into the grandes écoles or when he suggests that the description of the ruling class resulting from his work on the literary field in the second half of the nineteenth century and based on the opposition between the 'bourgeois' and the 'artist' corresponds to a state of society that belongs to the past (11 January 1983). In other words, it is important to remember that the fact that Bourdieu illustrates his theory with essentially French data does not mean that it would apply only to the situation in France. This kind of common-sense objection would reveal a certain, very French, flaw in theoretical reflection. For it would be absurd to say, for example, that the work of ethnologists would only be valid for the archaic societies that they study. In reality, nothing is less Franco-French than the analyses proposed by Bourdieu, where it is a question not of seeing transhistorical invariants or, conversely, specific historical events, but the 'particular case of one possibility among others'. We must do the exercise to which he invited the readers of *Distinction*'s English-language translation,[54] which consists in discovering structural equivalents for the phenomena that he analysed in a particular historical and national context. For him, sociology must undertake a precise and thorough analysis of historically situated facts, but in a totally different perspective from a historicizing narrative, or a journalistic discourse that is bound to disappear with the events that provoke it: what sociology seeks in the evocation of precise historical states is the discovery of deep social structures and the laws of their transformation.

At the end of 1985–6, Bourdieu brought the 'Course on General Sociology' to a close. It had lasted for five years, and was the first general introduction to sociology ever offered at the Collège de France. The following year, he took the opportunity of a sabbatical granted to members of this institution to temporarily suspend his teaching. He resumed his classes in March 1988, under a new title: 'On the State'. This was the beginning of a five-year cycle devoted to the analysis and deconstruction of this institution and, more generally, inaugurated a period when Bourdieu's lectures at the Collège de France would focus on specific themes: after the sociology of the state,[55] the sociology of the economic field, the sociology of domination, the sociology of a symbolic revolution in painting;[56] then, by way of a conclusion to his teaching, he came to analyse the research devoted to the sociology of science in general and to the sociology of sociology in particular,[57] as if to recall, in opposition to a certain radical relativism, that, subject to certain social conditions, precisely those that constitute the scientific field, it is possible to produce universal truths that are not reducible to the social world that produces them.

Appendix

Summary of lectures, published in the Annuaire du Collège de France

1981–1982

I first examined one of the procedures fundamental to the social sciences, that of naming and classifying. Sociologists encounter realities that are already named and classified, that bear titles, insignia and labels which are so many indicators of membership of a class. In order to avoid unwittingly adopting acts of constitution whose logic and needs escape them, sociologists should take as the object of their study the social procedure of nomination itself – especially nomination to an occupation and a professional position – and the rites of institution that enable it. Beyond that, they should examine the role played by language in the construction of social matters; or indeed, the role that the struggle for classification – which is an aspect of any class struggle – plays in constituting classes according to age group, gender identity and social class.

To discover what is specific to scholarly classification in the case of the social sciences, I compared the classification procedures practised by the sociologist to those practised in other sciences, like botany or zoology, but also to those that social agents actually use in practice, with a symbolic efficiency that varies according to their placing along the axis between the two extremes of the insult and an official nomination. Like biological classifications, the sociologist's classifications select a set of properties that correlate with each other and account for the optimal proportion of observed variation; this distinguishes them from practical classifications, of which the insult is an example, and which, being directed towards practical ends, favour one or other particular criterion. But the analysis of the practical procedures of classification reminds us that, unlike biology, sociology has to deal with agents who call classification into question, and not only as a conceptual problem: the properties that the sociologist treats as criteria for grouping, as indicators of objective distances between units or classes, function in reality as powers. This is why the hierarchy of criteria that the sociologist derives from objective measures is both the result of struggles and yet also an issue in a struggle aiming to preserve or transform the hierarchy. There is a class struggle over the existence or non-existence of classes. And our science should establish objective divisions without forgetting that the visible state of these divisions both now and in the future depends partly on the struggles between the individuals and the groups attempting to impose their *representation* of these divisions.

In the case of the social world, the neo-Kantian theory that grants language, and representation in general, a specifically symbolic efficiency in the construction of reality is very well founded: and social science should analyse the logic of the struggle for the symbolic power of nomination, constitution or institution that plays a part in creating social reality by naming it. In this context, we can refer again to the example of the insult, recently discussed by linguists: contrary to common nouns, and in particular the titles of professions (gendarme, teacher, etc.), which are supported by the common sense of the *consensus* or *homologein* of a whole group, as expressed in the social act of nomination whereby an official delegate confers a title, the 'qualifying nouns' (such as 'idiot') that the insult relies on have only a weak symbolic efficiency: their *idios logos* engages only its author. But the two poles share a common intention that we may call performative or, more simply, magical: the insult, like a nomination, belongs to the class of acts of institution or destitution, some more socially grounded than others, whereby an individual acting either in their own name or in the name of a group indicates to someone that they have a certain property, or that they grant them such a property. In other words, the insult and nomination both make some claim to symbolic authority as a socially recognized power to impose a certain vision of the social world, that is, the divisions of the social world.

Social science should include within its theory of the social world a theory of the theory effect which, in helping to impose an authorized manner of seeing the social world, helps to create the reality of this world: words, and *a fortiori* sayings, proverbs and all kinds of stereotypical or ritual expression, are programmes of perception. In the struggle to impose a legitimate vision, where science itself is inevitably engaged, agents wield a power proportionate to their symbolic capital, that is to the recognition accorded them by a group: the authority that grounds the performative efficiency of the discourse is a *percipi*, a being that is known and acknowledged, which enables it to impose a *perci-pere*. It is always the group that creates those who create the group.

In order to establish how the symbolic power to constitute and insti-tute is constituted and instituted, we may draw on the analyses of the historians of law (Kantorowicz, Post, etc.) who describe the magical procedure of transubstantiation by which groups establish their del-egates as the acknowledged depositories of the authority of the group. The mystery of the ministry (to borrow a play on words dear to the canon lawyers) can only be dispelled through a historical analysis of the logic of representation (in the different senses of the term) through which the representative creates the group that creates him: the spokes-man granted the full power to speak and act *in the name* of the group, and most importantly to act on the group itself through the magic of the slogan, is a substitute for the group, which exists only through this proxy; the group is made flesh, it is personified in a fictitious person who shakes it out of its condition as a simple series of separate indi-viduals, and allows it to act and speak through him as a single man. In return, the representative is granted the right to 'stand in' for the group, to speak and act in its name: *Status est magistratus, l'État, c'est moi*. He gives a body (his body) to a constituted body.

The representatives of the state have the *consensus omnium* on their side; they are the depository of common sense. An official nomination, like an academic qualification for instance, is universally valid in every market. We could say, after Leibniz, that the state is the 'geometral', the point of convergence of all the perspectives: in fact the act of nomi-nation (to the position of graduate, teacher or minister) overcomes the free-for-all symbolic struggle; it gives an authorized, acknowledged perspective over the social agents, while disguising the arbitrary nature of that perspectival truth. It is in this sense that we can see in the state the holder of the monopoly of legitimate symbolic violence.

Notes

Editorial note

1 Pierre Bourdieu, *Science of Science and Reflexivity* (Cambridge: Polity, 2004).
2 Pierre Bourdieu, *On the State: Lectures at the Collège de France 1989–1992*, trans. David Fernbach (Cambridge: Polity, 2014); Pierre Bourdieu, *Manet: A Symbolic Revolution: Lectures at the Collège de France 1998–2000*, followed by an unfinished manuscript by Pierre and Marie-Claire Bourdieu, trans. Peter Collier and Margaret Rigaud (Cambridge: Polity, 2017).
3 Bourdieu, *On the State*, pp. xi–xii.
4 [Where the sense is evident, I have translated the wording supplied without square brackets. – Translator.]

Lecture of 28 April 1982

1 See Pierre Bourdieu's inaugural lecture at the Collège de France entitled 'A lecture on the lecture', in *In Other Words*, trans. Matthew Adamson (Cambridge: Polity, 1990). As far back as 1962 he referred to the '*agrégation* exercise', especially in 'Systèmes d'enseignement et systèmes de pensée', *Revue internationale de sciences sociales*, 19.1 (1967), pp. 367–88. On the role of the *agrégation* in the French educational system, see *Reproduction* (London: Sage, 1977), esp. pp. 150–1. Later he would go on to develop his analysis of education 'in the French manner', as we find it in the preparatory classes for the grandes écoles, in *The State Nobility*, trans. Lauretta C. Clough (Cambridge: Polity, 1996), esp. pp. 71–127.
2 Nicholas of Cusa, *On Learned Ignorance*, 2nd edn (1440; Minneapolis: Arthur J. Banning Press, 1985).
3 Bourdieu published this book in the series he edited, 'Le sens commun': Émile Benveniste, *Le Vocabulaire des institutions indo-européennnes* (Paris: Minuit, 1969); translated as Émile Benveniste, *Dictionary of Indo-European Concepts and Society* (Chicago: Hau Books, 2016).
4 See for example the lectures by Georges Gurvitch, *Études sur les classes sociales* (Paris: Gonthier, 1966); Raymond Aron, *La Lutte des classes* (Paris: Gallimard, 'Idées', 1964).

5 Pierre Bourdieu, Jean-Claude Chamboredon and Jean-Claude Passeron, *The Craft of Sociology: Epistemological Preliminaries*, trans. Richard Nice (Berlin/New York: Mouton/de Gruyter, 2005).

6 On the question of classification, see Pierre Bourdieu, *Distinction: A Social Critique of the Judgement of Taste*, trans. Richard Nice (Abingdon: Routledge & Kegan Paul, 1984), esp. pp. 466–7, 471–3, 477–8. The comparison between biology or botany and the social sciences is not raised in *Distinction* but in 'Espace social et genèse des "classes"', *Actes de la recherche en sciences sociales*, nos 52–3 (1984), pp. 4–5, translated as 'Social space and the genesis of "classes"', in Pierre Bourdieu, *Language and Symbolic Power*, trans. Gino Raymond and Matthew Adamson (Cambridge: Polity, 1991), pp. 229–51. The question of what classification involves is also the subject of no. 50 (Nov. 1983) of *Actes de la recherche en sciences sociales*.

7 Here we recognize one of lines of force of Pierre Bourdieu's research in *Distinction*, where he affirms that 'taste classifies, and classifies the classifier'.

8 See Bourdieu, *Distinction,* esp. pp. 106–9 for the notion of a constructed class.

9 The enquiry which Bourdieu refers to here was published in Pierre Bourdieu, *Homo Academicus*, trans. Peter Collier (Cambridge: Polity, 1988) (see esp. pp. 6–21 for the points raised here).

10 [An *agrégé* is someone who has passed the *agrégation*, a highly competitive postgraduate diploma that qualifies them for a teaching post in a top lycée or university. – Translator.]

11 See Alphonse Allais, 'Un honnête homme dans toute la force du mot', in *Deux et deux font cinq* (Paris: Paul Ollendorf, 1895), pp. 69–72.

12 See Alvin W. Gouldner, 'Cosmopolitan and locals: toward an analysis of latent social roles', *Administrative Science Quarterly*, 2.3 (1957), pp. 281–307; see also Bourdieu, *Homo Academicus*, pp. 11–12.

13 Henri Bergson, *Matter and Memory* (1896; New York: Dover Press, 2006), p. 206. On the subject of this formula, see also Claude Lévi-Strauss, *The Savage Mind* (Oxford: Oxford University Press, 1996), p. 137: 'It is thus not grass but the difference between species of grass which interests the herbivore.'

14 See Nicolas Ruwet, 'Grammaire des insultes', in *Grammaire des insultes et autres études* (Paris: Seuil, 1982), pp. 239–314 (first published as 'Les noms de qualité en français. Pour une analyse interprétative', in C. Rohrer [dir.], *Actes du colloque franco-allemand de linguistique théorique* (Tübingen: Niemeyer, 1977), pp. 1–65).

15 Jean-Claude Milner, 'Quelques opérations de détermination en français. Syntaxe et interprétation', thèse de doctorat d'État, Université de Paris VII, 1975. Bourdieu here resumes in condensed form his analysis of the insult in *Ce que parler veut dire. L'économie des échanges linguistique*s (Paris: Fayard, 1982), esp. pp. 71–2, 100; republished in Bourdieu, *Language and Symbolic Power*, see pp. 75–6, 105, 121, 239, 243.

16 For more detail on this point, see the next lecture, for 5 May 1982, p. 18 and note 3.

17 The exact quotation (in Ruwet, 'Grammaire des insultes', p. 244) is: 'Les premiers auraient une "référence virtuelle" propre, dont les seconds seraient dépourvus. La référence virtuelle propre de *professeur, gendarme*, etc., définit une classe "dont les membres [sont] reconaissables à des caractères objectifs communs" (Milner, 1975, p. 368)' ('The former would have their own "virtual reference", which would be lacking in the latter. The specific virtual reference

of *teacher*, *gendarme*, etc., defines a class "whose members are recognizable from their objective common characteristics" (Milner, 1975, p. 368)').

18 John L. Austin, *How to Do Things with Words*, 2nd edn (1962; Oxford: Oxford University Press, 2009). Bourdieu discusses Austin's theses in *Language and Symbolic Power*, pp. 73–4, 107–15.

19 Milner, 'Quelques opérations', p. 368; quoted in Ruwet, 'Grammaire des insultes', p. 244.

Lecture of 5 May 1982

1 Nicolas Ruwet, 'Grammaire des insultes', in *Grammaire des insultes et autres études* (Paris: Seuil, 1982), p. 302, n. 14.

2 Harold Garfinkel, 'Conditions of successful degradation ceremonies', *American Journal of Sociology*, 61.5 (1956), pp. 420–4.

3 Heidegger emphasizes the fact that *katègoria* comes from *kata-agoreuein*, which means 'publicly accuse' (or, more precisely, 'accuse in the agora'). See Martin Heidegger, 'Ce qu'est et comment se détermine la *Physis*' ['Die Phusis bei Aristoteles' (1967)], trans. François Fédier, in *Questions II* (Paris: Gallimard, 1968), pp. 199–200.

4 Referring in particular to the example of the 'response of a mother to her son who has "dishonoured" a girl, and who must "atone": "You must marry that girl"', Oswald Ducrot speaks of an 'overt claim to possess a particular power'. Oswald Ducrot, 'Illocutoire et performatif', *Linguistique et sémiologie. Travaux du Centre de recherches linguistiques et sémiologiques de Lyon*, no 4 (1977), p. 36.

5 Jacques Cellard, *Ça ne mange pas de pain. 400 expressions familières ou voyoutes de France et du Québec* (Paris: Hachette, 1982).

6 See Pierre Bourdieu, 'Reading, readers, the literate, literature', in *In Other Words* (Cambridge: Polity, 1990), esp. p. 96.

7 See Max Weber, 'Charismatic authority', in *Economy and Society* (Berkeley: University of California Press, 1978), vol. 1, part 1, ch. III, iv, pp. 241–5.

8 Max Weber, 'Ascetism, mysticism and salvation', in *Economy and Society*, vol. 1, part 2, ch. VI, x, p. 542.

9 [Bourdieu may be thinking of Wittgenstein's formula: 'The world is all that is the case', in *Tractatus Logico-Philosophicus* (London, Kegan Paul, 1922), Proposition 1. – Translator.]

10 ['*Agrégé*' in French comes from the Latin *egregius*, 'outside the herd'. – Translator.]

11 [A *normalien* is a student or graduate of the École Normale Supérieure, a prestigious higher education institution. Recruitment is fiercely competitive. Successful candidates receive a grant for their studies and then a stipend after their university degree, in return for service as teacher or civil servant. Famous *normaliens* include Jean-Paul Sartre and . . . Pierre Bourdieu. – Translator.]

12 Bourdieu was about to publish, with Monique de Saint Martin, 'La sainte famille. L'épiscopat français dans le champ du pouvoir', *Actes de la recherche en sciences sociales*, nos 44–45 (Nov. 1982), pp. 2–53.

13 On this issue see 'Identity and representation', in Pierre Bourdieu, *Language and Symbolic Power*, pp. 220–8.

Lecture of 12 May 1982

1 The fuller quotation is as follows: 'An experimenter facing natural phenomena is like a spectator watching a dumb show. He is in some sort the examining magistrate for nature; only instead of grappling with men who seek to deceive him by lying confessions or false witness, he is dealing with natural phenomena which for him are persons . . . whose design he wishes to learn. For this purpose he uses all the means within his power. He observes their actions, their gait, their behavior, and he seeks to disengage their cause by means of various attempts, called experiments. He uses every imaginable artifice, and, as the popular expression goes, he often makes a false plea in order to learn the truth.' Claude Bernard, *An Introduction to the Study of Experimental Medicine* (1865; New York: Dover, 1957), pp. 31–2.

2 The exact quotation is: 'The flying buttresses of Caen and Durham, still hidden beneath the roofs of the side aisles, began by doing something before being permitted to say so. Ultimately, the flying buttresses learned to talk'. Erwin Panofsky, *Gothic Architecture and Scholasticism* (1951; Latrobe, PA: Saint Vincent Archabbey, 2005), pp. 54–7.

3 For more detail on the problems involved in the research into business executives and bishops, see Pierre Bourdieu and Monique de Saint Martin, 'Le patronat', *Actes de la recherche en sciences sociales*, no. 20 (1978), esp. p. 78, and P. Bourdieu and M. de Saint Martin, 'La sainte famille. L'épiscopat français dans le champ du pouvoir', *Actes de la recherche en sciences sociales*, nos 44–45 (Nov. 1982), pp. 2–53 (esp. p. 34, n. 51).

4 Erving Goffman, *The Presentation of Self in Everyday Life* (1959; London: Penguin, 1969).

5 There are examples in Pierre Bourdieu, *Distinction: A Social Critique of the Judgement of Taste*, pp. 193, 207–8. For a clear presentation of the problems in a 'contrary' case, see 'Postscript: A class as object', in *The Bachelors' Ball*, trans. Richard Nice (Cambridge: Polity, 2008), pp. 193–200. See also the presentation of self when faced with a camera, in *Photography: A Middle-brow Art*, trans. Shaun Whiteside (Cambridge: Polity, 1990), pp. 19–31, 80–3, and, with Marie-Claire Bourdieu, 'Le paysan et la photographie', *Revue française de sociologie*, 6.2 (1965), pp. 164–74.

6 See Pierre Bourdieu, *Homo Academicus*.

7 [An ironic reference no doubt to Descartes's motto, 'larvatus prodeo', indicating his caution when undermining the scholastic philosophy of the church. – Translator.]

8 Bourdieu is no doubt thinking of an article by Émile Poulat, 'Le catholicisme français et son personnel dirigeant', *Archives de sociologie des religions*, no. 19 (Jan.–June 1965), pp. 117–24 (see Bourdieu and de Saint Martin, 'La sainte famille', p. 4).

9 Sylvain Maresca, 'La représentation de la paysannerie. Remarques ethnographiques sur le travail de représentation des dirigeants agricoles', *Actes de la recherche en sciences sociales*, no. 38 (1981), pp. 13–18.

10 Friedrich Nietzsche, 'On the uses and disadvantages of history for life', in *Untimely Meditations* (1874; Cambridge: Cambridge University Press, 1997), pp. 57–123.

11 The reference is not certain, but this might refer to Paul Veyne's analysis of *Res*

gestae Divi Augusti in *Le Pain et le Cirque. Sociologie historique d'un pluralisme politique* (Paris: Seuil, 1974).

12 Bourdieu is no doubt thinking of studies like those by Fernand Boulard (1898–1977), the author in particular of a *Carte religieuse de la France rurale* (1947).

13 Bourdieu is probably thinking of the notion of 'serendipity'.

14 Robert Darnton, *The Business of Enlightenment: A Publishing History of the* Encyclopédie, *1775–1800* (Cambridge MA: Harvard University Press, 1987). Bourdieu returns to this example in the lecture for 11 January 1983.

15 See for example William Labov, *Sociolinguistic Patterns* (Philadelphia: University of Pennsylvania Press, 1973).

16 See Pierre Bourdieu, 'From the "rules" of honour to the sense of honour' (1960), in *Outline of a Theory of Practice*, trans. Richard Nice (Cambridge: Cambridge University Press, 1977), pp. 10–15.

17 Secretary General of the French Communist Party from 1972 to 1994.

18 [In English in the text. – Translator.]

19 A reference to the lecture given by Max Weber in November 1917, 'Wissenschaft as Beruf' ('Science as a vocation'). A French translation of this text has since appeared under the title *La Science, profession et vocation* (Marseille: Agone, 2005). The long essay by Isabelle Kalinowski that accompanies this translation, 'Leçons wébériennes sur la science et la propagande' (pp. 65–274) supplies information on the circumstances in which this lecture was given and on the forms of professorial vaticination against which Weber was reacting by stating the need for neutrality. For an English version and commentary see *Max Weber's 'Science as a Vocation'*, ed. P. Lassman, I. Velody and H. Martins (London: Routledge, 2015).

20 Bourdieu belongs to the population that he takes as his object in *Homo Academicus* (the graph of the space of the faculties of arts and human sciences on p. 276 includes his name at one point).

21 In Carl Linnaeus's *Genera Plantarum* (Leiden, 1774; London: Forgotten Books, 2017). (The phrase is quoted especially by Edmond Goblot in his *Traité de logique* (Paris: Armand Colin, 1918), p. 147.)

22 Bourdieu, *Distinction*, esp. pp. 106–9.

23 Bourdieu often refers to this 'geometral', or 'geometrical point or place' which corresponded for Leibniz to God's viewpoint (see for example Pierre Bourdieu, *Science of Science and Reflexivity* (Cambridge: Polity, 2004), p. 95), using Maurice Merleau-Ponty's interpretation: 'Our perception ends in objects, and the object, once constituted, appears as the reason for all the experiences of it that we have had or that we could have. For example, I see the neighboring house from a particular angle. It would be seen differently from the right bank of the Seine, from the inside of the house, and differently still from an airplane. Not one of these appearances is the house *itself*. The house, as Leibniz said, is the *geometrical plan* [*le géométral*] that includes these perspectives and all possible perspectives; that is, the non-perspectival term from which all perspectives can be derived; the house *itself* is the house seen from nowhere.' Maurice Merleau-Ponty, *Phenomenology of Perception*, trans. Donald A. Landes (1945; New York: Routledge, 2012), p. 69.

24 Raymond Aron's book, *The Opium of the Intellectuals* (1955; New York: Routledge, 2007), is a highly polemical criticism of left-wing intellectuals in general and Sartre in particular. For Bourdieu's commentaries on this book see

The Rules of Art, trans. Susan Emanuel (1992; Cambridge: Polity, 1996), esp. pp. 192 and 223.

25 This article by Simone de Beauvoir, written in response to Raymond Aron's book, appeared in two parts in *Les Temps modernes* in 1955 (nos 112–13, pp. 1539–75 and nos 114–15, pp. 2219–61). It was republished in *Privilèges* (Paris: Gallimard, 1955), and reissued as *Faut-il brûler Sade* (Paris: Gallimard, 1972), translated as 'Must we burn Sade?' in Simone de Beauvoir, *Political Writings* (Champaign: University of Illinois Press, 2012).

26 Ludwig Wittgenstein, *Philosophical Investigations*, trans. G. E. N. Anscombe (1953; Oxford: Wiley-Blackwell, 2010), §50, p. 29.

27 'Who may judge the legitimacy of the judges?' is the subtitle that Bourdieu gives to an article on the growing hold the journalistic field has over the intellectual field, published in 1984: 'Le hit-parade des intellectuals français, ou qui sera juge de la légitimité des juges?', *Actes de la recherche en sciences sociales*, no. 52 (1984), pp. 95–100 (republished in *Homo Academicus*, 'The hit parade of French intellectuals, or Who is to judge the legitimacy of the judges?', pp. 256–70).

28 The historian is Maurice Lévy-Leboyer (1920–2014) and the debate Bourdieu alludes to is probably the one that took place during a broadcast of 'Les Lundis de l'histoire' on *France Culture* on 15 December 1980, devoted to 'the management of the second era of industrialization' (this broadcast was based particularly on an issue of 'Cahiers du Mouvement social' which in 1979 had published several contributions to a round table organized at the Maison des Sciences de l'Homme on 22 and 23 April 1977 by Maurice Lévy-Leboyer and Patrick Fridenson). Bourdieu refers to this discussion again in an interview with Roger Chartier in 1988 (see P. Bourdieu and R. Chartier, *Le Sociologue et l'Historien* (Paris/Marseille: Raisons d'Agir/Agone, 2010), pp. 26–7, as well as in P. Bourdieu, *On Television and Journalism*, trans. P. P. Ferguson (1996; London: Pluto Press, 1998), pp. 61–2).

29 [*La Nouvelle Revue française*, a mainstream literary review. – Translator.]

30 [A left-of-centre intellectual review. – Translator.]

31 [A militant left-wing newspaper. – Translator.]

Lecture of 19 May 1982

1 See Paul F. Lazarsfeld, 'A conceptual introduction to latent structure analysis', in *Mathematical Thinking in the Social Sciences* (New York: Free Press, 1954).

2 Although seeming rather old-fashioned nowadays, 'scale analysis' designated a kind of statistical analysis developed in social psychology and sociology in the 1950s and 1960s. It consisted for example in studying the replies given by a group of people to a series of questions of opinion, by selecting a small number of ideal-typical patterns arranged along a scale (see, for example, Benjamin Matalon, *L'Analyse hiérarchique* (Paris: Mouton et Gauthier-Villars, 1965)). Scale analysis, which could appear to be 'a sort of factor analysis applied to qualitative variables', is in fact, in some respects, a precursor of the techniques of data analysis (correspondence analysis, methods of classification, etc.) which were developed in the 1960s and 1970s by Jean-Paul Benzécri and his collaborators and which Bourdieu employed quite widely for his work in social science.

3 Ludwig Wittgenstein, *Philosophical Investigations*, §50, p. 29.

4 See on this point Pierre Bourdieu and Jean-Claude Passeron, *The Inheritors*, trans. Richard Nice (Chicago: University of Chicago Press, 1979).

5 See Pierre Bourdieu, *Distinction: A Social Critique of the Judgement of Taste*, p. 21.

6 On the illusion of transparency, see Pierre Bourdieu, Jean-Claude Chamboredon and Jean-Claude Passeron, *The Craft of Sociology: Epistemological Preliminaries* (New York: de Gruyter, 1991), pp. 109–17, where they refer in particular to Émile Durkheim, *The Rules of Sociological Method*, ed. Steven Lukes (1938; Basingstoke: Palgrave Macmillan, 2013) [although Durkheim himself does not use these exact terms – Translator].

7 Bourdieu is no doubt thinking here of Lucien Goldmann's *The Human Sciences and Philosophy* (1966; London: Cape, 1969).

8 Bernard Guibert, Jean Laganier and Michel Volle, 'Essai sur les nomenclatures industrielles', *Économie et statistiques*, no. 20 (1971), pp. 23–36.

9 Laurent Thévenot, 'Une jeunesse difficile. Les fonctions sociales du flou et de la rigueur dans les classements', *Actes de la recherche en sciences sociales*, nos 26–7 (1979), pp. 3–18.

10 Daniel Bony and François Eymard-Duvernay, 'Cohérence de la branche et diversité des entreprises. Étude d'un cas', *Économie et statistique*, no. 144 (1982), pp. 13–23.

11 A statistical test used to infer an association between two categorical variables.

12 Spinoza set sensory perception, and opinions derived from 'hearsay' (the first kind of knowledge), as well as objective knowledge based on the use of reason (the second kind), in opposition to a 'knowledge of the third kind', that is intuitive, and accessible only to the philosopher: 'This kind of knowing proceeds from an adequate idea of the formal essence of certain attributes of God to the adequate knowledge of the formal essence of things'. Benedict de Spinoza, *Ethics* (London: Penguin, 1966), vol. 2, proposition 40, p. 57.

13 Pierre Bourdieu, *The Logic of Practice*, trans. Richard Nice (Cambridge: Polity, 1990), pp. 30–51.

14 On these points see Pierre Bourdieu, *The State Nobility*, pp. 264–72.

15 *Capésien*: a qualified secondary-school teacher, holder of the CAPES (Certificat d'aptitude au professorat de l'enseignement du second degré).

16 See Bourdieu, *The Logic of Practice*, esp. ch. 1 ('Objectification objectified'), pp. 30–41.

17 See Pierre Bourdieu, 'L'opinion publique n'existe pas', in *Questions de sociologie* (Paris: Minuit, 1980), pp. 222–35; translated as 'Public opinion does not exist', in *Sociology in Question*, trans. Richard Nice (London: Sage, 1993), pp. 149–57. Bourdieu also discusses this topic in *Distinction*, pp. 397–465, and in *In Other Words* (Cambridge: Polity, 1990), pp. 168–74.

18 The notion of 'knowing one's place' is taken from Erving Goffman; see esp. 'Symbols of class status', *British Journal of Sociology*, 2.4 (1951), p. 297; and *The Presentation of Self in Everyday Life* (1959; London: Penguin, 1969), p. 166.

19 See especially the collection edited by Stephen A. Tyler, *Cognitive Anthropology* (New York: Holt, Rinehart & Winston, 1969), and Marcel Fournier, 'Réflexions théoriques et méthodologiques à propos de l'ethnoscience', *Revue française de sociologie*, 12.4 (1971), pp. 459–82.

20 See Bourdieu, *The Logic of Practice*, esp. Book II, ch. 3 ('Irresistible analogy'), pp. 200–70.
21 See 'Associations: a parlour game', In *Distinction*, pp. 546–59.
22 Theorized by the Danish linguist Louis Hjelmslev, componential, or semic, analysis is based on the structural decomposition of words into lexical units of meaning, or semes. On its use in ethnobotanics, ethnozoology or more generally in the ethnosciences, see Tyler, *Cognitive Anthropology*. The enquiry that Bourdieu refers to was conducted by Yvette Delsaut in Denain, near Valenciennes, in 1978.

Lecture of 26 May 1982

1 For further development of this point, see 'On symbolic power', in Pierre Bourdieu, *Language and Symbolic Power*. On the theme of this lecture in general, see also 'Social space and the genesis of classes', in *Language and Symbolic Power*, pp. 229–51.
2 See the 'Conclusion' to Pierre Bourdieu, *Distinction: A Social Critique of the Judgement of Taste*.
3 Edward Palmer Thompson, *The Making of the English Working Class* (London: Vintage, 1963).
4 See Jean-Paul Sartre, *Critique of Dialectical Reason*, vol. 1: *Theory of Practical Ensembles*, trans. Alan Sheridan-Smith (1960; London: Verso, 2004).
5 Bourdieu will return to this point especially in his *Pascalian Meditations*, trans. Richard Nice (1997; Cambridge: Polity, 2000), pp. 202–5.
6 See Bourdieu, *Distinction*, esp. pp. 230–44.
7 [Paul Nizan (1905–40) was a friend of Sartre's and a militant communist. His essay *The Watchdogs* (1932; New York: Monthly Review Press, 1972) attacked the Idealist philosophy of Sorbonne professor Léon Brunschvicg (1869–1944), among others, for being mystical and bourgeois. – Translator.]
8 This is the article by Jean-Paul Sartre, 'Merleau-Ponty vivant', which appeared in the double number of *Les Temps modernes*, nos 184–5 (1961), pp. 304–76, republished in *Situations IV* (Paris: Gallimard, 1964), pp. 189–21, in honour of the philosopher, who died on 3 May 1961. Published in English as 'Merleau-Ponty', in Jean-Paul Sartre, *Portraits (Situations IV)*, trans. Chris Turner (New York: Seagull Books, 2017).
9 This is an allusion to the much discussed passage on 'das Man' in *Sein und Zeit* (Martin Heidegger, *Being and Time* (1927; Oxford: Blackwell, 1962), pp. 164–5), analysed by Bourdieu as a transfiguration of ordinary discourse into lofty philosophical terminology: 'L'ontologie politique de Martin Heidegger', *Actes de la recherche en sciences sociales*, nos 5–6 (1975), pp. 109–56. This article was developed in a book with the same title: Pierre Bourdieu, *The Political Ontology of Martin Heidegger*, trans. Peter Collier (Cambridge: Polity, 1991), esp. pp. 78–80.
10 Here Bourdieu is alluding to the experiments conducted by the theoreticians of gestalt psychology on the processes of perception and mental representation, of which one example is 'Rubin's vase': where the same image tends to appear either as two black faces in profile against a white ground, or a white vase against a black ground.
11 This is an allusion to a passage in Marx's *Critique of Hegel's Philosophy of*

Right, in which he refers to religion as 'the opium of the people': 'Religion is the
general theory of this world, its encyclopedic compendium, its logic in popular
form, its spiritual *point d'honneur*, its enthusiasm, its moral sanction, its solemn
complement, its universal basis of consolation and justification. . . . It is the
opium of the people.' Karl Marx, 'Critique of Hegel's Philosophy of Right', in
Early Writings (1843; London: Penguin, 1975), p. 244.

12 See Pierre Bourdieu, 'L'identité et la représentation. Éléments pour une réflex-
ion critique sur l'idée de région', *Actes de la recherche en sciences sociales*, no.
35 (1980), pp. 63–72; republished as 'Identity and representation: elements for
a critical reflection on the idea of region', in Bourdieu, *Language and Symbolic
Power*, pp. 220–8.

13 Bourdieu takes the term *allodoxia* from Plato: 'We describe false belief as
a sort of cross-believing, when the mind exchanges something that is for
something else that is, and one is claimed to be the other.' Plato, *Theaetetus*
(London: Penguin, 1987), 189c, p. 95. Bourdieu uses the term to designate a
false judgement or a misunderstanding – when a social agent's perception of
an object misrepresents what it is objectively. He uses the notion for instance
to refer to the self-taught who take an operetta to be 'classical music', or
first-generation students expecting their academic qualifications to give them
rewards they no longer provide (see Bourdieu, *Distinction*, pp. 155, 323, 326–7,
428).

14 The word 'theory' comes from the Greek *theorein* (to observe, to contemplate),
theoria (contemplation, viewing a scene, an intellectual view).

15 On this notion of *Vielseitigkeit* and its relation to the theory of the field,
see also Pierre Bourdieu, 'Fieldwork in philosophy', in *In Other Words*,
p. 21.

16 See, in particular, Max Weber, 'The nature of prophetic revelation: the world
as a meaningful totality', in *Economy and Society* (Berkeley: University of
California Press, 1978), vol. 1, part 2, ch. VI, iii, 6: 'prophetic revelation
involves for both the prophet himself and for his followers . . . a unified view
of the world derived from a consciously integrated meaningful attitude toward
life. To the prophet, both the life of man and the world . . . have a certain systematic and coherent meaning' (p. 450).

17 Kenneth Burke, 'Literature as equipment for living' (1938), in *The Philosophy
of Literary Form: Studies in Symbolic Action* (1941; Berkeley: University of
California Press, 1973).

18 Bourdieu returns to this notion of *Öffentlichkeit* in the lecture of 9 June 1982,
p. 106.

19 Émile Benveniste, *Dictionary of Indo-European Concepts and Society* (Chicago:
Hau Books, 2016), pp. 391–4.

20 Bourdieu is referring here again no doubt to Laurent Thévenot, 'Une jeunesse
difficile. Les fonctions sociales du flou et de la rigueur dans les classements',
Actes de la recherche en sciences sociales, nos 26–7 (1979), pp. 3–18.

Lecture of 2 June 1982

1 Bourdieu discusses this theory later, in the lectures of 7 December 1982 and 11
January 1983, as well as in *The Rules of Art*, pp. 138–40, 196, 200–1, 205, and
in *Manet: A Symbolic Revolution*, pp. 239–43.

2 On this point, see Pierre Bourdieu and Mouloud Mammeri, 'Dialogue sur la poésie orale en Kabylie', *Actes de la recherche en sciences sociales*, no. 23 (1986), pp. 51–66.

3 The original quotation is 'La Nature a lieu, on n'y ajoutera pas.' Stéphane Mallarmé, 'La musique et les lettres', in *Oeuvres complètes*, ed. Henri Mondor and Jean Aubry (1894; Paris: Gallimard, 1945), p. 647.

4 On the state as the agency that successfully claims the monopoly of symbolic violence and acts as the 'bank of symbolic capital', see the lectures at the Collège de France for the years 1989 to 1992, published as Pierre Bourdieu, *On the State* (Cambridge: Polity, 2014).

5 See in particular the end of the lecture for 16 June 1982, starting at the section on 'The problem of the truth of the social world', p. 127.

6 Pierre Bourdieu, 'Identity and representation', in *Language and Symbolic Power*, pp. 220–8.

7 Émile Benveniste, *Dictionary of Indo-European Concepts and Society*, pp. 307–12.

8 See Émile Durkheim, 'The two forms of the sacred', in *The Elementary Forms of the Religious Life*, trans. Karen E. Fields (New York: Free Press, 1995), Book III, ch. 5, §4, pp. 412–17.

9 An allusion to Pascal's famous aphorism: 'Truth lies on this side of the Pyrenees, error on the other side', in Blaise Pascal, *Pensées and Other Writings* (Oxford: Oxford University Press, 1995), p. 23.

10 See Pierre Bourdieu, 'Les rites comme actes d'institution', *Actes de la recherche en sciences sociales*, no. 43 (1982), translated as 'Rites of institution' in *Language and Symbolic Power*, pp. 117–26.

11 On the example of Occitania, see Bourdieu, 'Identity and representation'.

12 This phrase, which Bourdieu alludes to on several occasions, is probably: 'Reputation of power is power; because it draweth with it the adherence of those that need protection'. Thomas Hobbes, *Leviathan* (1651; Cambridge: Cambridge University Press, 1996), ch. X, p. 62.

13 On this point see Pierre Bourdieu, *Distinction: A Social Critique of the Judgement of Taste*, especially the chapter 'Cultural goodwill', pp. 318–71.

14 This is an allusion to the notion of 'mystical participation' used by Lévy-Bruhl to attempt to understand the identity relations, arising, he argued, from a 'primitive' or 'prelogical' mentality, in certain societies between peoples or individuals and, for example, their doubles or their ascendants/ancestors in the animal kingdom. See Lucien Lévy-Bruhl, *How Natives Think* (1910; Eastford, CT: Martino Fine Books, 2015), and *Primitive Mentality* (1922; London: Forgotten Books, 2017*).* See also the lecture for 5 October 1982.

15 Victor Karady and Istvan Kemeny, 'Antisémitisme universitaire et concurrence de classe. La loi du *numerus clausus* en Hongrie entre le deux guerres', *Actes de la recherche en sciences sociales*, no. 34 (1980), pp. 67–97.

16 See Max Weber, *The Protestant Ethic and the Spirit of Capitalism* (1904–5; London: Penguin, 2004).

17 This refers to Plato's *Meno*, whose point of departure is the following question (W. K. C. Guthrie translates *arétè* as 'virtue'): 'Can you tell me, Socrates, is virtue something that can be taught? Or does it come by practice? Or is it neither teaching nor practice that gives it to a man but natural aptitude

or something else?' Plato, 'The Meno', in *Protagoras and Meno* (London: Penguin, 1986), p. 115.

18 [The Cathars, also known as the Albigensian heretics, were a medieval Christian sect (twelfth to fourteenth centuries) in the South of France that rejected most of the trappings of Catholicism, including priests and churches. – Translator.]

19 See Pierre Bourdieu, 'From the "rules" of honour to the sense of honour', in *Outline of a Theory of Practice*, trans. Richard Nice (Cambridge: Cambridge University Press, 1977), pp. 10–15.

20 An allusion to the saying 'Caesar's wife must be above suspicion' (alleged to have been spoken by Julius Caesar to justify his repudiation of his wife Pompeia, who was suspected of infidelity, on very tenuous grounds).

21 In 'From the "rules" of honour to the sense of honour', Bourdieu gives a different version of this Kabyle expression, no doubt closer to his sources: 'his women can walk out on their own, with a crown of gold on their heads, without anyone dreaming of attacking them'.

22 An allusion to the *Revue des études grecques*, founded in 1888, and a symbol of learned classicism, which Bourdieu assimilates here to the title of its bibliographical section, the *Bulletin épigraphique*, which is often used to refer to the review.

23 This is probably an allusion to the 'rediscovery' of the writer Boris Vian (died 1959), whose work, republished from the middle of the 1960s, met with enormous success among the rebellious youth of May 1968 and became an emblem for the subversion of the literary canon (for example, *Le Magazine littéraire* devoted an issue to him in April 1968).

24 Benveniste, *Dictionary*, pp. 391–4.

25 Benveniste, *Dictionary*, pp. 324–7.

26 Benveniste, *Dictionary*, pp. 423–30.

27 See Max Weber, 'Charismatic authority', in *Economy and Society*, vol. 1, part 1, ch. III, iv, pp. 241–5.

28 Bourdieu develops this problem later in his lectures at the Collège de France from 1989 to 1992, published as *On the State*.

29 Georges Duby, *The Three Orders: Feudal Society Imagined*, trans. A. Goldhammer (1978; Chicago: University of Chicago Press, 1982).

30 See Pierre Bourdieu, 'The lengthening of the circuits of legitimation', in *The State Nobility*, pp. 382–9.

31 Pierre Bourdieu is no doubt thinking of Francis Ponge's appearance on the literary television programme *Apostrophes*, broadcast on 8 April 1977. The presenter introduced his guest in these terms: 'His name is Francis Ponge, he has just celebrated his seventy-eighth birthday, he has been writing and publishing for over fifty years, and yet you have hardly ever seen him on television or seen his name in a list of bestsellers.'

Lecture of 9 June 1982

1 Auguste Comte, *A General View of Positivism*, trans. J. H. Bridges (London: Routledge, 2015), ch. 3, 'The action of positivism upon the working classes'.

2 Émile Benveniste, *Problems in General Linguistics* (1966; Miami: University of Miami Press, 1971), pp. 236–8.

3 The notion of 'speech acts' is taken from J. L. Austin, *How to Do Things with Words*, 2nd edn (1962; Oxford: Oxford University Press, 2009).

4 Jean-Jacques Rousseau, *The Social Contract* (1762).

5 Ernst Hartwig Kantorowicz, *The King's Two Bodies: A Study in Medieval Political Theology* (Princeton: Princeton University Press, 1957); and Gaines Post, *Studies in Medieval Legal Thought: Public Law and the State, 1100–1322* (Princeton: Princeton University Press, 1964).

6 Montesquieu, *The Spirit of the Laws* (1758; Cambridge: Cambridge University Press, 1989), Book 23, ch. 4, 'On laws in their relation to the number of inhabitants', p. 429.

7 See Pierre Bourdieu, 'Les rites comme actes d'institution', *Actes de la recherche en sciences sociales*, no. 43 (1982), translated as 'Rites of institution', in *Language and Symbolic Power* (Cambridge: Polity, 1991), pp. 117–26.

8 Bourdieu, 'Rites of institution'.

9 Bourdieu will return to this difficulty in *On the State*, p. 3.

10 See Martin Heidegger, *Being and Time* (1927; Oxford: Blackwell, 1962), pp. 164–5, and Pierre Bourdieu, *The Political Ontology of Martin Heidegger*, p. 79.

11 Following Émile Durkheim in *The Elementary Forms of the Religious Life* (New York: Free Press, 1995), Book I, ch. 1, 'Definition of religious phenomena and of religion', pp. 21–44.

12 Luc Boltanski and Pascale Maldidier, 'Carrière scientifique, morale scientifique et popularisation', *Informations sur les sciences sociales*, 9.3 (1970), and *La Popularisation scientifique et son public. Contribution à une sociologie des cultures moyennes* (Paris: Centre de Sociologie de l'Éducation et de la Culture, 1973).

13 This may be a reference to Schopenhauer's Stratagem 28: 'Persuade the audience, not the opponent': 'If you have no argument *ad rem*, and none either *ad hominem*, you can make one *ad auditores* . . . particularly if the objection which you make places him in any ridiculous light', in *The Essays of Arthur Schopenhauer: The Art of Controversy* (1864; Fairford: Echo Library, 2006), p. 21.

14 This is an allusion to the hit parade published by the magazine *Lire* in April 1981. Bourdieu was to develop this analysis in 'The hit parade of French intellectuals, or Who is to judge the legitimacy of the judges', in *Homo Academicus*, pp. 256–70.

15 Immanuel Kant, 'The conflict of the faculties' (1798), in *Religion and Rational Theory* (Cambridge: Cambridge University Press, 2001), pp. 237–62.

16 Max Weber, *Economy and Society*, vol. 1, part 1, ch. I, p. 32.

17 See Pierre Bourdieu, 'The interest of the sociologist', in *In Other Words*, p. 93.

18 Norbert Elias, *The Court Society* (Dublin: University College Dublin Press, 2006), esp. the chapter 'Etiquette and ceremony', pp. 32–95.

19 See Pierre Bourdieu, 'Modes of domination', in *The Logic of Practice* (Cambridge: Polity, 1990), pp. 122–34.

20 Post, *Studies in Medieval Legal Thought*.

21 Kantorowicz, *The King's Two Bodies*, p. 101, and E. H. Kantorowicz, 'Mysteries of state: an absolutist concept and its late mediaeval origins', *Harvard Theological Review*, 48.1 (1955), p. 65. Bourdieu was to develop this analysis in particular in 'Le mystère du ministère. Des volontés particulières à

la "volonté générale"', *Actes de la recherche en sciences sociales*, no. 140 (2001), pp. 7–11.

22 See Weber, *Economy and Society*.

23 See Claude Lévi-Strauss, *Structural Anthropology* (1949; London: Allen Lane, 1968), ch. IX, 'The sorcerer and his magic', pp. 167–85.

24 Kantorowicz, *The King's Two Bodies*, p. 438.

25 Kantorowicz, *The King's Two Bodies*, p. 438.

26 In fact this is a phrase attributed to a Father of the Church, Cyprian of Carthage (*c.*200–*c.*258): 'The Bishop is in the Church, and the Church in the Bishop' (quoted by Kantorowicz, *The King's Two Bodies*, pp. 215, 440).

27 Kantorowicz, *The King's Two Bodies*, pp. 8–9.

28 On the notion of 'collective consciousness', see Durkheim, *The Elementary Forms of the Religious Life*.

29 Post, *Studies in Medieval Legal Thought*.

30 This does not seem to be an exact quotation from Post, *Studies in Medieval Legal Thought*, but rather a summary of the first chapter ('Parisian masters as a corporation, 1200–1246') of the first part ('Corporate community, representation, and consent') of the book, pp. 27–60.

31 See Bourdieu, *The Political Ontology of Martin Heidegger*, on the subject of *Fürsorge* in Heidegger, *Being and Time*, pp. 76, 79.

32 Jean-Paul Sartre, *Critique of Dialectical Reason*, vol. 1: *Theory of Practical Ensembles*.

33 Percy Ernst Schramm, *A History of the English Coronation*, trans. Leopold G. Wickham Legg (Oxford: Clarendon Press, 1937).

34 Blaise Pascal, *Pensées and Other Writings*, 'Cause and effects', pp. 29–34. See Pierre Bourdieu, *Pascalian Meditations* (1997; Cambridge: Polity, 2000), pp. 168–9, 171.

35 On the 'discours d'importance' ('language of self-important significance'), see Pierre Bourdieu, 'La lecture de Marx ou quelques remarques critiques à propos de "Quelques remarques à propos de Lire le Capital"', *Actes de la recherche en sciences sociales*, nos 5–6 (1975), pp. 65–79; republished as 'Le discours d'importance' in *Ce que parler veut dire. Langage et pouvoir symbolique* (Paris: Fayard, 1982), pp. 207–26. [Not reproduced in the English edition *of Language and Symbolic Power*. – Translator.]

36 'Social functions are social fictions', in 'A lecture on the lecture', in *In Other Words*, p. 195.

37 Pascal, *Pensées and Other Writings*, 'Cause and effects', pp. 29–34.

Lecture of 16 June 1982

1 Pierre Bourdieu, *The Political Ontology of Martin Heidegger*, on the word *Fürsorge*, which Bourdieu translates as 'social assistance', see esp. pp. 76–9.

2 Pierre Bourdieu, 'Rites of institution', in *Language and Symbolic Power*.

3 Durkheim defined sociology as 'the science of institutions': 'In fact, without doing violence to the meaning of the word, one may term an *institution* all the beliefs and modes of behaviour instituted by the collectivity: sociology can then be defined as the science of institutions, their genesis and their functioning.' Émile Durkheim, *The Rules of Sociological Method* (1895; London: Simon & Schuster, 2014), Preface, p. 15.

4 Bourdieu develops this reflection on the religious or artistic faith that works may inspire in different historical periods, or inspire in different publics in the same period, in 'Piété religieuse et dévotion artistique. Fidèles et amateurs d'art à Santa Maria Novella', in *Actes de la recherche en sciences sociales*, no. 105 (1994), pp. 71–4.

5 John of Salisbury, *The Polycraticus* (*c.*1159), quoted by Gaines Post, *Studies in Medieval Legal Thought,* p. 356.

6 'Status, id est, magistratus'; Post, *Studies in Medieval Legal Thought*, p. 353.

7 Bourdieu is probably alluding to the place that Austin, in his analysis of performative utterances, reserved for 'infelicities', where the speaker makes false promises, such as someone who says 'I bet' but does not intend to pay (p. 40) or someone who does not have the required authority (as in the case of some absolute nonentity who names a ship the *Mr Stalin*; p. 23); he points out that 'part of the procedure is getting oneself appointed' (p. 24) and 'the particular persons and circumstances in a given case must be appropriate for the invocation of the particular procedure involved' (p. 34). J. L. Austin, *How to Do Things with Words*.

8 Bourdieu went on to develop the question of political delegation in 'Delegation and political fetishism', *Actes de la recherche en sciences sociales*, nos 52–3 (1984), pp. 49–55; republished in Bourdieu, *Language and Symbolic Power*, pp. 203–19.

9 Pierre Bourdieu, 'Questions de politique', *Actes de la recherche en sciences sociales*, no. 16 (1977), pp. 58–9 (this is the first version of the chapter 'Culture and politics' in *Distinction: A Social Critique of the Judgement of Taste*, pp. 397–465); see also Pierre Bourdieu, 'Les doxosophes', *Minuit*, no. 1 (1972), pp. 26–45.

10 Jean-Paul Sartre, *Critique of Dialectical Reason*, vol. 1: *Theory of Practical Ensembles* (1960; London: Verso, 2004). On the example of the storming of the Bastille as forming a fused group, see 'The fused group', pp. 345–73.

11 For the historical context in which Bourdieu's investigations are set, we can consult Pierre Bourdieu, *Interventions 1961–2001*, texts chosen and presented by Franck Poupeau and Thierry Discepolo (Marseille: Agone, 2002).

12 A quotation from Hegel's preface to *Elements of the Philosophy of Right* (1821; Oxford: Clarendon Press, 1957), p. 13.

13 An allusion to the definition by Max Weber of the contemporary state as 'that human community which (successfully) lays claim to *the monopoly of legitimate physical violence*, within a certain territory'. Max Weber, 'The profession and vocation of politics', in *Political Writings* (Cambridge: Cambridge University Press, 1994), pp. 310–11.

14 See lecture of 12 May 1982, section on 'The geometrical point of convergence of all perspectives' and n. 23.

15 See n. 13 above.

16 Bourdieu returns to this point at length in his lectures for 1989–92 published as *On the State*, esp. pp. 231, 346.

17 Friedrich Nietzsche, *The Gay Science* (1882; Cambridge: Cambridge University Press, 2001), esp. §333, 'What knowing means', pp. 185–6: 'Before knowledge is possible, each of these impulses must first have presented its one-sided view of the thing or event', and §374, 'Our new "infinite"', pp. 239–40: 'The human intellect cannot avoid seeing itself under its perspectival forms, and *solely* in

these'. Perspectivism does not mean 'to everyone their own truth' but that the pluralism of perspectives is a condition of the manifestation of the truth.

18 Leo Spitzer, 'Linguistic perspectivism in the *Don Quijote*', in *Linguistics and Literary History: Essays in Stylistics* (Princeton: Princeton University Press, 1948), pp. 41–85.

19 Vilfredo Pareto, *The Mind and Society: A Treatise on General Sociology* (Mineola NY: Dover, 1963), chs 11–13.

20 Mikhaïl Bakhtin (V. N. Vološinov), *Marxism and the Philosophy of Language* (1929; Cambridge MA: Harvard University Press, 1986), esp. p. 23 on the 'social *multiaccentuality* of the ideological sign'.

21 See Pierre Bourdieu, 'The production and reproduction of legitimate language', in *Language and Symbolic Power*, pp. 43–65, esp. pp. 44–9.

22 The nomenclature of the socio-occupational categories by INSEE whose first version was devised for the census of 1954 was revised with effect from 1982.

23 Immanuel Kant, 'The transcendental aesthetic', in *Critique of Pure Reason* (1787; Cambridge: Cambridge University Press, 1998), pp. 153–92.

24 See Austin, *How to Do Things with Words*.

25 The word *taxis* means organization or arrangement and, in military affairs, the disposition of troops, the place reserved for each soldier (whereas *tagmata* designates what is organized, and, in particular, the troop formations).

26 Gaston Bachelard, *The Philosophy of No: A Philosophy of the New Scientific Mind* (1940; New York: Orion Press, 1968), p. 20.

Situating the Course on General Sociology in the work of Pierre Bourdieu

1 Most of these lectures have been or will be published: *On the State* (lectures for 1989 to 1992), *Manet. A Symbolic Revolution* (lectures for 1998 to 2000), *Science of Science and Reflexivity* (lectures for 2000), *Anthropologie économique* (lectures for 1993), *Le Champ juridique* (lectures for 1986), *Sociologie de la domination* (lectures for 1995).

2 See, for example, Pierre Bourdieu and Yvette Delsaut, 'Sur l'esprit de la recherche. Entretien', in Yvette Delsaut and Marie-Christine Rivière, *Bibliographie des travaux de Pierre Bourdieu, suivi d'un entretien sur l'esprit de la recherche* (Pantin: Temps des Cerises, 2002), pp. 204–5.

3 The dates in brackets refer to the lectures from which the quotations are taken.

4 We can quote two examples, taken from the last years, where, for obvious reasons, the risk of misunderstanding is greatest: 'I sometimes return to the same point by a different route' (17 April 1986); 'I have said this in a previous lecture, but I am now going to discuss the same topic in another context' (18 April 1985). We can also note themes that recur (for instance, the discussion of finalism and mechanicism, broached in 1982 and then in 1986) or the examples drawn on (like the careers of regionalist writers in the nineteenth century – 25 January 1983 and 12 June 1986) at different times, to illustrate different arguments.

5 A phrase used in Pierre Bourdieu, Jean-Claude Chamboredon and Jean-Claude Passeron, *The Craft of Sociology* (1968; Berlin/New York: Mouton/De Gruyter, 2005), pp. 53–4.

6 See *Pascalian Meditations*, p. 8.

7 See Pierre Bourdieu and Yvette Delsaut, 'Sur l'esprit de la recherche', p. 193.

8 For this reason, the first year is much shorter than the others, while the second is distinctly longer.

9 On the election of Pierre Bourdieu to the Collège de France, see Christophe Charle, 'Collège de France', in Gisèle Sapiro (dir.), *Dictionnaire international Pierre Bourdieu* (Paris: CNRS Éditions, forthcoming).

10 Published under the title of *Leçon sur la leçon* ('A lecture on the lecture', in *In Other Words: Essays Towards a Reflexive Sociology*, pp. 177–98).

11 On the election and teaching of Marcel Mauss at the Collège de France, see Marcel Fournier, *Marcel Mauss* (Paris: Fayard, 1994). On the election of Maurice Halbwachs, see Jacqueline Pluet-Despatin, 'Halbwachs au Collège de France', and Maurice Halbwachs, 'Ma campagne au Collège de France', *Revue d'histoire des sciences humaines*, no. 1 (1999), pp. 179–88 and 189–229. We should also mention Pierre Bourdieu's text on 'L'assassinat de Maurice Halbwachs' (in *La Liberté de l'esprit*, no. 16 (1987), pp. 161–8).

12 Johan Heilbron, *French Sociology* (Ithaca: Cornell University Press, 2015).

13 'Propositions pour l'enseignement de l'avenir élaborées à la demande de Monsieur le Président de la République par les professeurs du Collège de France' (Paris: Collège de France–Presses du Palais-Royal, 1985); for the history of the report, see Pierre Clément, 'Réformer les programmes pour changer l'école? Une sociologie historique du champ du pouvoir scolaire', doctoral thesis in sociology, Université de Picardie Jules Verne, 2013, pp. 155–240.

14 Charle, 'Collège de France'.

15 Remi Lenoir, 'Duby et les sociologues', in Jacques Dalarun and Patrick Boucheron (dir.), *Georges Duby. Portrait de l'historien en ses archives* (Paris: Gallimard, 2015), pp. 193–203.

16 Pierre Bourdieu, *Sketch for a Self-Analysis* (Cambridge: Polity, 2007), pp. 79–82.

17 Bourdieu mentions this ceremony in *Manet*, pp. 318–19.

18 Pierre Bourdieu, 'Le plaisir de savoir', *Le Monde*, 27 June 1984; 'Non chiedetemi chi sono. Un profilo di Michel Foucault', *L'Indice*, October 1984, pp. 4–5.

19 Pierre Bourdieu and Monique de Saint Martin, 'Le patronat', *Actes de la recherche en sciences sociales*, no. 20 (1978), pp. 3–82.

20 Pierre Bourdieu and Monique de Saint Martin, 'La sainte famille. L'épiscopat français dans le champ du pouvoir', *Actes de la recherche en sciences sociales*, nos 44–5 (1982), pp. 2–53.

21 A specific feature of the French educational system is the existence alongside the universities of elite institutions that play a major part in the recruitment and reproduction of the social elite.

22 Pierre Bourdieu, 'Political representation: elements for a theory of the political field', in *Language and Symbolic Power*, pp. 171–202.

23 Pierre Bourdieu, 'Social space and the genesis of "classes"', in *Language and Symbolic Power*, pp. 229–51.

24 See Pierre Bourdieu, *Homo academicus* and 'La force du droit', *Actes de la recherche en sciences sociales*, no. 64 (1986), pp. 3–19 (Bourdieu returns to the analysis of the legal field in his lectures for 1987–8).

25 See Pierre Bourdieu and Rosine Christin, 'La construction du marché. Le champ administratif et la production de la "politique du logement"', *Actes de la recher-*

che en sciences sociales, nos 81–2 (1990), pp. 65–85 (republished in *Les Structures sociales de l'économie* (Paris: Seuil, 2000), pp. 145–94); Pierre Bourdieu, 'Esprits d'État. Genèse et structure du champ bureaucratique', *Actes de la recherche en sciences sociales*, nos 96–7 (1993), pp. 49–62; 'Le champ économique', *Actes de la recherche en sciences sociales*, no. 119 (1997), pp. 48–66; *Sur la télévision* (Paris: Raisons d'Agir, 1996) (*On Television and Journalism*); 'Le fonctionnement du champ intellectuel', *Regards sociologiques*, nos 17–18 (1999), pp. 5–27; *Propos sur le champ politique* (Lyon: Presses Universitaires de Lyon, 2000).

26 Pierre Bourdieu, 'L'institutionnalisation de l'anomie', *Les Cahiers du Musée national d'art moderne*, nos 19–20 (1987), pp. 6–19; 'La révolution impressionniste', *Noroît*, no. 303 (1987), pp. 3–18.

27 Bourdieu, *Manet*.

28 'The hit parade of French intellectuals, or Who is to judge the legitimacy of the judges?', in *Homo Academicus*, pp. 256–70.

29 '"Meanwhile, I have come to know all the diseases of sociological understanding": an interview with Pierre Bourdieu, by Beate Kreis', in Bourdieu, Chamboredon and Passeron, *The Craft of Sociology*, p. 247.

30 Pierre Bourdieu, 'L'invention de la vie d'artiste', *Actes de la recherche en sciences sociales*, no. 2 (1975), pp. 67–94.

31 The analysis of *The Trial* resulted in a paper presented at the end of the university year 1983–4 at a multidisciplinary colloquium organized at the Centre Pompidou on the occasion of the sixtieth anniversary of Kafka's death; Pierre Bourdieu, 'La dernière instance', in *Le Siècle de Kafka* (Paris: Centre Georges Pompidou, 1984), pp. 268–70.

32 Bourdieu also mentions Dostoyevsky's *The Gambler,* more briefly, in the lecture for 29 March 1984. During the same period, he published a text on Francis Ponge: 'Nécessiter', in 'Francis Ponge', *Cahiers de L'Herne*, 51 (1986), pp. 434–7.

33 Pierre Bourdieu, *Images d'Algérie. Une affinité élective* (Arles: Actes Sud/Sinbad/Camera Austria, 2003), p. 42.

34 Pierre Bourdieu, 'N'ayez pas peur de Max Weber!', *Libération*, 6 July 1982, p. 25.

35 Pierre Bourdieu, 'La force du droit'.

36 Pierre Bourdieu, *On the State: Lectures at the Collège de France (1989–1992)*.

37 Pierre Bourdieu, 'La domination masculine', *Actes de la recherche en sciences sociales*, no. 84 (1990), pp. 2–31; and *Masculine Domination*, trans. Richard Nice (Cambridge: Polity, 2001).

38 'L'emprise du journalisme', *Actes de la recherche en sciences sociales*, nos 101–2 (1994), pp. 3–9.

39 Pierre Bourdieu, *On Television and Journalism*.

40 See *Pierre Bourdieu et les médias. Huitièmes rencontres INA/Sorbonne, 15 mars 2003* (Paris: L'Harmattan, 2004).

41 For a detailed analysis of the philosophical field at the time when these lectures were delivered, see Louis Pinto, *Les Philosophes entre le lycée et l'avant-garde. Les métamorphoses de la philosophie dans la France d'aujourd'hui* (Paris: L'Harmattan, 1987).

42 See also Pierre Bourdieu, 'Sartre', *London Review of Books*, 2.22 (1980), pp. 11–12.

43 See Pierre Bourdieu, *Homo Academicus*, pp. 105–12.

44 Luc Ferry and Alain Renaut, *La Pensée 68. Essai sur l'anti-humanisme contemporain* (Paris: Gallimard, 1985).

45 This model is that of the intellectual who combines properly intellectual recognition with celebrity among a fairly wide cultivated public. At the beginning of the 1980s, publishers of works in the humanities started to deplore the dearth of scholarly authors attracting mass sales, in a context where university specialization seemed to be on the increase.

46 Pierre Bourdieu, *Questions de sociologie* (Paris: Minuit, 1980).

47 Alain Accardo, *Initiation à la sociologie de l'illusionnisme social. Invitation à la lecture des œuvres de Pierre Bourdieu* (Bordeaux: Le Mascaret, 1983; republished Marseille: Agone, 2006). This book was accompanied by a selection of texts commented on by Alain Accardo and Philippe Corcuff: *La Sociologie de Bourdieu* (Bordeaux: Le Mascaret, 1986).

48 Pierre Bourdieu and Jean-Claude Passeron, *The Inheritors*, trans. Richard Nice (Chicago: University of Chicago Press, 1979); Pierre Bourdieu, *Reproduction* (London: Sage, 1977). On Raymond Boudon, see esp. Heilbron, *French Sociology*, pp. 193–7.

49 Bruno Latour and Steve Woolgar, *Laboratory Life: The Social Construction of Scientific Facts* (London: Sage, 1979).

50 Pierre Bourdieu, 'La spécificité du champ scientifique et les conditions sociales du progrès de la raison', *Sociologie et sociétés*, 7.1 (1975), pp. 91–118; and 'Le champ scientifique', *Actes de la recherche en sciences sociales*, nos 2–3 (1976), pp. 88–104.

51 Pierre Bourdieu, *Science of Science and Reflexivity*, esp. pp. 22, 54, 76.

52 See the section '1981–1986', in Pierre Bourdieu, *Interventions 1981–2001. Science sociale et action politique*, texts chosen and presented by Franck Poupeau and Thierry Discepolo (Marseille: Agone, 2002), pp. 157–87.

53 See, for example, Pierre Bourdieu, *Acts of Resistance* (Cambridge: Polity, 1998), p. 40.

54 'Preface to the English-language edition', in Pierre Bourdieu, *Distinction*, pp. xi–xiv.

55 Pierre Bourdieu, *On the State.*

56 Pierre Bourdieu, *Manet.*

57 Pierre Bourdieu, *Science of Science and Reflexivity.*

Index